CBS
NBC } Forerunner in tv n[...]

ABC came along some time later, and have been
in the formative years "trying to catch up."

Wed: 230 March 5th

The Decade That Shaped
Television News

THE DECADE THAT SHAPED
TELEVISION NEWS

_____ CBS in the 1950s _____

Sig Mickelson

PRAEGER

Westport, Connecticut
London

PN
4888
.T4
M43
1998

Library of Congress Cataloging-in-Publication Data

Mickelson, Sig.
    The decade that shaped television news : CBS in the 1950s / Sig
Mickelson.
        p.   cm.
    Includes bibliographical references (p.) and index.
    ISBN 0–275–95567–2 (alk. paper)
    1. Television broadcasting of news—United States—History.
2. CBS Television Network—History.   I. Title.
PN4888.T4M43   1998
070.1'95—dc21   97–32044

British Library Cataloguing in Publication Data is available.

Library of Congress Catalog Card Number: 97–32044
ISBN: 0–275–95567–2

First published in 1998

Praeger Publishers, 88 Post Road West, Westport, CT 06881
An imprint of Greenwood Publishing Group, Inc.

Printed in the United States of America

The paper used in this book complies with the
Permanent Paper Standard issued by the National
Information Standards Organization (Z39.48–1984).

10 9 8 7 6 5 4 3 2 1

For my extended family:

Elena
Ann and Alan; Alberto and Ina
Alan, Michael, Trevor, Lars, Alexa

If man could learn from history what lessons it might teach us . . . the light which experience gives is a lantern on the stern.

SAMUEL TAYLOR COLERIDGE
T. Allsop's Recollections

Contents

Acknowledgments

The source of most of the information in the volume that follows were files in my home office or the Mickelson Archive at the Library of the Wisconsin Historical Society in Madison. Special credit is due to Ms. Janice O'Connell, then a member of the library's staff, who arranged for the acquisition of my files and supervised their classification and filing.

Among my colleagues at CBS News during the late 1940s and the 1950s who cheerfully and exhaustively recalled for me their experiences in the formative period of television news were Walter Cronkite, Chet Burger, Don Hewitt, Phil Scheffler, and Joe Wershba. Other important and useful sources of background included Dr. Frank Stanton and Jack Cowden. The research department of CBS Television was particularly helpful in searching out data regarding television news ratings and growth in television set density through the entire period from 1946 through 1961. The CBS Law Library arranged access to *CBS Annual Reports* for the same years and made copies for me of pages that were useful in carrying out the project.

Jesse Sheppard combed through files of the *New York Times* and other periodicals, making copies of significant items relating to the development of the thesis of the book. The clippings he delivered are in themselves an interesting running history of television news broadcasting in the 1950s.

Introduction: The Decade
That Shaped Television News

Like Caesar's Gaul, the history of network television news can be divided into three parts: the start-up phase beginning with tentative, experimental steps as early as mid-1946 and continuing to full maturity by the end of 1960; the period of consolidation and refinement leading to peaks in audience size and prestige between 1961 and 1980; and the era of decline in both ratings and influence beginning in 1981. The concentration here will be on the first of these periods, recounted largely through the growth to maturity of CBS News.

The largely experimental CBS television operations date from 1946, when there was an expectation that receivers would shortly be back on the market after a wartime shut-down. The first experimental postwar efforts to broadcast news began that same year. CBS's news staff grew from a total of six recruited in late 1946 to more than 400 by the end of 1960. The network was not alone in experimenting with news. NBC in 1946 was farming out its once a week news programming to an outside contractor. The first regularly scheduled five nights a week network news broadcasts began on both NBC and CBS in the fall of 1948. The first national political conventions to be covered by television were transmitted to a network extending from Boston on the north to Washington, D.C., on the south and Pittsburgh on the west in the summer of 1948.

In 1948 there were only approximately 400,000 television homes in the entire nation, concentrated largely in the Northeast. By January 1, 1950, there were more than 3 million and by 1960 more than 46 million, scattered across the entire nation.

By 1961, patterns for news and information broadcasts had been formulated, staffs employed, and audiences built, and prestige was running high. The news consuming public was apparently reasonably well pleased by what it saw. The start-up phase was over.

There may have been a decade in American history that witnessed more profound changes in American life than the 1950s, but one would have to look long and hard for its equal. A little more than four years had passed since the conclusion of a long and brutal war that had converted the nation from a civilian-based economy to a wartime footing. Now normality had returned and the good life was reappearing in unprecedented measure.

Factories were reconverting to civilian goods from concentration on war material. Luxuries were reappearing on market shelves. And society was changing dramatically. Center cities began losing population as city dwellers rushed to the suburbs. Colleges and universities were engulfed in a flood of new students, many of them war veterans. A network of superhighways began to reach out across all portions of the nation, and motels mushroomed at their junctions. A web of air routes followed a similar pattern and airports were expanded or new ones built to accommodate a growing army of air travelers. As air traffic boomed, passenger trains suffered from the swift competition. Dress became less formal and recreational facilities boomed.

Not one of these startling transformations in American life, however, exceeded the impact stimulated by a new medium of entertainment and information that suddenly began to capture attention by the end of the decade of the 1940s. There had been some sporadic television before manufacturing was shut down shortly after Pearl Harbor but it had been a costly toy for a few wealthy residents of large metropolitan areas.

By early 1947 a few television receivers were beginning to find their way to the marketplace and into shop windows and some homes. By early summer 1948, those few Americans with access to television receivers and living within the limited range of the coaxial cables linking nine northeastern cities were able for the first time in history to watch a national political convention without personally being in the hall. By early autumn, both NBC and CBS had inaugurated weeknight fifteen-minute news broadcasts. By the beginning of the new decade on January 1, 1950, television had become a tidal force there was no stopping.

Swift as was the growth of the new medium the pace was overshadowed by its impact on society. The nation had never seen a decade that represented so dramatic a change in all aspects of national life. Television was not the sole responsible stimulus, but it surely was a major contributor.

Change was particularly evident in political and governmental affairs. Government could not overlook the new medium. As the decade opened only a handful of Americans had seen live transmission of government in action. That limited minority had watched some meetings of the United Nations Security Council and some hearings conducted by committees of the United States House of Representatives, but only set owners in the narrow Northeast quadrant of the nation had access to the signals. Once it had established a solid foothold, television quickly became the tool most essential to getting elected, and for officeholders, to winning public support for specific programs or getting reelected. Presidents and members of Congress quickly learned that it was the most effective medium within reach.

Television was a key player in converting news from a largely local commodity to a national service. There was still no national newspaper. Although the wire services were national and international in scope, the principal source of news and information for most Americans was the local newspaper. The newsmagazines, *Time* and *Newsweek*, were delivering a national service but on a weekly, not a daily, schedule. Radio was the first service that was truly national, but no network news program ever approached the audience levels gained by television. As early as autumn 1951, both the Douglas Edwards quarter hour on CBS and the John Cameron Swazey program on NBC were outrating the most popular radio news programs.[1]

By the end of the decade, with television signals available live from coast to coast and set density at nearly a 90 percent level, the White House began to communicate frequently with the national electorate, not the Congress. The problem was not television, it was the House leadership, which barred live TV until several decades later. Live sessions of the United Nations Security Council and General Assembly were available from the late 1940s, as was programming on local stations from many of the nation's state capitals. The impact on the process of governing has never been fully measured.

Sports promoters, after giving away rights to their events in the start-up period, began to look at television as both enemy and potential cash machine. They moved both to bring the monster under control and to turn it into a money maker rather than a drain. Professional football, once it learned that television could be an ally rather than an enemy, was soon rivaling baseball if not exceeding it as the "nation's pastime." The Olympic Games, which had existed since 1896 as a quadrennial curiosity, suddenly became an international passion. And both professional tennis and golf rose from status as sports with small followings among the wealthy to major audience builders.

Television was the stimulant. As the new medium of entertainment and information continued its expansion across the nation, television households were added at a breathtaking rate. As station programming expanded from limited nighttime schedules into both day and late night hours the number of hours viewed in the American home soared with it.

The growth of television during the 1950s was so swift that the medium grew from novelty to virtually full maturity in that short ten-year span. There were only a handful more than 3 million television homes in the entire United States as the decade of the 1950s opened; when it ended, the count had grown to more than 45 million, an increase of nearly fifteen times. There were television receivers in approximately 9 percent of American homes in 1950, in more than 86 percent in 1960.[2] As the decade opened there were 108 television stations in operation, in 1960 more than 600. In 1960 live coverage was available to very nearly every city in the nation.

While growing at a very rapid pace, the medium was forced to face up to the pressures imposed by the wave of postwar blacklisting. It had to contend with congressional investigations, McCarthyism, the reverberations from the quiz scandals, and constant threats of punitive actions from a government that always had the latent power to revoke licenses. Even though it is now commonly assumed that news was a loss leader that never had to pay for its full keep, pressures to hold down budgets were intense and budget hearings painful for news executives.

The impact on government was particularly apparent. The process of campaigning was revolutionized. Political advertising budgets soared. Political campaign consultants proliferated. Candidates were selected as much for their capability in communicating on the television screen as for their competence.

Government, too, felt the sharp impact of the new medium. The response time between policy formulation and public support was sharply reduced. Many serious issues were trivialized in an effort to cater to the presumed interests of the viewers. Emphasis in political campaigning was frequently shifted from serious policy matters to superficial, sometimes trivial, solutions. Efforts were made to reduce complicated explanations to the lowest common denominator, avoiding the difficult to understand in favor of the simplistic approach. Emphasis frequently shifted to issues that lent themselves to consensus rather than disputation. Likewise, response time between policy formulation and action was frequently dramatically shortened.

The defining event in the accession of television to a dominant role in the political process was the Nixon-Kennedy debates in the closing months of the decade. Some 100 million Americans watched some part of one or more of the debates, and it is widely assumed that they were largely responsible for Senator Kennedy's victory over Vice President Nixon.[3]

It was a remarkable, almost unbelievable, decade. It is now buried so deeply in communications history that it may seem ancient. Yet it was so vibrant and is such essential background to the enormous changes in communications that have occurred since and continue that its history bears telling. It may also furnish tools for better understanding the communication revolution that is well under way as this is written. ·

The rapidly spiraling growth impacted almost all facets of society. Television turned sports into a megamillion-dollar commercial complex, revolutionized the film industry, destroyed the newsreels, drove the picture magazines *Life* and *Look* out of business. The new medium drastically changed the life-style of nearly everyone living within range of a television transmitter or, more recently, a cable outlet. It was a juggernaut, laying waste to everything that got in its way or, if not destroying it, dramatically changing it. Most of the shock effect had been registered by the time of the Kennedy inauguration.

To some old-line institutions the impact of television, at least during the temporary period of adjustment, was devastating. The motion picture industry was hit hard. Many of the old movie theaters, the Taj Mahals built in the 1920s and 1930s, went dark. They were gradually replaced by multiscreen cinemas. Some were even converted into television offices and studios. Hollywood production suffered, not to recover until at least a decade later. Evening newspaper circulations began to slide as television rounded out its late afternoon, evening, and late night news programs. The four evening newspapers in New York City in 1950 were down to two at the end of the decade and to one a decade later. In Philadelphia, where the promotional slogan "Nearly everyone reads the *Evening Bulletin*" was not entirely an idle boast, the *Bulletin* started a downward slide that eventually led to its demise. The same fate befell the *Washington Star*, which for many years had boasted of selling more advertising lineage than any American newspaper.

Collier's and the *Saturday Evening Post* both died and *Look* and the original weekly *Life* suffered damaging blows that were eventually to lead to their following suit. Vaudeville was in a weakened condition when television began to invade American homes, but once the new medium began its meteoric rise there it quickly expired. As early as 1948, without leaving their living rooms, viewers could see the vaudeville stars at no cost and at home. They could watch a full hour of Milton Berle every Tuesday at 8:00 P.M. And Jack Benny, George Burns and Gracie Allen, Ed Wynn, Red Skelton, and Phil Silvers followed in the early fifties.

In the decade of the fifties television news and documentaries grew most rapidly, established themselves securely, and created the patterns and procedures that were to prevail through the remainder of the century. Succeeding years saw refinements, extensions of both depth of coverage and geographic range, and the introduction of new technologies that vastly simplified coverage and transmission. But the pioneering period was over. Many of the changes that occurred in the subsequent years diluted the product, catered to the commercial interests of advertisers, and reduced standards to win the race for ratings. And the proliferation of local television stations created new and formidable competition for the networks.

The carefree days of gambling with untested techniques, of daring to defy convention and laws of probability, of flaunting established procedures were largely finished. There continued to be significant evolution of methods and procedures. Technologies coming on stream, including videotape, satellites, camcorders, jet airplanes, and electronic editing, made everything easier. The ratings book, however, rather than the mission to deliver information to the viewer, became the Holy Grail and the product began to soften. The 1950s may not have been the "Golden Years," but they certainly were the formative years. There would continue to be growth but not at the same dizzying pace.

1 •

The Search for a Road Map

There had been some limited television before the war but it was little more than a rich man's toy. A minimal broadcasting schedule continued after Pearl Harbor but set manufacturing was shut down in early 1942. When it resumed in 1946 programming had to begin almost from scratch. There were only seven thousand television receivers in the entire country, approximately three thousand of them in New York City. Nobody knew how many were still in operating order. There was hardly a large enough audience base to interest advertisers in investing in what programming was available. And there was no evidence that television was more than a costly toy.

Some news and information programs had been broadcast before the war. In fact, on the day Pearl Harbor was bombed the CBS news staff began broadcasting shortly after the Japanese attack was announced in early afternoon New York time and continued until late into the evening, reading the latest bulletins and illustrating them with still photographs, maps, and charts. But by 1946 that small staff had been dispersed by war and it was necessary to start anew.

There was not much to start with. There had been no enduring patterns established before the war. Prospects in 1946 looked pretty grim. Receiver manufacturers had been granted permission to resume production, but factories had to be outfitted, assembly lines geared up, sales and merchandising strategies devised, and pipelines filled before the new production could make any dent in the abysmally low receiver count. Only a trickle reached the marketplace before mid-1947. By the end of that year the number of receivers in use, according to one estimate, had risen to approximately sixty thousand. The number of stations on the air had grown to twelve.[1] This was hardly deep enough penetration to constitute a profitable market. There was one upbeat note, however. A coaxial cable link had been completed between Boston and New York.[2] This marked a first small step toward interconnecting the entire country.

Technology, a critical element in further progress, was likewise making rapid forward strides. Videotape recorders were first used in the late fifties. Film quality was vastly improved. Professional film cameras were beginning to replace the amateur equipment that had dominated the market in 1950. Film processors were yielding higher quality. Increasing numbers and capacity of AT&T transmission lines not only enabled most populated areas of the nation to receive live signals but made "back haul" transmission (transmission from the field to central headquarters) relatively easy and inexpensive. This helped deliver coverage of major news in the field to broadcast headquarters in a fraction of the time required in the early fifties. Jet aircraft were gradually replacing propeller-driven planes, thus speeding film shipments. They were flying from more and larger airports and on enhanced schedules. As recently as the early 1950s shipment by train or bus was frequently more efficient than that by air.

All these changes combined to simplify the reporting and recording process and reduce time elapsed between event and transmission. It also enabled producers and reporters to experiment with new devices and new processes to make their reports more interesting and attractive.

In the early 1950s CBS had relied almost entirely on Telenews, an independent contractor, for film coverage. By 1960 it had its own camera teams in the field working with its own correspondents to develop integrated news reports. Hard-hitting reporting was beginning to replace soft features that sometimes had to be used because hard news was in short supply. Where it had no personnel of its own it was able to rely on exchange agreements with other television or film organizations or on stringers (part-time camera personnel or reporters who might service several clients on a piecework basis).

Early in the decade television was rarely able to rely on members of the famed CBS correspondent team to add depth to coverage. They were largely restricted to radio, and some looked on television with disdain. When the radio and television staffs merged in middecade, the problem was solved and some of the disdain melted as opportunities for television exposure became increasingly tempting.

The increased amount of viewing, the growing impact on society, and the growing interest demonstrated by the government reflected the developing attractiveness, efficiency, and sophistication of the medium. But never again would television news reach the percentage of available audience that it had reached in 1950. A total count of a phenomenal 45 percent of all homes within range of the signal has never since been exceeded or even approached, except for short periods during major crises. The reason can probably be found in the fact that in the early fifties there was little competition on the air to divide the audience. Local stations carried very little news. Many communities were served by only one station, many others by only two, so it was a matter of watching the news or turning off the set. NBC, with the best lineup of stations, started off with a big lead. CBS gradually caught up, and when ABC finally entered the field as a third contestant, the three-network race began.

No decade since has seen a fraction of the progress achieved during those ten years. It wasn't all error-free. There were ludicrous moments when inexperienced staffs overreached. There were experiments that did not pay off. Gambles were taken that would not even be considered today. Improvisation did not always yield positive returns, but it demonstrated a vitality if not maturity that helped the medium grow.

The inexorable direction was forward. Failed experiments led to more efficient approaches. During the decade patterns were set and methods developed that would constantly be modified but never completely abandoned in the next thirty-five years.

Although the daily fifteen-minute news broadcast was the centerpiece of the early television news effort, the real glamour lay in the special events that television covered during the decade. The Japanese Peace Conference in San Francisco in September 1951, from which the networks delivered the first West Coast television signal seen on the East Coast; the exciting and dramatic political campaign of 1952; the coronation of Queen Elizabeth II in June 1953; early efforts by NASA to conquer space in the late 1950s; and the first presidential candidate debate in 1960 all took a solid grip on an enthusiastic public.

There were, however, anxious moments. News and public affairs programs were somewhat slower to mature than entertainment shows. Their audience base at the outset could hardly compare to the millions reached every Tuesday night by Milton Berle or, starting in the autumn of 1951, by "I Love Lucy." By midsummer 1952, however, the nation had been given a sample of what television could do with live coverage of major public events. More than 60 million Americans looked in on the two political conventions in Chicago that summer.

The total head count in the CBS Television News department on January 1, 1950, showed only fifteen employees: one on the air broadcaster, two studio directors, three writer-editors, four film editors who doubled as cameramen on local New York City stories, three graphic artists, one special events director, and a director of news.

A Washington bureau, existing primarily to serve CBS Radio, helped out

The author with Walter and Betsy Cronkite aboard the USS *United States* prior to departing for London to cover the coronation of Queen Elizabeth. The small boy in the foreground is the author's son Alan. Photo courtesy of Sig Mickelson. Used by permission.

occasionally, principally on special events such as presidential messages or congressional hearings in which service was delivered to both television and radio. The largely radio-focused orientation of the earliest news on television was soon facing stiff competition from the young television novices who began to introduce innovation geared to television's unique capabilities.

The early television news program was an experimental hybrid. But TV personnel were beginning, even in those earliest days, to give the medium a character of its own. They began tentatively at first to experiment with storytelling devices conceived by their own imaginative personnel.

No one involved at the beginning was quite sure what television news should be. The pioneer television news personnel preferred not to produce radio with pictures but had no clear-cut notion of what they really wanted or what they were creating. They just went ahead innovating from day to day, searching for new ways to tell a news story in a new medium with drastically limited resources. To add pictorial content CBS experimented with film shot by its one cameraman. To broaden coverage CBS purchased a film service from a fledgling news film syndicator named Telenews. NBC started hiring its own camera crews. It was soon obvious that a syndicated service was not the answer. Not only was the film quality inadequate, but, worse, what was delivered was essentially an old-time newsreel product. It was geared to the motion picture screen, not to the introduction of a news service in the living room, a more intimate setting than a motion picture theater. Furthermore, it was simply impossible to deliver a daily news report without coordinating film product with daily news flow. The film assignment editor could not go one way and the television personnel another. It was clear at an early date that one assignment editor had to coordinate both news assignments and film coverage. The objective of the television staff was to find a new way of conveying news and information to a growing audience. The end product would likely be much more responsive to viewer interests if reporters could work directly with camera teams. That was unlikely when working with an outside supplier.

Growth by 1960 had been enormous. The fifteen-person staff at CBS in 1950 had grown to nearly four hundred, including production teams working on special projects and documentaries, an increase of more than twenty-five times in ten years. In contrast to the insularity of 1950, when the entire staff was New York–based, there were now staff members and contract personnel in eight major capital cities outside the United States and in six cities within the country. Washington had become a major bureau point manned by editors, correspondents, writers, cameramen, film editors, a special events staff, and a bureau chief. The entire radio news and public affairs operation had been absorbed by television and the newly formed CBS News division had been given special status as an autonomous unit within the CBS corporate structure.

The eastern United States did not see live television from the West Coast until the broadcasting of live pictures from the Japanese Peace Conference in San Francisco in early September 1951. Nor did the West Coast see television from the East Coast until October 1 that same year, when a National Baseball League championship play-off between the Brooklyn Dodgers and the New York Giants was broadcast nationwide. Ironically, before the decade was over both those teams would be West Coast–based, and television was a major inducement for the westward move.

It was October of the same year before the transmission lines crossing the whole country were fully established for regular service. The microwave facilities used to carry the signal across the country were still so limited, however, that they could carry only one program at a time. This led to complicated time sharing arrangements.

While growth in the volume of network service was multiplying, the number of stations available to carry the programs was static. The Federal Communications Commission had imposed a freeze on granting new licenses in spring 1949. As a consequence the 108 stations that been licensed prior to the freeze had the field to themselves for nearly four years.

The freeze was lifted in the spring of 1952, but it was months before additional stations could complete their license applications, move them through the commission, acquire studio and transmission equipment, employ and train personnel, and begin to broadcast. Once the new licensees began to come on the air, though, a trickling stream quickly became a torrent. In contrast to the 108 stations on the air at the beginning of the decade, the total count in 1960 was growing to the 1,000 level. By 1995 it had topped out at 1,699, including UHF and public stations.[3]

Through most of the first three years of the decade CBS's only major news program was fed to a network lineup that hovered between 18 and 20 stations. By 1960 the total had exploded to more than 200. The two networks, CBS and NBC, that were reaching measurable audiences for their news programs in the 1950–51 season were watched regularly in a remarkable 5 million homes. That represented 45 percent of the entire market. By 1960 the number of homes reached, boosted by ABC's becoming a factor in a three-network race, had soared to more than 16 million.

Whereas personnel in network newsrooms in 1950 had drifted into television largely by accident, the pattern in 1960 was quite different. New recruits had been imported by design from newspapers, wire services, newsmagazines, picture magazines, newsreels, still picture services, and documentary production companies. An amalgam of varied talents and experiences was replacing the largely radio-oriented programming of the earlier days. It was reasonably certain, even at this primitive stage in television's development, that news and news-related programming would ultimately constitute an important element in television schedules, but critical decisions had to be made before news broadcasts could be expected to build the audience. There was no pattern for a fledgling news department to follow and there were no experienced personnel to create the patterns. The prewar news show was not much more than radio dressed up with a few stills and maps and some scratchy film.

When the first news broadcasts were scheduled, network executives charged with creating program schedules were confronted by a number of questions regarding news on the new medium. It had been pretty well decided that something more was needed than a radio news program with a camera fixed on the broadcaster or a daily newsreel with off-camera narration. If the latter, where would one obtain the news footage? And in what form? Would having a news reporter on the screen add enough interest to justify the effort and cost? The newsreel idea had the merit of saving the viewer the price of admission and the time to travel to and from the motion picture theater. But conventional newsreels would not serve the purpose because ordinarily they were released only once a week and ran for only about ten minutes, too little time to cover more than a fraction of significant events. They concentrated on items that were loaded with theatricality at the expense of the day-to-day information that was harder to pictorialize. And they were designed for a large screen and a captive audience, not for a small screen and a family setting.

In fact, producing a daily news report with a newsreel format was not practical: Delivering a weekly, or even twice weekly, report was one thing; producing sufficient volume to follow current developments on a daily basis would require an enormously expanded operation. To complicate the problem further, newsreel crews were tied down by heavy and bulky equipment that restricted their flexibility. They were accustomed to using 35-millimeter (mm) cameras that were too unwieldy to transport to fast-breaking, unanticipated events. They simply could not move fast or have the flexibility required on the scene. In addition, the film stock was more costly and processing required much more time.

Using the much lighter 16-mm photographic equipment would help but there was no 16-mm camera with a sound-on-film capability. Silent film would be a valuable asset in some circumstances but useless in events in which sound was critically important. A viewer could hardly be attracted to a news broadcast featuring a silent film of President Truman announcing the initiation of the Marshall Plan or Winston Churchill delivering his "Iron Curtain" speech at Westminster College in Missouri. There would be a place for stills but only as a poor man's substitute for motion.

Even if highly mobile high-quality sound-on-film cameras were available and there were competent crews to operate them, transportation was a problem. No available telephone lines had sufficient bandwidth to accommodate a moving picture, much less one with sound. Coverage outside the largest population centers was difficult, if not impossible. Airlines scheduled only infrequent flights and many areas had no commercial air service.

Planes were slow and stops frequent. Except for very long distances, trains and buses at this stage were more effective and reliable in transporting completed film reports.

Producing a daily newsreel was quickly dismissed; something comparable to the popular radio news broadcast seemed more promising. An on-camera personality could preside over the program, introduce pictorial or graphic elements, narrate news items for which illustrative material was unavailable, and serve as a guide through the day's news. But there were still unanswered questions regarding both content and format; there were no guidelines. Should television try to cover the significant news of the day comprehensively like first-class daily newspapers? Or should it restrict itself to reporting events for which it had film or other illustrative materials? When film or graphics were not available should they use the "talking head" format and read the story straight into the camera? And where would they find personnel with the ambition, imagination, and creative skills to face dismaying realities and make the system work?

It was assumed that news would be a significant part of television once it got under way. Both CBS and NBC had discovered that news, if it accomplished no other purpose, was an invaluable builder of prestige. It helped create an image that was useful in attracting audiences and stimulating commercial sales, not to mention maintaining favorable government relations. The Federal Communications Commission in granting station licenses had no legal mandate to prescribe that news be included in schedules, but it made it clear that public service broadcasts, news among them, would be a critical factor in deciding among applicants for licenses and in granting license renewals. Even though the networks were not directly licensed, they owned stations that were and served as a program source for affiliated stations that depended on them for balanced schedules. News met the test of "public service."

It was pretty well understood from the beginning that news and information would play a part in network television schedules as it had in prewar programming. Facilities were not available in the late 1940s for much more than illustrated lectures buttressed by still photographs, maps, charts, and interviews. There were no experienced television journalists and only the limited prewar experience to serve as a guide.

The real birth of postwar television can be placed some time in mid-1947, when postwar receivers began to come onto the market. During the remainder of the 1940s TV was building the foundation for a meteoric ascent. By January 1, 1950, the preliminaries were over, and TV was ready for the main event. Formats were being tested and adopted; program schedules expanded; personnel recruited, hired, and trained; and audiences were exceeding the most optimistic expectations. Income, though still negligible, was showing signs of gathering momentum. Television was on the threshold of a breathtaking decade that would see its rise to a dominant phenomenon in society.

As the medium began to scratch out a foothold in the late 1940s there was still little news in the abbreviated schedules except for the early evening weeknight broadcasts that began in September 1948. There was, however, an abundance of live coverage of sports. Sports programs were inexpensive. Sports promoters had not yet learned that there was gold to be mined in selling rights to television programmers. No studios were required, no rehearsal time to book, no script to pay for. The only performer required was a play-by-play broadcaster and perhaps an aide. A mobile unit with a minimum of personnel could program two to three hours of excitement and thrills at minimum cost. And sports interested men, who in the late 1940s were still the family breadwinners. It was they who would buy the new box that would put live sports events into their homes. Bar owners simultaneously discovered that play by play coverage attracted additional customers, mostly men, and kept them at the bar longer. The television receiver became almost standard equipment.

NBC in 1946 made a preliminary move into postwar television news. It hired a former newsreel employee, Paul Alley, to produce a weekly news program, largely patterned after the theatrical newsreels that were still a staple at motion picture theaters. CBS was also producing a once a week news program. It was a little more innovative in that it attempted to create something new and better adapted to home viewing. It employed a six-man news department, a legacy of its efforts to build a well-rounded news schedule in 1941 before the war shut down most of its live programming. CBS had a news director, an assistant director, a special events expert, a "visualizer," a cameraman, and a secretary. It is notable that there were both a "special events expert" and "visualizer." Inclusion on the roster of these positions suggests that thought was being given to using the special capabilities of television to create something new in news broadcasting that would go beyond still pictures, silent film, or "talking heads."[4]

There was no designated "anchorman." That came later. The network was still experimenting with talent. Should there be on-camera narration? If so, should the central figure be a ringmaster to drive the program forward or a guide and interpreter? Should the person selected be a father figure, a show business personality, a star, a widely known reporter, or a competent news reader? No one was quite sure. The staff tried an elderly man with a beard, an aggressive young sportswriter from a New York daily newspaper, and finally a number of staff announcers who were professional performers. It was quickly determined that they still did not have the answer.

By midsummer 1948, when the Republican party opened its national convention in Philadelphia, the number of homes with television had grown to more than 400,000; AT&T had interconnected cities from Boston to

Washington and Pittsburgh. Westinghouse tried to fill in the gap in the Midwest by feeding a signal through what it called "stratovision," an airplane carrying a television receiver and a transmitter. The plane picked up the signal from Pittsburgh on the receiver and relayed it back on the transmitter to an area across central Indiana and parts of Illinois and Ohio. The system did not prove very effective.

Chicago and Los Angeles, still islands with no connection with the East Coast network, were becoming television centers with their own production facilities. Other cities across the country, including San Francisco, St. Louis, Cleveland, Kansas City, Minneapolis-St. Paul, and Miami, were beginning to develop their own programs and their own audiences, awaiting the day when they could be interconnected with networks operating out of New York or Los Angeles. Like the networks, they were experimenting with news.

The real birth of the television news era can be dated from the 1948 political conventions. Television had then its first real opportunity to prove to masses of Americans that it could deliver a service unlike anything that had ever been available. The geographical area in which the signal could be seen was limited. The number of persons with access to television receivers was still minute, but the enthusiasm of those who had access to sets could hardly be kept secret. The contest for the presidential nominations was the center of attention, but television was the new element on the scene. Newspaper reporters were fascinated by it. It was so omnipresent that radio could not avoid mentioning it.

At the end of the summer NBC had decided to take the full plunge into news. It assigned the central role to John Cameron Swayze, who quickly became identified by his sign-off line, "Glad we could get together." R. J. Reynolds Tobacco Company bought full sponsorship of the program, which was known henceforth as the "Camel News Caravan."

CBS quickly followed suit. By this time CBS executives had concluded that they had had enough of experiments in their effort to find the ideal master of ceremonies. They decided that rather than a slick MC what they really needed was a reporter who was articulate, friendly, warm, and able to communicate. There wasn't much chance they could assign one of the stars of their famed cadre of correspondents who had won their laurels during the war. There was so much distaste, whether feigned or real, for the upstart medium among the elite corps that there was little hope of attracting any one of them.

It was clearly necessary to select one of the lesser lights who would feel that he had nothing to lose by being identified with an environment that was considered too frivolous by the elite of the staff. Management picked Douglas Edwards. Edwards had had some choice radio assignments but was not one of the haughty inner circle of "The Murrow Boys." He had achieved some national standing, but his real strength lay in the fact that he appeared likable, modest, warm, friendly, and knowledgeable. Olds-mobile shortly later assumed full sponsorship of the five day a week program, and the duel between NBC and CBS was on. ABC carried news, but its ratings were so low that it was not a factor until the 1960s. DuMont was never really in the running.

By autumn 1948 both networks were grinding out Monday through Friday fifteen-minute news programs to the handful of television homes able to receive the signal. It was a period for both experimentation and expansion. Sponsorship added new pressures but also new resources. NBC continued building its own film gathering organization to support its Swayze show. To bolster its coverage it sent a German-American photojournalist, Gary Stindt, to Europe to start building a film structure there. CBS relied on Telenews, a news film supplier staffed largely with former newsreel personnel, to furnish a daily service. A pattern was beginning to develop. A ringmaster, Edwards on CBS or Swayze on NBC, introduced film or still pictures, sometimes maps or charts, and sometimes he just read the news item when no illustrative material was available. Sometimes crude animations or jerry-built props were used to illustrate stories when no film or stills were available.

Apparently the haphazard process was working. The growth of television news, once TV set sales began to boom, was rapid. News broadcasts went from obscurity in the late 1940s, a novelty shunned even by radio news personnel, to a dominant role in electing a president in 1952. Only a handful of Americans had even seen a television screen prior to the opening of the 1948 Republican convention in Philadelphia. By mid-July 1952, only four years later, as many as 55 million had watched simultaneously as Senator Taft and General Eisenhower dueled for the GOP nomination at the International Amphitheater in Chicago and Adlai Stevenson rose from relative obscurity to win the top spot for the Democrats. The total number of the curious who had looked in on some part of either of the conventions was estimated at more than 60 million.[5]

When the gavel fell to open the Republican convention on July 7, 1952, there were more than 18 million receivers in American homes, a gigantic increase from the 7,000 in mid-1947 and the 400,000 in midsummer 1948. In 1948 there were only nine interconnected television markets; in 1952, fifty-two.[6] Microwave and coaxial cable facilities capable of carrying a television signal that had reached only as far as Pittsburgh in midsummer 1948 by 1952 had crossed the continent. Through the 1950s AT&T lines continued pushing outward, not only driving television's Golden Spike to bind East and West coasts into a single network but also reaching into more remote areas. Receiver manufacturers continued to pour out torrents of sets and the public kept buying them.

In the early 1950s the networks, still restrained by the FCC's freeze on licensing, were engaged in fierce competition to place their programs in single- or two-station markets. It was a particularly serious problem for ABC and CBS since NBC had acted swiftly to sign primary affiliation contracts. By 1961 there were three going networks (ABC, CBS, and NBC) and the race for program acceptance was a matter of history (DuMont had dropped out in 1953).

Studies on public attitudes toward news media made by the Roper Organization show that by 1959 television was already far ahead of radio and nearly on a level with newspapers as the primary source of news. By 1962 it had caught and passed print.[7]

In a little more than a decade television had moved from a novelty to a major force in journalism. Patterns had been established that were to guide further expansion in subsequent years, but the expansion would be more deliberate, without the carefree élan and bursts of chance-taking energy that characterized the fifties. It was a period of trial and error, on-the-air experimentation, serious analysis of strengths and weaknesses, and intense desire to create a new medium for dissemination of news and information. All available evidence suggests it was succeeding. By the end of the decade experimentation and risk taking were decelerating. By January 20, 1961, the date of President Kennedy's inauguration, television news was out of its adolescence. It continued to mature and to experiment, but it was the experimentation of a mature organization, not the rash risk taking of the fifties or the late forties. Still to come were President Kennedy's assassination, the Viet Nam War, the introduction of satellite transmission, the coming of cable, and the birth of CNN; but by the JFK inauguration, patterns were established and the set count was near enough to saturation to indicate that the period of explosive growth was over.

2 •

The First Awkward Steps

Television's coming out party was the 1948 national political conventions. The quadrennial rites of politics starting with the Republicans in June in Philadelphia gave television news the perfect venue for its introduction to thousands of viewers. The conventions were exciting. They had suspense and drama. A race to the wire between New York governor Dewey and Ohio senator Taft for the Republican presidential nomination and an explosive walkout by southern delegates protesting Minnesota senator Humphrey's fiery civil rights speech at the Democratic convention kept tension high. Even a third convention scheduled by the Progressives after the Republicans and Democrats had left town served to keep the excitement level high.

The audience in end of the century terms was not very large. Only fourteen stations were interconnected and able to receive the convention signal.[1] It was television's first chance, however, to show off its new muscle. The receiver count, too, was misleading as a measure of total viewership. Television sets in bars and in department store windows captured large audiences and viewing parties in homes added to the total count. *Broadcasting* magazine, in a series on television history published in early 1981, estimated (perhaps a little optimistically) that up to 10 million viewers may have seen some part of one or more of the conventions.[2]

Americans living within range of the television signals were given their first chance to look in on the boisterous process by which candidates for

The CBS News staff assigned to cover the national political conventions in Philadelphia in 1948 pictured in the Convention Hall the week before the convention. Photo courtesy of Sig Mickelson. Used by permission.

the nation's highest offices are chosen. They could sit in their living rooms and look in on the sometimes tedious, sometimes apparently lunatic, but nevertheless highly significant and frequently exciting process.

Few concessions were made to the infant medium by convention planners. No delegate in the hall or on the streets or in downtown hotels, however, could fail to note the presence of the television cameras on platforms in the Convention Hall and television crews with their bulky gear roaming the Philadelphia streets. Monitors in the corridors of the Convention Hall permitted delegates and guests play-by-play views of the action. In those few cities that had coverage, crowds gathered in bars and in front of department store display windows, where enterprising store managers had discovered a novel marketing device. They found that television receivers carrying pictures from Convention Hall or candidate headquarters could draw curious crowds so large that they blocked traffic. No more effective way could have been found to stimulate receiver sales than these impromptu TV set demonstrations.

Camera and sound facilities in the Convention Hall were pooled. Temporary studios had been constructed in auxiliary space by both CBS and NBC. They were used for interviews, analysis, and background pieces. NBC had contracted with *Life* magazine to produce its coverage. The producer was Andrew Heiskell, later publisher of *Life* and board chairman of Time Inc. Heiskell, given free rein by network executives and surprised to have so much latitude, not only covered the proceedings inside the Convention Hall but sent roaming camera crews to pursue the Taft campaign's baby elephant striding through Chestnut and Walnut streets, march with Governor Warren's parade down Broad Street, and look in on Harold Stassen's followers gorging themselves on Wisconsin cheese in the candidate's headquarters suite.

Print and radio reporters quickly discovered that there was a more comfortable spot from which to watch the proceedings than their stiff, straight-back seats in the steaming Convention Hall. They could do just as well sitting in overstuffed furniture, a mug of beer in hand, in the air-conditioned railroad lounge watching television receivers conveniently placed throughout the room. The lounge was a public relations gesture of the Association of American Railroads. Whether the railroads or television profited more is still a question. This was an audience that whether or not it approved of the new competition could not fail to give television a big boost.

Radio and newspapers reached far larger audiences and were able to go where television cameras failed to go. Inside the Convention Hall television did not have the resources to do much more than relay the action from the rostrum, supplemented by limited analysis from some of the correspondent personnel.

The Democratic convention also had plenty of fireworks. Minneapolis mayor Hubert Humphrey's stirring civil rights speech was covered by the television cameras, which also followed the southern delegations as they angrily stalked from the hall. But it was radio and newspaper reporters who were able to probe for the motivations that led to walkout. Television was not quite ready to do a thorough reporting job, and still had too small an audience to have much impact. It was the newspapers that showed the haunting picture of President Harry Truman sitting forlornly on the back steps of the Convention Hall awaiting his belated postmidnight cue to enter the auditorium to make his acceptance speech. Except for NBC's portable unit roaming Philadelphia's streets, television lacked the mobility at this stage in its development to move its bulky cameras and the hundreds of feet of coaxial cable required to capture a picture except from prepared sites. Nor did it have access to the reporting staffs attached to radio, who derived more satisfaction from reporting for the much larger radio audience. But for those Americans able to see a television set, even without many of the technological improvements that would come later, television had made its mark.

The fast-growing new medium had demonstrated in Philadelphia, particularly through the imaginative NBC coverage, that it could excel in showing actual public events to the American people, or at least that it would be able to do so when signals could travel from coast to coast and when the number of receivers in American homes would be sufficient to justify the effort.

It was significant from the beginning that management's goal was to create television news as a new information medium. The character of television at CBS was in large measure a legacy from the two men who were responsible for nurturing it in its earliest stage, Gilbert Seldes and Worthington (Tony) Miner, both imports from Broadway, who saw TV not as radio with illustrations but as a new art form closely related to the stage and motion pictures.

CBS recruited a miniature news department in late 1946. Only Henry Cassirer, the assistant news director of this new unit, had a radio background. Leo Hurwitz, the news director, had been a documentary film producer. Larry Racies, the only cameraman, came from CBS Technical Operations but had been in the Signal Corps during the war and was familiar with motion picture cameras. Chester Burger was employed to fill a job with a title that showed some managerial foresight: He was designated "visualizer," but he had no background for the assignment. Burger had been a CBS page briefly in 1941 but had had no broadcast experience; nor had Fred Rickey, who was assigned as studio director.

This small cadre began with the notion that they were creating something new. There were virtually no constraints except those imposed by a meager budget and inadequate equipment. They could try anything reasonable to create a new type of service, but photographic facilities were in short supply. They had a Bell and Howell 70 DL silent film camera that Racies used to cover local news. Sound on film was not available until 1949, when Auricon started marketing a camera with sound capability. Burger conceived of story approaches and went along on assignments as reporter and scriptwriter. There was a premium among the staff on developing ideas for illustrating major news stories with the limited resources available. Staff members were willing to try anything within reason if it would illustrate a complex news item.

On one occasion during the period when Soviet aggression in Central Europe was rapidly changing the map of the Continent, the news staff asked for help from an innovative member of the television production staff, Rudy Bretz. Bretz, who had a reputation for being willing to take a gamble if he thought it might effectively illustrate a complicated story, had been assigned to assist from time to time in developing new approaches to the news. He suggested a novel approach: Maps of Europe, one without the Soviet-forced changes, the other reflecting the new de facto boundaries, were placed on a table covered by a black cloth. Members of the staff found a wooden arrow that could be painted white to show up on camera. Burger was then sent to Bergdorf Goodman to buy a pair of long silk ladies gloves. The plan was designed to exploit a weakness of the old orthicon studio camera, a forerunner of the more effective image-orthicon that was introduced several months later: Because it had a limited sensitivity to light the camera would only convey images that were brightly illuminated. Burger was to put on the gloves and move the arrow on cue. With its limited capability for showing dimly lighted images the camera would not be able to reproduce Burger's hand encased in the black glove nor the black cloth on the table. It would appear that the arrow was moving under its own power. By this process Bretz hoped to produce what amounted to crude animation. The sequence, however, never got on the air. The International Brotherhood of Electrical Workers (IBEW) protested that only union members could move sets and props. Arguments were futile. The gloves and arrow went into storage.

The 1947 World Series involving the New York Yankees and the Brooklyn Dodgers, a series made to order for New York television viewing, was carried in its entirety, sponsored by Gillette. Brooklyn Dodgers home games and college basketball from Madison Square Garden were sponsored by Ford, and Columbia University home football games by Knox, the Hatter.[3]

Also in 1948 arrangements were made to begin some networking of programs. It would not be much of a network. Signals would be able to go only to Boston, Philadelphia, Baltimore, and Washington, but it was a beginning, and it would enlarge the audience, thus reducing the cost per viewer and making the medium more attractive to advertisers.

As television expanded so did news operations. The rapid upward spiraling of viewer counts suggested that the time had come to give some serious thought to television's basic objective in delivering a news service. Once these decisions were made it would be easier to determine the sources from which future personnel would be recruited. Since there was no existing talent pool from which to draw, it was clear that inexperienced personnel would have to be trained. The best available course would seem to be enticing restless talent from a variety of other media: newsreels, newspapers, radio, wire services, picture magazines, still picture services, or an amalgam of all.

The conclusion was gradually being drawn that television news was to be a new art form, an amalgam of existing news media, with a substantial infusion of showmanship from the stage and motion pictures. The role of the limited news staff was to mix all the ingredients in proper proportions and deliver a product that was distinctive, employing all the capabilities of the electronic medium. That was the long-range goal; in the shorter term a medium struggling even to get a start could not be very selective. It would have to look to younger recruits willing to gamble on the future.

The source of motion picture film to support its news posed another problem. There were two options, either discover an outside supplier able to serve the unique requirements of television or develop its own service. If it were to develop its own service, its IBEW contract would lead it into an inevitable union conflict. Newsreel crews were members of the International Alliance of Theatrical and Stage Employees (IATSE). CBS was tied to its IBEW contract for all its technical services, including film.

An assignment issued to the news staff's "visualizer," Chester Burger, on one spring day in 1948, illustrates the problems facing television news in its efforts to film important local stories.[4] Burger was assigned by the assistant news director, Henry Cassirer, to accompany the cameraman, Larry Racies, on a venture in New York Harbor. They were to board a Coast Guard cutter, which would take a cadre of news personnel out into the harbor to meet the Cunard liner *Queen Mary* arriving from London. Their objective was to film the Duke and Duchess of Windsor arriving for a New York visit. The film story would be fitted into the news program broadcast on WCBS-TV.

It was not an easy assignment for a fledgling television news reporter. It was a scene made to order for newsreel personnel to demonstrate their contempt for the new competition and the rival union. Television cameramen belonging to IBEW were regarded as "scabs" and were sitting targets for a wide range of dirty tricks. They were accustomed to being bumped and shoved and their electrical power suddenly shut off.

The duke and duchess, affable and charming, appeared on schedule, made their little speeches, answered a few questions, and said their goodbyes. Burger, meantime, discovered that an electrical plug had been pulled and the CBS camera had nothing. He caught the duke before leaving and asked for a repeat, preferably on the deck away from the newsreel crews.

The duke graciously agreed, even though there was a rain shower in progress. And Burger had his story. The newsreel men could not have foreseen it then, but it would be only a very few years before television personnel would have the field to themselves. The newsreels would vanish under the avalanche of television.

The year 1948 marked a watershed in the history of television news. After the conclusion of the political conventions, CBS management decided that the medium had grown to the point where it could obtain advertiser support for a daily news program. It was time to assign a full-time broadcaster to what later became the anchor position. Full promotion was to be given to the effort and the program put on the market for possible sponsorship.

Douglas Edwards was selected, partly by default, as the on-air reporter. Most of the highly regarded stable of correspondents expressed no interest in the assignment. They couldn't see television competing with radio and it was too closely related to show business to interest them. Franklin Schaffner, who had done his apprentice work in the Program department, was selected to direct the program in the studio. He stayed only a year before moving back to directing drama.[5] Don Hewitt was recruited from Acme News Pictures to be his assistant and succeeded him on his departure. Schaffner brought professionalism, style, and quality; Hewitt, flair, energy, creativity, inventiveness, and imagination that have never been duplicated. His "60 Minutes," created after he left the evening news, is frequently referred to as the most successful television program series ever broadcast.

Burger became one of three writers assigned to the program. Technicians with some experience with film, mostly home movies, were transferred from technical operations to edit film and, on occasion, to function as cameramen. A contract was signed with Telenews to supply film. Telenews was staffed for the most part by experienced newsreel personnel but had made one major concession to television: It used 16-mm cameras adapted to television rather than the 35-mm units used by the newsreels and delivered service daily, rather than weekly. The news stories photographed on 16 mm were easier to edit and project. Camera crews could respond to fast-breaking stories and submit film for immediate processing.

There were, however, discouraging aspects to depending on a syndicated service. The News department had to accept what was delivered. Its personnel had little impact on the product and there was little opportunity to coordinate the efforts of its reporters with Telenews crews. It could, on occasion, suggest stories for coverage but had no real control over the output. The net effect was that Telenews, even though more flexible than traditional newsreels, was more newsreel-oriented than television would have liked and, more important, less responsive to television's specialized news requirements.

The CBS staff established two procedures to overcome the weakness: The combination film editors-cameramen who had been transferred to News by the Technical Operations department were increasingly sent out on local assignments, usually with Burger as the reporter. Later, as the staff was enlarged, reporter contacts were trained for this function. But this only took care of the New York metropolitan area.

An effective process for developing specially tailored coverage of events out of New York was struck on almost by accident. In spring 1948 the nation was in danger of being crippled by a strike of the Brotherhood of Railway Engineers. The brotherhood's headquarters was in Cleveland and its president, A. F. Whitney, managed the strike from his office there. Whitney was obviously the key to any meaningful coverage. When his office announced that he would issue a statement regarding the union's position later the same day, Burger's news instincts were aroused. This was not the type of news Telenews could or would cover.

It was a challenge, however, to Burger, who immediately searched out a Cleveland Yellow Pages directory. In it he found listings for a number of freelance cameramen, one with sound equipment. He dialed a number and within minutes had his quarry. The freelancer was instructed to go immediately to Whitney's office, film the statement, and, when his assignment was completed, pack up his film and deliver it to the conductor of a New York Central train at Cleveland's central railroad station. There he was to hand it to the conductor with instructions to turn it over to a CBS representative who would meet him at Grand Central Station the next morning.

The Whitney episode triggered a series of experiments with freelance camera personnel scattered across the country. Burger accepted the responsibility for building a master list of available freelancers, particularly those who had invested in sound gear. Many of them proved adequate only in emergencies but the exercise unearthed some real gems: Wendell Hoffman in Lincoln, Nebraska, and Manhattan, Kansas; Fred Lawrence in Dallas; and Mario Biasetti in Boston, among others, were subsequently on regular call.

The neophyte news organization was also lucky to discover a highly imaginative graphic artist willing to take a gamble on joining the new venture. Aaron Ehrlich had, besides good taste, a willingness to gamble with Hewitt and the news staff in discovering graphic approaches to making news interesting and understandable to a growing audience.

No one discovered the magic formula for solving all the problems of television news but there was constant experimentation. Crude animation, notwithstanding the failure of the Rudy Bretz effort, was the subject of ongoing innovation. Ehrlich and Hewitt together tried various combinations using still cameras and fusing negatives and positives to create interesting superimpositions to illustrate difficult stories. Maps and charts were spread out on the floor, where cameras could achieve novel effects. After the Korean War broke out, Hewitt went to a store specializing in toy soldiers and bought a set, along with tanks, guns, trucks, and planes. He spread out his toy armies on the studio floor to recreate major battles. His daring and inventiveness, coupled with his fertile imagination, kept the news staff alert. No one could anticipate what implausible stunt he would try next.

Two technological developments introduced during 1949 greatly simplified production: One was the acquisition of a 16-mm sound-on-film camera. Prior to the introduction of the Auricon Pro in 1949 reporters wrote scripts to accompany silent pictures. Natural sound could be recorded by audiotape recorders, but synchronization was out of the question. The second was a device called a TelePrompTer, which projected script alongside the lens of the studio camera, enabling the broadcaster to appear to be ad libbing.

TelePrompTer didn't add to the impact of the news, but it immeasurably improved the comfort of the broadcaster and even more so the program assistant, who was assigned to hold the heavy cue card. Entire scripts had to be printed by hand on long, narrow cardboard panels that a member of the staff held up alongside the camera lens. The person holding the cards had to be alert enough to keep the line the broadcaster was reading alongside the lens to create the illusion that the entire narration was spontaneous. He had to be muscular enough to hold the card steady and had no time to relax. There were no middle commercials at that time.

The political conventions were clearly the major television event of 1948 but there was another breakthrough. For the first time television was able to broadcast directly from Congress. One of the most compelling stories of the year featured an odd assortment of highly newsworthy characters. The principals were Alger Hiss, one of the most widely known and respected diplomats in the State Department, who was charged with having worked with Communists, and Whittaker Chambers, *Time* magazine editor and admitted former party member. One of the key House members on the investigating panel was a young first-term congressman from California, Richard Nixon. Cameras and microphones were able to capture the tense scenes as Chambers directly confronted Hiss under the interrogation of Congressman Nixon and his colleagues. Scenes caught on television included the famous "pumpkin papers" episode and the controversy over the typewriter that Hiss was charged with using to copy secret government documents. Television, although its geographical range was still sharply limited and its potential audience minimal, was beginning to make its mark on government and politics. In January 1949 it carried its first picture from the House chamber in the national Capitol when it covered President Harry Truman's State of the Union address.

Most of the excitement generated by television in the late 1940s originated in the Northeast, where receivers were concentrated, but one of the most dramatic stories of the early era occurred in California. Since there were no facilities available to carry the signal beyond the state borders, television viewing was limited to Los Angeles and San Francisco and to a lesser extent San Diego.

Californians huddled before their sets in fascination as a gripping and emotional story unfolded. Residents of the rest of country, without access to television signals, kept up with developments through radio and newspapers.

The object of the attention was three-year-old Kathy Fiscus, who had fallen into a thirty-foot well in the backyard of her home in fashionable San Marino, a close-in suburb of Los Angeles. The date was early April 1949. News personnel were alerted to the story shortly after it began and swarms of reporters from newspapers and radio stations converged on the scene. Banks of newsreel and still cameras and radio personnel with tape recorders surrounded the eerie setting as construction workers dug to free Kathy from her dank and narrow prison. The whole nation followed the story with rapt attention. It was an event that had all the elements calculated to grip the public: a child in desperate straits, suspense, frantic rescue efforts, grieving parents, sympathetic neighbors—and reporters with voracious appetites for any morsels of information that might be available.

Newspapers ran banner headlines. Radio broadcast blow by blow reports of progress of rescue crews digging frantically to reach Kathy at the bottom of the well. The little girl was the primary topic of conversation across the country. Wire services, national newspapers, and newsmagazines all covered the event.

An enterprising Los Angeles television pioneer who had a strong engineering background immediately recognized that the plight of the San Marino child was made to order for the infant television medium. Klaus Landsburg, general manager of station KTLA, was not only an aggressive manager, but a person knowledgeable enough about technology to push his equipment to undertake ventures that other managers would never consider. He had built a reputation for discovering innovative ways to use the still relatively primitive equipment available. And he was willing to experiment.

When he was first told of the Fiscus case Landsburg immediately dispatched a mobile unit to the scene. Getting the signal from San Marino to studios in Los Angeles was a problem that discouraged other broadcasters, but Landsburg had an idea. He had designed a device that could transport a signal from the site of the action to a receiving antenna that would in turn transport it to his transmitter. Remote broadcasts with similar devices soon were commonplace, but in 1949 they were a radical innovation. The required equipment was packed into a mobile unit and quickly dispatched to San Marino.

The Landsburg scheme worked and Angelenos sat before their ten- and twelve-inch screens transfixed as the tedious rescue efforts went on. The

[handwritten margin note:] The birth of the breaking News. The precursor of modern / Princess Diana's death CNN Breaking News, OJ Simpson, The DC snipers that have viewers / in Paris fixated on the screen for hours.

remainder of the country, though, was outside the signal range. Long-line transmission facilities could carry the program only as far as San Francisco.

KTLA remained on the scene for days while workmen struggled vainly to reach the child. The station furnished what amounted to a play by play account and the public remained transfixed until workmen finally recovered the body. Landsburg's efforts foreshadowed what might happen when the entire country would be interconnected by television. Eastern and mid-western viewers had followed baseball, football, the political conventions, and debates at the United Nations Security Council but no event matching the human drama of the Kathy Fiscus story.

Television had matured sufficiently by late 1949 that CBS was ready to invite its ragamuffin television group into the family. It had been a more or less free-floating function with only slender ties to the prosperous and bustling radio network. In late 1949 a reorganization within the CBS cor-porate structure gave it status roughly parallel with radio on organization charts. A television program director would report to a corporate vice pres-ident for programs, a television sales director to a corporate vice president for sales, and a television director of technical operations to a senior cor-porate executive responsible for both media.

News departments of the two were combined into a single unit under a director of news, who, in turn, would report to the vice president for pro-grams. Public affairs production units, including discussion and religious programs, documentaries, talks, and sports, were lumped together under a public affairs director, who also reported to the corporate vice president for programs. There was a bit of eyebrow lifting at this latter step; news and public affairs had previously reported through its own vice president directly to the president and chairman of the corporation, a structure cre-ated when Edward R. Murrow was brought back from the London bureau to become a corporate officer. His successor, Davidson Taylor, resigned rather than accept the decision, leaving news and public affairs in disarray as the decade of the fifties opened.

3 •

A New Star on the Horizon

By January 1, 1950, television had outgrown its infancy but was hardly a robust adult. The Federal Communications Commission suspension of the process of granting station licenses was still in effect, freezing the number of stations on the air at 108. The American Telephone & Telegraph Company was still extending its coaxial cables and microwave relays out into the country, but progress seemed excruciatingly slow to potential viewers beyond the range of the existing cable. Network signals could still not be seen south of Richmond or west of Chicago.

Television was, however, poised for a dramatic surge. It had built a large enough audience base in its limited geographical area to attract advertisers. It had experimented with viewer responses to program formats and stars. It had begun to establish patterns for program production, no small feat in a new medium that had to create its own methods and formats and to build the facilities in which to produce them. It had recruited and organized staffs to accommodate a growing program schedule. But mainly it had caught the public's attention. And the public was interested.

Milton Berle, who started his "Texaco Star Theater" in September 1948, had become a national icon, capturing 70 to 80 percent of all available viewers on Tuesday nights at eight o'clock in those communities with network service. One of his programs recorded a Hooper (the dominant audience measurement system in use at the time) rating of an astronomical

80.7.[1] This meant that more than four of every five homes with television receivers in interconnected areas watched his program.[2]

Worthington Miner's "Studio One" was giving high-quality drama to CBS viewers on a weekly basis. Arthur Godfrey, capitalizing on the enormous popularity of his daytime radio program, had both his "Talent Scouts" and "Arthur Godfrey and His Friends" on television in evening time. Ed Sullivan's "Toast of the Town" was a Sunday night fixture and plans were well advanced to introduce "Your Show of Shows" with Imogene Coca and Sid Caesar to Saturday night audiences on NBC. They were to be followed by Dean Martin and Jerry Lewis. In a little more than a year Desilu Productions would introduce "I Love Lucy" on CBS.

The portion of the public in interconnected markets had gotten a taste of big time sports through watching the World Series and a Joe Louis–Billy Conn heavyweight fight. They had sat in on sessions of the United Nations Security Council during the early stages of the Cold War. Douglas Edwards on CBS and John Cameron Swayze on NBC had had more than a year to polish their weeknight news broadcasts. Both were already building substantial audiences. In the 1950–51 season more than 45 percent of those with televisions were regular viewers.[3]

CBS opened the year with a news extravaganza. It brought together eight of its famed staff of correspondents in New York on the night of January 1 for a one hour discussion program, "The Challenge of the Fifties—Years of Crisis." Five were from foreign posts, London, Paris, Berlin, Rome and Tokyo; one from Washington; and one from the United Nations. The moderator was the star of the staff, Edward R. Murrow, and calling the shots in the control room was Don Hewitt, director of the Edwards news program. This was the first exposure on television for a number of the correspondents, many of whom had serious reservations about the relationship of television and news. To some of them the picture tube tarnished the image of the reporter.

Steered by Murrow, who had achieved fame as a reporter in London during the war, the discussion was concerned almost entirely with international affairs. This preoccupation with overseas developments for some years diluted efforts at CBS to achieve similar dominance for its domestic news product. Significantly, Douglas Edwards, the only CBS News staff member appearing regularly on television, was nowhere to be seen.

Obtaining film support for news programs continued to perplex CBS News leadership. There was general agreement that television could not be content with talking heads. Since the medium was capable of projecting pictorial representations of people and events with full sound and motion, it seemed a waste of a valuable resource not to exploit its capabilities. Its aim was to discover how it could best obtain high-quality, full-motion pictorial representations of major news events with natural sound. Telenews, it was agreed, was not the answer. It was adequate, but barely, in covering events for which it had ample warning for setup time, but there was little opportunity for coordination with the assignment desk. The stringer system set up by Chet Burger could perform adequately in special circumstances, but it was cumbersome and only a handful of the correspondents on Burger's list were professionally capable and possessed the creative skills required to create a genuinely new service. Notwithstanding these deficiencies, CBS continued to build an audience. Oldsmobile appeared satisfied with the results.

An experiment had been undertaken in late 1949 to buttress foreign coverage and draw the CBS correspondents more fully into the television spectrum. Sixteen-millimeter Bell and Howell silent cameras were sent to each of the bureaus with instructions as to how bureau chiefs might supplement their regular voice coverage with motion picture film. The plan was doomed to failure. The correspondents were amateurs at best and resented being requested to perform what they regarded as a mechanical function. Since the cameras had no capability for recording sound, they were useless in interviews and coverage of events in which sound was of critical importance. Some film pieces, however, shot not by the correspondents but by freelance crews, were delivered to New York headquarters and went on the air. The 1949 *CBS Annual Report* for 1950 boasts, "Such film-tape reports prepared by CBS correspondents have been shown several times on CBS-TV programs."[4] The author of the paragraph was more enthusiastic about the plan than the staff of the Edwards program or of Howard K. Smith, the London bureau chief, who wrote to Murrow of his distaste for the whole idea "I frankly think it is about the goddamdest idea I ever heard of. It's about as absurd as asking a surgeon to fill a few of his victim's teeth after an appendectomy—medicine and dentistry being about the same thing."[5]

News programming suffered from another crippling problem. Production personnel were using what is called "reversal" film with optical sound. Reversal film eliminates the processing of a negative. The exposed film goes directly from camera to processor to editing bench for cutting. Since there is no negative, the use of reversal is practical only when there is no need for multiple prints. The sound was "optical." The sound recording mechanism in the camera made perforations alongside the exposed film. The perforations were converted into sound when played back on a projector. It was a relatively simple system, quick to process, easy to edit, and relatively inexpensive, but it delivered sound quality that the news staff regarded as atrocious. Hewitt and his colleagues insisted that the sound was even worse than the grainy and indistinct pictures that they got from the Auricon cameras. In fact, it made the pictures seem even worse than they were. Hewitt's staff were sure that the ultimate hope for their television news programs would be for CBS to create its own professional news film service and promote the production of a high-quality 16-mm camera.

A relatively uneventful spring and summer of 1950 suddenly exploded into a flurry of activity on the morning of Sunday, June 25. Shocking information came through the wire services that North Korean military forces had burst through South Korean defense lines and were moving almost unchecked on Seoul, the South Korean capital. Since many American troops were stationed in South Korea the United States was involved. CBS had at year's end, over strong protests from its correspondents, closed its Far East bureau. As a consequence it had no full-time staff member anywhere near the scene of the action. Telenews had established a film bureau in Tokyo and was in a position to deliver some motion picture coverage once enough order could be restored in South Korea to move personnel to the scene, but it was unclear on June 25 and for several days thereafter when that might be.

Delivering film to New York from Korean battle lines, once it was available, would be a complicated and time-consuming operation. The camera team, after fighting the military bureaucracy to get permission to photograph meaningful scenes of action, would have to scout up transportation to get exposed film to Japan. It would then have to be transshipped to the West Coast of the United States by conventional propeller-driven aircraft. Commercial jets were still some years in the future, as were long-range aircraft capable of crossing the Pacific without refueling either in the Aleutians or in Hawaii. Once film arrived at Seattle or San Francisco, another transshipment would be required for crossing the United States, necessitating another fuel stop. Rarely could a film story from the Korean battle front find its way to the air in less than ninety-six hours. The news staff, however, made an interesting discovery. A ninety-six-hour-late film story had just about as much impact as a much more recent one, if it provided pictorial coverage that had not previously been seen by viewers.

The CBS News department quickly began to assign stringers and move staffers to the scene. By late July the star of the staff, Edward R. Murrow, was on his way for a look at the combat zone. In an effort to buttress the news staff to meet the new war challenge, Ed Chester, the news director, sought to hire a veteran war correspondent who was in Washington operating a syndicated radio news service for a number of midwestern radio stations. Walter Cronkite had compiled a distinguished record as a war reporter. He had covered the Eighth U.S. Air Force for the United Press, had landed with American troops on a glider to cover the ill-fated Arnhem-Nijmegan campaign in Holland, and had flown on several bombing missions over Germany. Murrow had at one time tried to recruit him to join the CBS London staff. After the war he served as United Press's (UP's) correspondent covering the Nuremberg war crimes trials and as bureau chief, first in Amsterdam and then in Moscow.

Cronkite accepted the CBS offer and was prepared to take off for Korea at short notice but he never went. His wife, Betsy Cronkite, was momentarily expecting the birth of a second child, and CBS found an alternative solution to the Korea problem. That left him with a CBS contract but without an assignment. An assignment appeared quickly. Cronkite started a ten-minute daily network radio news program. At this time CBS's Washington radio outlet was its wholly owned WTOP. Its television affiliate was station WOIC, owned by the Bamberger Broadcasting Corporation, a subsidiary of the Bamberger department stores. Eager to get into television, the *Washington Post* arranged to buy WOIC from Bamberger and traded 45 percent to CBS in return for a 55 percent interest in WTOP radio. It then renamed WOIC, WTOP-TV. The new majority owners contracted with CBS to deliver a full local news service: both radio and television.

One of the first objectives of the new ownership was to deliver a television news service. The *Washington Post* could hardly fail to broadcast at least one local television news program from its new facilities. In early autumn Cronkite became WTOP-TV's first news broadcaster.

Facilities and raw materials were in short supply. Cronkite set about producing a show his way. He hired a recent college graduate, Neal Strawser; arranged to have a still picture service supplemented by maps and charts delivered to his office; used what Telenews product was available; and proceeded, with Strawser's aid, to deliver what amounted to a military briefing every weeknight at eleven o'clock. Since the conflict in Korea dominated the day's events, Cronkite could afford to spend the bulk of his time on war news. Maps, charts, and stills selected by Cronkite and Strawser were installed on blackboards and easels. Walter confidently played the role of the briefing officer, moving about the room from chart to chart or map to map, ad libbing as he went, a process that seemed natural to him but was anathema to news directors and station managers, who trust only scripts. The Washington audience liked what they saw. If there were errors they were minimal and ratings soared. Cronkite became an overnight star.

My own role at this time was director of public affairs at network headquarters in New York, an assignment embracing discussion and talk shows, documentaries, education, religion, and sports, but no hard news. In this role even though I had no direct connection with news I traveled to Washington frequently and when there made it a point to watch the eleven o'clock news on WTOP. Since Cronkite and I had been friends before the war it was easy to renew our acquaintance and to see him from time to time both at the office and in a social setting. His easy competence on the air, the strength of his personality, and his ability to explain complex events simply and interestingly convinced me that when we needed a strong personality with finely honed news sense, widely varied experience, and a capacity to ad lib coupled with an intense desire for perfection, Cronkite would be a very likely candidate. That time would come, and relatively soon.

Murrow's trip to Korea, reported solely on radio, added a dimension to

CBS coverage that only a Murrow could provide. He reported with color and vigor from the frontlines, exposing himself to dangers that many correspondents would have avoided. But one of his radio reports never made it to the air. The refusal of the network to broadcast it opened a rift between him and Chairman Paley that would widen and probably contributed to his angry departure from CBS some ten years later.

In a cable sent to New York news headquarters, Murrow harshly criticized the American military leader. The editor on duty in the news room was concerned about what he regarded as a possible violation of CBS policy. He sent it on for checking by his superiors, Edmund Chester and Wells Church. They saw the piece as a clear policy violation and decided to consult corporate counsel, who ultimately referred it to President Stanton and Chairman Paley. All agreed that Murrow's strong position transgressed stated policy and recommended that the piece be killed. Murrow on his return to New York was clearly irritated but kept his resentment under control. Eventually all seemed to be forgiven.[6] Three years passed before the next confrontation, but the warm relationship between chairman and the star of the news staff had suffered its first rift and it is reasonable to assume that the chairman's memory was long and conflict could arise again.[7]

The Korean War and the shock waves that followed encouraged the television Public Affairs department to try its hand at more complicated programming than it had previously undertaken. It had produced interview, discussion, and debate programs on television but nothing more complex. The perilous state of international affairs and what appeared to be a genuine threat of war now seemed to call for a more aggressive approach, including some risk taking.

Korea, of course, was the source of the most immediate tension, but the Cold War was still raging, the Soviet Union was moving aggressively to subvert the political systems of Western Europe, and Soviet agents were active in undermining democratic governments the world over. No area seemed safe from turmoil. America's role in international affairs, fueled by the Korean War, was becoming more complex by the day. Television, it appeared to CBS executives, should be able to make some contribution to achieving a higher level of understanding.

Since the source of much of the turbulence lay in international relations, the State Department was asked to participate in an effort to clarify some of the murky issues. The department responded by making ten coming stars of the Department of State, all of whom had had significant experience in foreign posts, available for an eleven-week series, "Diplomatic Pouch." The program analyzed the many points of tension around the world and concluded with Secretary of State Dean Acheson's first television appearance. Production techniques were primitive but the program marked an effort to use television as a more varied and complex information tool than its regular news broadcasts. "Diplomatic Pouch" was a forerunner of many more sophisticated long-form television programs broadcast in subsequent years, including the acclaimed "See It Now" and "CBS Reports."

The recurrent fear that the Korean War might give the Soviet Union a provocation to launch a bomb attack on American cities motivated CBS to produce "Primer for Survival" in cooperation with the American Red Cross. The program was designed to inform American viewers how to behave in the event Russian bombs fell on American cities. It seems nearly a half century later to reflect extreme paranoia, but at the time the fear was quite real. One episode informed city dwellers how to deal with poison ivy if they were dislodged from the city and forced to wander in suburban and exurban areas where it grew abundantly.

By January 1, 1951, television had made giant strides toward self-sufficiency. The total receiver count had more than doubled during the year, from a little more than 3 million to in excess of 7 million.[8] More new households had been added in that twelve months than in all the previous years of television's existence. AT&T lines had extended south to Jacksonville, west to Omaha and Kansas City, and northwest to Minneapolis and St. Paul. CBS boasted in its 1950 *Annual Report*[9] that forty-six affiliated stations were now able to receive live programs and another fifteen were serviced with kinescopes, a film made by photographing the face of the picture tube while it was projecting a program. The picture delivered by kinescope was grainy and fuzzy, the sound mushy, but viewers at this stage were willing to accept the inferior signal without much complaint.

The CBS annual report, in boasting of the forty-six stations in its live affiliate lineup, did not reveal that many were in single-station markets. A competing network, usually NBC, frequently held the primary affiliation contract, thus giving that network first call on filling time periods. CBS or ABC could get access to the station only if it could demonstrate that its offering was clearly superior. A number of large and important markets were in this position, among them Buffalo, Pittsburgh, Indianapolis, Milwaukee, St. Louis, and Grand Rapids/Kalamazoo. Getting superior ratings was almost impossible if major American population centers were unavailable for network lineups. This lack of primary affiliates in major markets seriously penalized CBS in its efforts to build the Douglas Edwards news program to parity with John Cameron Swayze's program on NBC. The inability to guarantee acceptance in major markets would continue to hamper the network until the FCC freeze on licensing was lifted and additional licensees were able to complete construction of new facilities.

The Edwards news, meantime, was continuing to make progress. Even with its inferior station lineup it was moving steadily toward catching NBC and Swayze. In the 1950–51 season it had been 15 points behind NBC. In 1951–52 it had reduced the margin to 10 points and was closing the gap.[10]

In order to prepare itself for the competitive struggle ahead CBS began to rethink its structural organization. During the early experimental period television had been treated as an orphan with separate quarters and little contact with the company's main focuses, radio broadcasting and phonograph records. Effective January 1, 1950, it had been merged with radio in corporate organization charts creating what was, in effect, a broadcasting division. By early 1951 it had become clear that radio and television were not really complementary; they were competitive and could progress more effectively if left to fight their own battles independently. Plans were shortly under way to split the two into separate and competitive autonomous divisions, each with its own executive officers reporting to the corporate president and chairman. By mid-July the structural reorganization was announced. News and public affairs, which had been so laboriously sliced into separate units in January 1950 with each having responsibilities in both radio and television, were now to be shuffled again, this time to what appeared to be a more orderly arrangement. Radio public affairs would join radio news in a single department. Television news would be spliced together with television public affairs. A director of radio news and public affairs would report to a radio division vice president for programs and a television director of news and public affairs to a vice president for television programs.

Ed Chester was appointed to head the radio department and I was given command of the television side. Chester's assignment was clearly the more important, but the rate at which television was growing suggested that it wouldn't be many years before it would catch or even surpass the older medium. The reorganization was announced in mid-July and took effect immediately. With events throughout the world moving so rapidly there was no time for contemplation and long-range planning. Action was required immediately on a number of fronts.

4 •

Driving Television's Golden Spike

Almost from its earliest days television recognized that it would not be fully competitive with other national media until it spanned the continent. It needed access to the major population centers of the West Coast to create a truly national audience, and it needed to be able to tap the vast show business resources of the Los Angeles area if it ever hoped to build a full program service.

Its enthusiasm for spanning the continent and establishing a direct link between east and west was not a new phenomenon in American history. The urge to move the frontiers west had begun well before the Revolutionary War. Even before President Thomas Jefferson had completed the Louisiana Purchase in 1803 he had arranged to send Captains Meriwether Lewis and William Clark on an expedition to explore routes to the Pacific coast. Wagon trains, the famed Pony Express, and packet ships sailing around the tip of South America constituted the only means of contact between coasts until 1869. In that year the first transportation link tying east and west into a single geographic unit was sealed with the driving of the Golden Spike on Promontory Point extending into the Great Salt Lake in Utah. The joining of the Central Pacific and Union Pacific railroads made rail service between the coasts a reality.

Television desperately needed a comparable Golden Spike to continue its accelerating expansion and permit unimpeded program flow across the nation. News departments needed it to provide national service advertisers to reach the entire nation.

In midsummer 1951 television's growth was still rapid, but its westbound signals stopped abruptly at Omaha and Kansas City. There was still no television in Denver and only a few receivers in Salt Lake City. The real bonanza would materialize when the networks were able to mine the rich markets of San Francisco, Los Angeles, and San Diego. In midsummer 1951 there were approximately 1.4 million television homes in these three metropolitan areas, three and a half times as many as in the entire country when the political parties met in Philadelphia for their 1948 national conventions.

A new transcontinental link would not only open up new markets. Los Angeles would yield a treasure trove of producers, directors, writers, actors and actresses, musicians, sound stages, film laboratories, cutting rooms, and skilled technical personnel. Tapping this rich resource would change the whole process of program production. It would allow the merger of the vast show business resources of Hollywood with the television pioneers and theater veterans of New York. As a bonus it would enable the national government to communicate simultaneously to the entire nation with both sound and picture, not an insignificant step with the Korean War still in progress. When the first transcontinental television signal could flow unimpeded from coast to coast television would have its equivalent of the Golden Spike.

By midsummer 1951 the new facility was nearing the testing stage. It was the Department of State, though, not the television industry, that succeeded in convincing the telephone company to open the new facility before it would be fully ready for commercial use. The department had been working for months preparing for a peace conference at which all the fifty-one participants in the war against Japan would meet in San Francisco to sign a peace treaty officially ending the war some six years after Japan's surrender. Negotiations for the final draft were well enough along by midsummer that dates could be set for the largely ceremonial event. The dates selected were Tuesday, September 4 through Saturday, September 8.

A prestigious New York lawyer, John Foster Dulles, had been appointed by President Truman as his personal emissary to negotiate details. His assignment was to negotiate terms with each of the fifty-one nations that had been at war with Japan. The end result was to be a document formally ending the conflict, which would be debated, amended as required, and formally signed at a conference including all combatants. San Francisco's Opera House, where the United Nations had been born six years earlier, was chosen as the venue.

State Department leadership was eager to get as much exposure as it could for the ceremony. It was particularly interested in television coverage, but that would require completion of AT&T's monumental effort to build

located @ Omaha, Neb

microwave towers across the high plains and the Rocky Mountains. In *to complete the continental link* midsummer the work was close enough to completion that formal opening of the service had been scheduled for approximately October 1, four weeks too late for the event, but company officials were wary about putting it into use without adequate testing. State, however, made a persuasive case for opening the facility on a temporary basis and company officials finally yielded. After adjournment it would be shut down until the start of commercial service approximately a month later.

State Department officials jubilantly informed the networks of their coup. Within hours the chief news executives of the four television networks met to begin planning. ABC was represented by News Director Thomas Velotta, DuMont by Special Events Director Tom Gallery, and NBC by Director of News and Public Affairs Davidson Taylor; I, as Director of News and Public Affairs, represented CBS Television. The decision to proceed with coverage of the entire conference was unanimous and fully supported by senior management.

Since there would be sufficient bandwidth for only one television channel the networks would have to pool their coverage. The pool would assume responsibility for organizing facilities and producing the broadcast. It was the committee's function to decide which network would be assigned the responsibility for producing the pool signal. Drawing straws seemed the fairest method for making the choice.

Gallery of DuMont drew the short straw but quickly admitted that his network lacked the resources and personnel to undertake a project of this magnitude. He recommended that since DuMont and CBS shared affiliation in San Francisco with station KPIX and since the support of a local affiliate was essential CBS be assigned the responsibility. There was no dissension so as the meeting broke up I had assumed responsibility for producing television's first megaevent, which would make television, still in its infancy, a truly national institution.

Since this would be a CBS production, it was my responsibility to choose the person to serve as what would later come to be called "anchorman." I had no doubts whom I would choose. Several months earlier I had earmarked Walter Cronkite for just such an assignment. He did not have a national reputation; in fact, he had never been seen on the screen outside Washington, but he had a quality that seemed to be ideally suited for the assignment. He was warm and friendly and had the unusual knack of being able to communicate with his viewers. Above all he was knowledgeable, articulate, a skilled ad libber, and, I was sure, would fully prepare himself for the assignment. Freeing him up from his Washington assignment, however, was not likely to be easy. The general manager of station WTOP-TV was reluctant to release his newly discovered star from the 11:00 P.M. news assignment. It took some persuasion but he finally relented. Cronkite immediately began familiarizing himself with the issues and the personnel on

Cronkite to anchor the peace conference in S.F.

whom he would be reporting. Even learning the proper pronunciation of the names of some of the newly independent countries and training himself to recognize their flags demanded study.

Those of us concerned with television production assumed that the conference would turn out to be a largely ceremonial event with plentiful doses of pageantry and color but little startling news. That assumption was given a severe jolt during the week prior to departure for San Francisco. As a result of his primary role in planning the peace conference Dulles was invited to be a guest on the CBS radio interview program "Capitol Cloakroom." When he accepted I decided that being present at the broadcast in Washington might furnish an opportunity to discuss arrangements with him.

The strategy worked. After the half hour question and answer program Dulles consented to spend a few minutes with Ted Koop, the manager of CBS's Washington news and public affairs operations, and me. It turned out to be a surprisingly candid conversation. If we had assumed that we were going to San Francisco to cover a cut and dried ceremonial event, Dulles informed us, we were dead wrong. There might be more excitement than anyone expected; it was possible, he told us, that during the opening minutes of the conference, the Soviet Union's chief of delegation, Andrei Gromyko, might force his way to the rostrum and demand adjournment. There was even some risk, Dulles added, that Gromyko's intervention would be the signal for the Soviets to launch a bomb attack on Japan. He spelled out the scenario in such stark terms that both Koop and I were stunned. It seemed totally unthinkable that only six years after a long and bloody war had been brought to an uneasy conclusion we would find ourselves in another one, one much larger than the Korean conflict that was now in its fifteenth month. We were so fully occupied with the Korean War, he suggested, that we would have little strength to fend off an attack. The British and French would be of little help; they were still so devastated by the war that they had neither the strength nor the will to contribute. Furthermore the Soviets, he said, would rather destroy Japan than permit it to be absorbed into the Western camp.

The scenario did not seem very plausible but Dulles was surely better qualified to speculate on world events than we were. His predictions could not be entirely discounted even though they sounded farfetched. They would surely add suspense to the opening ceremony. 1951

The program, as planned by the State Department, specified that the conference be opened on Tuesday, September 4 at 10:30 P.M. Eastern Daylight Time (7:30 P.M. in San Francisco). When the director of the television program gave the signal to throw the switch opening television's historic first transcontinental broadcast the Marine Band would be playing. As soon as the music stopped and after a moment of silent prayer, the San Francisco mayor, Elmer Robinson, would welcome delegates on behalf of the host

Japanese Peace Conference

city, then Secretary of State Dean Acheson, the conference chairman, would introduce President Harry Truman. The most likely point at which Gromyko might demand the floor and throw the whole conference into disarray would be immediately after Mayor Robinson's greeting and before Secretary Acheson's introduction of the president. That would be the moment of greatest suspense.

There was also a characteristic behavior pattern of Soviets at international conferences that called for careful planning. Soviet delegations had frequently demonstrated that whenever they were displeased by proceedings they would simply get up and walk out. If such a walkout were to take place we felt it imperative that we be prepared to cover it every step of the way.

The KPIX staff proved to be flexible, cooperative, and enthusiastic. It was decided that seven cameras would be used to cover the event, five within the Opera House, one in the lobby, and one on the sidewalk outside. The five inside the hall were positioned to cover what we considered all reasonable contingencies. Two were installed in boxes on the mezzanine at the rear directly facing the stage. Two more were on the left mezzanine in a box a little forward of a point midway from the rostrum to the rear mezzanine. The fifth camera was stationed in a box in the right mezzanine a little to the rear of a midway point between the stage and the back wall. One of the two in the center rear box could maintain a tight shot on the rostrum and whatever speaker might be there. The other could use a wide-angle lens to keep the entire stage area in focus. The two on the left were positioned to cover much of the floor area including the Russian delegation, which was seated on the right side of the hall about midway from stage to rear. One would maintain a close-up of Gromyko and the other a wider angle on the right side of the hall. The camera operator could narrow his focus if required, limiting it largely to the Soviet delegation. The lone camera on the right side had the entire left side of the hall within range plus the double door at the rear through which most of the delegates would arrive or leave. With this positioning we assumed that we had enough flexibility to keep cameras focused on nearly any movement on the stage or in the delegate section on the main floor.

The two additional cameras not stationed within the auditorium were positioned to observe any movement in the lobby or on the street outside, one in the lobby, the other on the sidewalk. Both were on tripods and both had enough cable to move freely. The camera in the street could cover both the main entrance and a limousine entrance around a corner at the side of the auditorium. The tripods, however, suffered from one basic weakness. The cameras were in a fixed position at about shoulder height and could not be raised or lowered. In a crowded area we could expect to see only a sea of heads and shoulders.

The preparations seemed thorough enough to assure coverage of any unusual activity by the Soviet delegation. We could also show viewers virtually any action on the stage or on the floor. A rehearsal prior to each session was designed to cause each cameraman to snap to attention in response to the cue "He's taking a walk."

Preparing for the seemingly unlikely eventuality that Gromyko might seek to disrupt the conference during its opening minutes posed problems over which we had little control. The best that could be done was to work with the State Department to ensure that the Marine Band would play its loudest and that the mayor of San Francisco would keep his remarks brief. Secretary Acheson, we assumed, would be at the podium ready to introduce the president the moment the mayor was finished. A camera would stay focused on Gromyko in the event he moved toward the stage to disrupt proceedings. There was no way of knowing how many persons on the stage or in the audience were aware of the potential disruption, but tension in the broadcast control room ran high. There was the possibility of witnessing more history in the making than the calm in the Opera House reflected.

The rehearsal before the opening ran smoothly. Each camera responded promptly to the cue "He's taking a walk." The camera designated to remain focused on Gromyko was ready to follow whether he headed for the stage to demand the floor or for the rear exit.

Promptly at 7:30 P.M. the technician in charge opened the switch. The picture of the interior of the San Francisco Opera House was live on television screens from Boston to Jacksonville on the East Coast and as far south as San Diego on the Pacific coast. Viewers could see a panoramic view of the interior of the Opera House including the stage. The Marine Band was in the orchestra pit playing a loud march. There was a brief moment of silent prayer. The moment it was finished the mayor of San Francisco moved to the rostrum and began his welcome to the delegates. He followed his instructions and spoke for less than a minute. In the control room we anxiously watched the monitor focused on the Soviet delegation. There was no sign of movement. When the mayor finished Secretary Acheson was at his side to begin the customary introduction, "The President of the United States." There was still no motion in the Soviet delegation. The president began to speak and the control room relaxed. Dulles's fears had proved groundless. There was no disruption and apparently there were no Soviet bombers over Tokyo.

The suspense was apparently not confined exclusively to the control room. The *New York Times* that morning had called attention in a front page story to the fact that "the opening of the peace conference . . . will be one of the most precisely planned operations in history." It added, that "Everything will be timed out to a split second," and it "might even be necessary to short change the opening minute of silent prayer by a few seconds." The *Times* story explained that part of the "exactitude" was due to technical problems and "part to a lurking apprehension that the Russians

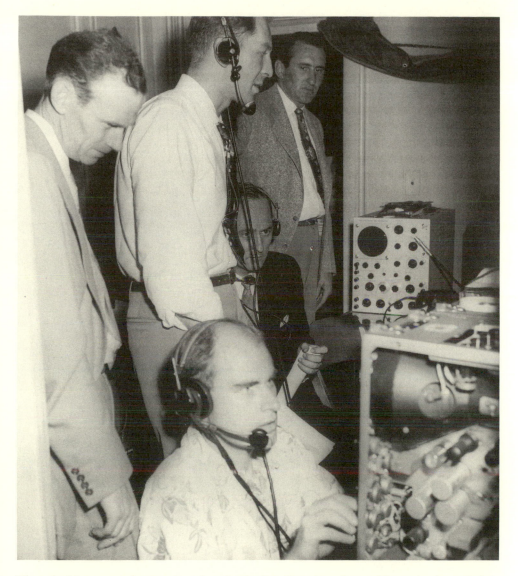

The television control room in a box in the San Francisco Opera House as the switch is opened to send the first television signal to cross the continent on September 4, 1951. Photo courtesy of Sig Mickelson. Used by permission.

may try to grab the floor from the Mayor of San Francisco."[1] Leonard Mosley, in his biography of the Dulles family, makes an even more direct reference to possible Soviet sabotage of the conference: "A last attempt was made by the Russians to wreck it," he wrote, "but it was overcome by the skillful maneuvering of Dean Acheson."[2]

When President Truman finished his address the conference recessed until the next morning. The first potential crisis had passed without any evidence of Soviet intentions to disrupt the proceedings. But there were four days to go.

The *New York Times* the next morning headlined the president's address on page 1. Directly under the five-column, three-line headline was a three-column picture of President Truman as he was photographed off the face of a television screen in the *Times* newsroom. The cutline read, "Mr. Truman is seen here while addressing the opening session of the Japanese Peace Conference in San Francisco last night." Immediately below the photograph was a critical review of the coverage of the opening session written by Jack Gould, the newspaper's television critic. Gould noted, "Television spanned the United States for the first time at 10:30 last night when viewers from Boston to Atlanta simultaneously watched President Truman as he made the principal speech at the Japanese Peace Treaty conference in San Francisco." The *Times* critic also noted, apparently with some surprise, "The images reproduced in the New York area, nearly 2,000 [*sic*] miles away from the scene, had excellent clarity and compared favorably with programs of local origin."[3]

The second day, Wednesday, passed uneventfully. The camera assigned to keep an eye on the Soviet delegation kept Gromyko in tight focus but the delegation's chairman made no move toward the center aisle. The third day, Thursday, also started uneventfully. The delegation had been surprisingly quiescent. Gromyko had spoken a number of times, arguing in favor of several amendments, but these were orderly interventions with no evidence of acrimony. Otherwise he sat impassively. Suddenly, when it was least expected, the operator on camera three barked, "He's taking a walk." Every cameraman snapped to attention. Camera one at the rear focused tightly on Chairman Acheson. Camera two widened his picture to encompass the whole stage. Camera three on the left side of the auditorium held a close-up of Gromyko as he moved through the row toward the center aisle. Camera four alongside three maintained a wider shot on the whole Soviet delegation. Camera five in the mezzanine above the Soviet delegation maintained a wide shot of the portion of the auditorium it could see, then panned slowly to the rear door, toward which Gromyko was walking. Camera six in the lobby moved toward the double door, through which the leader of the Soviet delegation would exit the hall. Camera seven, in the street outside, saw two limousines wheel into the drive on the right side and move toward the limousine entrance. The operator pushed his tripod toward the corner of the building to keep them in camera range. It looked ominously like a walkout. The program director switched from camera to camera to keep an eye on developments from several perspectives, including the arrival of the two limousines.

At this point our failure to have the camera in the lobby on an elevated stand disrupted our plans. The lobby suddenly filled with curious onlookers. All the camera could see was a mass of heads milling about in no particular pattern. Inside the auditorium, the conference, oblivious to the commotion outside, proceeded as if nothing had happened. In approximately five minutes camera five caught the Soviet chairman returning through the rear door and camera three followed him back to his seat.

What happened remains a mystery. The *New York Times* headlined the episode on page 1. It reported that the Soviet head of delegation "gave the diplomatic walk out a new twist today. He staged one with reverse English." The story related that a Czech woman delegate had followed him to the lobby with a bulging briefcase in hand. She apparently expected some kind of conference. Rather than confer with her, the *Times* reported, Gromyko gave what appeared to be a quick brush-off.[4] When he returned to his seat there was no evidence of any change in strategy. He sat as stony faced as he had before.

There was one more day of discussion of fine points of the treaty. On the final day, Saturday, September 8, the heads of all of the fifty-one delegations filed onto the stage to sign the final document in a ceremony made to order for television. Flags of all the nations, many of them unfamiliar to viewers, decorated the stage. By midafternoon, the ceremony was finished, the documents had been signed, the stage was clearing, and the war that ended six years earlier was formally an item for history books. Cameras were turned off, lights were turned down, and the microwave relay to Omaha and the East Coast shut down for a period of refining and testing until the anticipated reopening on October 1.

Broadcasting magazine reported in its issue of September 10, 1951, that 94 of the nation's 107 television stations had carried the broadcasts and that the programs were available to approximately 40 million viewers.[5] It was a major milestone in television's already meteoric growth, the successful culmination of the driving of its Golden Spike. Millions of citizens, from coast to coast, had watched live an international conference with all the ceremony, panoply, flags, and rigid formality characteristic of the conduct of foreign affairs. Some had previously watched the Hiss-Chambers hearings, the Kefauver hearings featuring Frank Costello and his nervous hands, the Kathy Fiscus tragedy, and Security Council sessions, but television transmission facilities carried them only to portions of the nation. But now television set owners from coast to coast had simultaneously watched an international event that they could only have read about or listened to on radio in previous years. It was as if they could have been present at Compiegne, Versailles, or Vienna or Utrecht deeper in the historical past.

Television had broken a new trail across the continental divide and had become national. And in Walter Cronkite viewers had discovered a new personality, with whom they would become much more familiar in years to come.

5 •

A New Species of Documentary: The Birth of "See It Now"

Anything other than regular news broadcasts and live coverage of significant public events including sports was beyond the reach of early television news personnel. They simply did not have the manpower or facilities to undertake documentary programs or those requiring superior camera and editing equipment. Nor was there financial support. The exception was regular news, but even there financial support was meager, sufficient to maintain a competitive position, but hardly lavish.

It was assumed that television would eventually produce some kind of long-form news-related programming at least remotely related to film and radio documentaries. But as 1950 opened that day seemed remote. There were too many obstacles, among them the lack of ideas and the range of personnel to execute them.

CBS among the networks had compiled the most conspicuous record for programming radio documentaries. On the evening of VE Day the network had broadcast Norman Corwin's widely acclaimed "On a Note of Triumph." A year later CBS, with a flurry of publicity that blanketed the nation, scheduled the first of a series of socially oriented, hard-hitting documentaries that commanded widespread attention. A sixty-minute program, "The Eagle's Brood," dealing with the widespread concern with juvenile delinquency, was backed by an intense nationwide promotional campaign. The campaign utilized the well-honed skills of the highly regarded CBS Promotion and Advertising department. The program's producer, Robert Louis Shayon, gained national recognition and CBS earned a reputation for the best in documentary broadcasting. Television was given an auspicious model to follow when it was ready.

None of the publicity fallout accrued to television, which was just gearing up for a restart after the war and was simply not ready to try anything similar. It did not have the personnel, the equipment, the financial resources, or the large enough potential audience base. As television entered the 1950s, CBS maintained its radio documentary unit, but the unit's efforts to develop a theme for a radio documentary that could win plans board support were futile. It was evident that CBS management felt it had squeezed the radio documentary for all the value it could get and was not interested in scheduling additional programs simply to keep the unit busy. Charges that former contributors to the unit had "been soft on communism" or contributors to "liberal causes" may also have made corporate management squeamish. Eventually television would be a likely outlet, but in early 1950 documentaries were a costly luxury television could not afford.

As the executive to whom the documentary unit reported I was concerned that progress seemed to be stalemated, but I also had some serious reservations about the technique used in producing "The Eagle's Brood" and its successors. The theme of each program was developed through a fictionalized treatment, with key roles played by professional actors and actresses. There was a reason for using this device in 1946 when audiotape was still in a primitive stage, but in the intervening years field recorders had been reduced in size and become portable, sound quality had improved, and editing had been simplified and made more precise. Furthermore, it seemed obvious that recorded reality would register more impact than fiction.

One day in mid-July 1950 Frank Stanton called to inquire whether I could meet with him and Mr. Paley. The topic was documentaries. The concern was with radio, not with television. They were interested in probing my ideas regarding directions we might take to revive documentary production. I explained my reservations regarding the fictionalized approach and argued for substituting taped actuality for reconstruction of events. They asked me to develop some proposals and prepare to meet again in a few days. Following up on their request I submitted a memo outlining three possible topics. It was apparent as the meeting began that they had read the proposals and agreed that we should proceed as I had recommended.

At that point they raised a question I was not prepared for: Who would produce the programs? I quickly answered that there was a young producer at NBC who had just completed a taped series on nuclear energy in which he parlayed the erudite science editor of the *New York Times*, William L. Laurence, with the comedian Bob Hope as twin narrators. The series had elicited rave reviews from media critics. Friendly had also, I pointed out, worked with Ed Murrow on the record album *I Can Hear It Now*. With no hesitation, Paley said, "Go get him." I returned to my office; placed a call for Friendly, whom I had never met; and arranged to dine with him the next night at the Chinese Rathskeller on West Fifty-second Street. Murrow at this time was in Korea.

Friendly's response to coming to CBS on a contract basis was favorable, even enthusiastic. He was quite willing to work on radio documentaries. His long-range goal, however, he said, was to produce a "*Life* Magazine of the Air." That, I explained, was a bit premature. We still lacked the audience base, the financial resources, and the technology to undertake anything as costly and complicated as a filmed newsmagazine. We would certainly encourage him, though, to think along those lines and prepare to move when the time was right. We sealed our agreement with a drink at the old Ritz Hotel bar within less than an hour of the time it was closed forever. Demolition crews would be there in the morning.

By late September negotiations had been completed and contracts signed. Almost immediately Friendly began to assemble staff to begin production of a one-hour weekly radio news program featuring Murrow. It was not to be a documentary but rather a long-form treatment of the news. Scheduled for late fall, it would be called "Hear It Now." Although it was not exactly what I had proposed to Paley and Stanton it promised to bring some excitement to the radio network and perhaps eventually lead to a breakthrough in television.

Friendly worked intensively on the radio program through a six-month run, December through May, and continued to plan mentally for a "*Life* Magazine of the Air." He had begun to steep himself in film techniques. He spent hours at the Museum of Modern Art studying documentaries in the museum's film archive. He familiarized himself with each of the old-line newsreels and sought out experienced film documentarians to study their attitudes and techniques. He analyzed the operating methods of the newsreels and acquainted himself with their personnel. And he thoroughly checked out the technical equipment they were using.

By the end of the run of "Hear It Now" he was ready to move full bore into preparations for the fall start of a half hour television program that would bear some similarity to the radio series he had just completed. Full management support enabled him to proceed to employ personnel and contract for services. It was assumed from the start that Ed Murrow would be a part of the package as he had in "Hear It Now."

The project Friendly had in mind had no counterpart in film, radio, or print. If he started by thinking in terms of a *Life* magazine of the air, he soon found that route static compared to what he might be able to accomplish if he could discover a process for harnessing the full potential of television. Dealing with both sound and motion would give him new dimensions and new opportunities that were not available to the static photographs of *Life*. He began thinking of a new art form that would borrow from print, sound broadcasting, film, and live television blended in a way that was unprecedented. Film documentaries normally took weeks or months to produce; Friendly's intention was to produce one program each week. Such an ambitious schedule would impose unprecedented pressures on whatever staff he might build. Newsreels were able to maintain a weekly schedule, but their total running time was limited to ten minutes and there was relatively little synchronous sound except excerpts from speeches. Friendly planned something much more ambitious. Running time would be a half hour. In a sense it would be more closely related to radio than to film. Exploiting the inherent flexibility of television, he hoped, might enable him to produce a program of substance that did not need months of preparation.

What Friendly had in mind was not a documentary in the sense that "The River" and "The Plow That Broke the Plains," the two Depression-era classics produced by the WPA film project, were documentaries. He envisioned a project that was more closely related to a newsmagazine in content and a radio news roundup in form, enhanced by motion picture film.

One of the factors inhibiting freedom to produce a high-quality product at CBS was the network's exclusive contract with the International Brotherhood of Electrical Engineers (IBEW) for both live and recorded programming. IBEW personnel were experienced in operating the electronic equipment associated with broadcasting but few had any acquaintance with film. And what limited film equipment the television network owned at this stage was designed for 16-mm production. Friendly was convinced that the program he wanted to produce would have to be done in 35 mm because of its vastly superior quality. The upshot was that the program that he envisioned could not be done "in house."

The only alternative was contracting with an outside organization. There would be no shortage of companies interested in bidding on the project but most would want to deliver a finished product, not turn over facilities and personnel to the buyer. Friendly wanted full control. It was his intention to use a subcontractor's personnel and equipment under his direction. He intended to be the producer in fact as well as name. Fortunately for him, the newsreels were beginning to feel the pinch of television; the Hearst Metrotone News/MGM News of the Day combination was ready to start cutting back. It was willing to turn over, on a contract basis, camera teams, photographic equipment, and full production facilities. Its employees would, for a fee, be available to serve exclusively under the direction of Friendly and Murrow, thus bypassing the CBS contract with IBEW and eliminating the necessity of a major investment in equipment. Camera teams for the project would be included in the contract, but the project would still need reporters and a European cameraman/producer.

Friendly discovered that a very able young Pathé film reporter based in Paris was temporarily in New York and might be willing to switch to his team. After one meeting with Friendly and Murrow, Bill McClure signed on and went immediately to Pathé to submit his resignation. An able free-lancer, Palmer Williams, showed up looking for an assignment and quickly became Friendly's operations manager and general executive.[1] Long after Friendly had left CBS and Don Hewitt had begun producing "60 Minutes" Palmer Williams was still on the CBS payroll and serving as Hewitt's second in command and senior producer. The remainder of the staff quickly fell into place, including two superior reporters, Joe Wershba and Eddie Scott. Both were graduates of "CBS Views the Press," a highly regarded press critique program that had run on WCBS in New York. A full team was quickly rounded out, cutting rooms and projection facilities leased, and Don Hewitt selected as director. After some prolonged discussions "See It Now" was selected as the program's title.

Friendly then introduced two innovations that deviated dramatically from normal newsreel practice. He wanted the high quality that he could get from separate sound and picture tracks but would not have time for the tedious process involved in matching the tracks and fusing them into a single film. By checking with engineer friends he discovered that it might be possible, by gambling with an untried process, to eliminate the time consumed by fusing the two tracks. He found that with luck he could project them separately and synchronize them as they were going on the air rather than matching them in the cutting room before show time.

The second innovation was equally radical. He wondered why, since he was producing a film program, he had to use a studio. Why not put Murrow in the control room along with the director and the full control room crew? Cameras could be positioned in the rather cramped space to focus on the narrator with the program showing on the monitor behind him. Fitting Murrow and the cameras into the control room was a tight squeeze but worth trying both for novelty value and saving of time. A three-minute test was run and the offbeat approach was successful. Again television had broken ground and created new processes.

One critical element remained to be solved. The program would be costly and revenues in the autumn of 1951 were still minimal. Fortune smiled on them again: The Aluminum Company of America (Alcoa) had been having trouble with the federal government. Its reputation had been damaged by an antitrust suit and it needed some bold stroke to win public goodwill. It may not have anticipated just how controversial "See It Now" would become, but for the time it was willing to concentrate on the commercials and leave program content to the production staff. It signed on as sponsor.

Friendly now had his staff, his 35-mm production unit, his system for synchronizing sound and picture on air, and his novel control room setting for Murrow's narration. The Alcoa order gave him a sponsor but he still had a surprise left for the opening program. At 3:30 P.M. Sunday, November 18, 1951, viewers were shown something that would have been unthinkable as recently as the beginning of September. "See It Now" used a split screen to show simultaneously live pictures of both the Pacific and Atlantic oceans. It was not a difficult feat with the technology that had recently become available but it took someone with the imagination of Fred Friendly to use it so skillfully to attract public attention. It was the feature that caught the headlines and started people talking.

"See It Now" was a hit from the first program. Critics hailed it as a demonstration of what television could do when it used imagination and editorial judgment. It was the first successful effort of television to produce a long-form news-related program that was pure television, not a feeble copy of techniques used in either radio or newsreels, though it borrowed from both.

The Business Affairs department at CBS Television, though, was somewhat less enthusiastic than the critics. The program consistently ran over budget, not marginally but grossly. Budget control personnel came to me as the executive under whose jurisdiction the program fell, insisting that I take whatever steps were required to get the costs under control. A meeting of the principals seemed to offer the most effective process for bringing the controversy out into the open and searching for a solution. Accordingly I distributed a memo to Murrow and Friendly and to the appropriate representatives of the Business Affairs office asking that we meet as soon as possible to discuss the matter.

For several days I heard nothing from Murrow or Friendly. Then after approximately a week had elapsed a senior executive of the television network told me that Murrow had taken my memo to the chairman of the board. He told the chairman, according to my informant, that he was not going to be badgered by money counters. He and Friendly would take care of the production of the program and the financial affairs people should stay out of the way.

This was mid-February. The primary election campaign was heating up in New Hampshire. Preparations for the political conventions in July were commanding my full attention. And the fledgling news department was still sorely understaffed and needed time and attention. I decided that Murrow and Friendly were quite competent to manage "See It Now" without my participation. I could use my time more effectively if I concentrated on the areas that desperately needed attention. From that point on CBS possessed, in effect, three news departments: one for radio, one for television, and "See It Now." Friendly and I talked frequently. He and Murrow generally kept me informed of their plans but I made no effort to exercise any authority over them; nor would I have been likely to succeed had I tried.

The program quickly picked up momentum. It was moved from its Sunday afternoon position to Tuesday night at 10:30 and Alcoa stayed with it even though it became more controversial almost by the week. With its success television news had carved out a beachhead in production of long-form news-related programming. It had from its beginnings struggled with the complex problems of delivering a regular news service and was making notable progress. It had also dispatched its electronic cameras and mobile units outside the studio to permit viewers to participate vicariously in congressional hearings, political conventions, and major sports events. Now it had added a third string to its bow, extended news with a documentary twist. And it had done so with astonishing success.

6 ·

Breaking New Ground

While "See It Now" was developing a new documentary form and launching it to applause by the critics, the Television News department was moving ahead vigorously on its own. It had had broken free of radio in midsummer 1951, but it still had only limited resources. Most of its personnel, including on the air performers, were still carried on the CBS Radio payroll. Administratively, however, it was now free of radio control and reported to the television Network Program department. In a sense it was back in the same independent position it had occupied in the late 1940s, but it was now part of an aggressive television network, not a lightly regarded experimental unit.

For the first eighteen months of the 1950s TV news had been almost an orphan. The network's acclaimed Radio News department got the major share of both attention and resources. Television was regarded as a secondary nuisance, hardly a primary service.

It was not much larger as it began operating under the aegis of a full-fledged television division in July 1951, but it attracted more attention from senior management and with it more flexibility to experiment with new techniques and methods. Resources were still limited but there were signs that as the television network grew and began to deliver a profit, support for news would increase. At the very least it would be in an improved position to gamble with techniques exclusive to television.

One early goal of the news unit was to become fully independent of radio news leadership. It was also determined to end its dependence on an outside film supplier for most of its pictorial coverage. Its leaders were convinced that television could win respect only if it created a distinctive product and that the conventional newsreel was not the answer.

The only competition for video news came from the newsreels. Technically they had done very well. They were using high-quality 35-mm cameras with faithful sound recording units. Their camera personnel and film editors were professionals whose standards were high, but newsreel management had never had much freedom to furnish a complete news package.

The newsreel's role in the motion picture theater was to furnish an overture to a feature film, not to function as stand-alone purveyor of news. In that sense it was more closely related to show business than to journalism. Its function as an add-on to a feature film had to prevail over journalistic judgment in making assignments and editing the reel. The reporting, too, was lacking in enterprise. It was common practice to set up cameras and sound recorders where news was expected to take place and invite persons in the headlines to come to them or to join pools for presidential speeches or press conferences. Coverage based on enterprise was limited. No one ever confused a newsreel with the front page of the *New York Times*. The reels did very well on fires, tornadoes, floods, and other natural disasters, particularly when they had ample warning, but their prime function was to furnish material for a weekly ten-minute release, not for the fifteen or thirty minutes each day required by television schedules. In short, the newsreel was a news-related feature that added substance to the bill in a motion picture theater, not an independent news medium.

That was not enough for television. Don Hewitt and the staff of the CBS evening news were determined to deliver a full daily news report, not with the detail of the *New York Times* but with at least a smattering of most significant stories, even those that offered few obvious picture possibilities. Visuals, both motion and still, would be used to attract viewers but more than that to add meaning and to aid in understanding. In that sense television news was more closely related to radio than to newsreels. Its goal was to give viewers as much coverage of important news as could be crammed into the fifteen-minute format. Film would be used, not as an end in itself, but rather as a device for illustrating and illuminating stories in the news and making them more comprehensible. The use of film would enable television to tell stories in a new way. Fewer words would be required if pictures were used judiciously to illustrate stories. The objective was to go to the locale where news was being made or to the people who were making it and photograph them on the spot with sound, recording as much substance as possible and supplementing it with narration in the studio. The television news pioneers in the late 1940s had struggled with the same set of objectives but were restricted by a lack of resources. Resources, though not plentiful in midsummer 1951, were improving. The network was stronger economically and playing to an audience three or four times as large as that only eighteen months earlier. Advertising support was growing rapidly.

The staff charged with creating a news product in this rapidly changing environment was not greatly enlarged. One notable change was the addition of a recent Columbia University graduate who had worked in the CBS newsroom during his final year in college. Phil Scheffler began to go out with camera crews from the limited CBS news staff to cover important stories in the New York metropolitan area. Not satisfied to be a "contact" man, he was determined to be a reporter. And television, competing with newspapers and radio, needed stories to be reported, not just filmed. Scheffler added the reporting component to the film function and with it gave new depth to the news report.

Innovation and *imagination* were watchwords in the newsroom. During the 1952 nationwide steel strike President Truman seized the nation's steel plants to ensure that they would keep turning out raw material for military hardware needed to prosecute the Korean War. During a tense period of negotiations the president of the Steel Workers Union, Philip Murray, called a press conference in his headquarters hotel, the Commodore, in midtown Manhattan. Following normal procedure, the newsreels would set up their cameras and sound recording equipment in a room in the hotel, then wait for the union president to appear.

Hewitt and Scheffler were not satisfied with this passive approach. They wanted more than a run of the mill press conference. Their goal was a personalized news story that would feature Murray's statement but would not be duplicated by every other news service. In order to deliver the coverage they wanted they had to improvise on equipment. Their 16-mm units were more portable than the 35-mm cameras used by the newsreels but were still heavy and awkward to move and required a nearby power source. Their objective was to be able to move freely with a complete sound-on-film unit and a power source.

One possible alternative to the power requirement was to use a large high-capacity automobile battery, but such batteries are not light and portable. The problem was solved by transporting the battery on a two-wheeled luggage cart. Another cart was borrowed to transport the sound recording hardware. The cameraman would carry his own camera. With the equipment problem solved a four-man crew; cameraman, sound man, reporter contact, and porter; set out for the Commodore. They did not, however, go directly to the room selected for the press conference. They went instead to the union president's suite. Their plan was to interview Murray before he went to the formal press conference. Their ingenuity paid off. They got their interview, a much less formal one than they would have had at the press conference, and with much more newsworthy information.

When Murray terminated the interview to meet his schedule at the press conference the four-person caravan with both camera and recording equipment still running followed him down the corridor and into the elevator. At the door to the suite where the newsreels waited they broke off and headed back to the newsroom. Their audacity, a little ingenuity mixed with imagination, and a willingness to experiment provided a real television story and set a pattern for similar innovations to follow. As Scheffler puts it, "We took the camera to the story rather than wait for the story to come to the camera."[1]

The still limited news staff gradually began to take on some form and shape. It still was not adding much personnel but it was starting better to define duties. Hewitt as director also became the de facto producer. Of the three writers on the staff Chet Burger, who had been hired as a "visualizer" five years earlier, assumed the role of assignment editor. The writer David Zellmer was assigned to be editor and Alice Weel remained a writer. The staff now boasted three graphic artists, four directors, four combination cameramen-film editors, and a number of program assistants. Scheffler, no longer a copyboy, was now designated reporter-contact. The addition of the word *reporter* was recognition that television needed something that newsreels did not have—reporting.

The emphasis on reporting, however, demanded sophistication in film editing, something the primitive editing tools were unable to provide. The semiprofessional sound readers the film editors were using were adequate for the simplest sound takes but were totally inadequate for anything more complex. The editors could get satisfactory results on speeches, interviews, scenes with natural sound, or straight stand-up reports from correspondents but on nothing more complicated. In order to use a reporter's talents fully, something more complex was required. It would be essential to intercut between the reporter's own commentary, and interviews, background scenes of the location where the story took place, and such other scenes as might be pertinent. Building such a complicated story would be no problem with the more sophisticated editing equipment used by newsreels and documentarians and with the elimination of time constraints but out of the question with the simple sound reader.

Hewitt devised an answer, a two-projector system that used two cameras in the field and two telecine projectors in the control room. After thoroughly researching his story the reporter or correspondent would prepare a script flexible enough to allow for intercutting with scenes reflecting details essential to illuminating the story. The script would be recorded as a "talking head" on the first camera, the supplementary scenes on camera number two. The two tracks, once fully edited, would be racked up on separate projectors in the control room. Hewitt would then be able to intercut at will between the two tracks. It was a simple system that took advantage of the flexibility of television to accomplish results that would have required much more sophisticated equipment and many more hours of labor using traditional methods. The system would be particularly useful once the foreign correspondents were fully integrated into television news.

Logistics continued to plague the small staff. The only CBS studio with telecine projection equipment adequate to support a news program was at Liederkranz Hall, a former German turnverein, distinguished principally by its having the longest oak bar in New York. CBS had leased it to house a production facility. Both the studio and the telecine installation were quite adequate for the news program but there was a problem, a major one. Liederkranz Hall was on Fifty-eighth Street between Park and Lexington avenues, six blocks north and a long block and a half east of the newsroom in the CBS building at Fifty-second Street and Madison Avenue, where the news was edited and assembled. The news staff had to write script, edit film, prepare graphs and charts, and complete preparations in the newsroom; then compete with thousands of home-bound office workers for a taxi for the last-minute dash to the studio. It was troublesome enough in good weather but in rain or snow cabs were scarce and time was short. There were times when the staff had to make the run on foot, dodging raindrops or snowflakes en route.

Even though facilities were primitive and no one had yet written a textbook on how to produce television news, the young and relatively inexperienced staff tackled new problems on a daily basis with vitality, exuberance, and daring. As Scheffler explains it, "There were no guide posts, no experience to relate to. We made it up as we went along. We never once sat down to talk about what we were doing. I don't think that Don and I ever took time to consider a plan on a calculated basis. We tried stunts that had never been tried before because we didn't know what could not be done."[2]

It was relatively easy, for example, to cover the Korean War in a conventional way. Telenews and special correspondents were able to send back film from frontline areas. Even though it arrived as late as four or five days after the action it described, it gave viewers pictorial evidence of the nature of the war. The news staff, though, wanted to bring it a little closer to home. Producers and editors developed a plan to follow a new army recruit through basic training from his first bewildering days to graduation thirteen weeks later. Scheffler was sent to Fort Dix, New Jersey, about an hour's train ride from New York, to produce the story. Every Monday for thirteen weeks he and a camera team went to the fort to chronicle the experiences of the private they had selected. And every Monday night at 7:30 the progress of the soldier as he advanced through basic training was chronicled on "Douglas Edwards News." Viewed from the perspective of five decades later, the venture doesn't seem either novel or daring, but in 1951 it was precedent-shattering.

There was a persistent and irritating lag, however, in that early period. The imaginations of the practitioners frequently ran far ahead of the ability *[handwritten margin notes: National Live coverage were feasible due to mic relay problem. (except in local area) Video technology wasn't available until 1957]*

of technology to deliver the desired product. Live coverage was still out of the question except close to New York or Washington. It took time for the microwave relays that would eventually interlink the entire nation to become generally available, and where they were available they were costly. Local stations, too, were slow to come on line after the three-year freeze on licensing and even slower to build news departments and acquire equipment that would enable them to feed local news into the network. Videotape that would allow network news production staffs to store incoming materials and retain them for later use would not be available until 1957, and even then both tape machines and tape were cumbersome and costly and technicians to operate them needed time for training and experimentation.

Ingenuity, however, made up for some of the inadequacy of the hardware. Harry Truman, after he left the presidency in January 1953, was a frequent New York visitor. One of the former president's routine activities was a daily walk on Fifth Avenue. Each morning as he left his hotel he was met by a corps of reporters, still cameramen, and newsreel photographers. The former president chatted amiably and often colorfully as he proceeded on his walk, and much of what he had to say was faithfully reported by the printed press.

Television, however, was at a distinct disadvantage. It needed sound to catch the flavor of the former president's running commentary, but the Auricon sound cameras were heavy, designed to be used on tripods, and not adapted to picking up sound from a moving target. The CBS news staff went to work to solve the problem. The plan devised for the Philip Murray interview was a model. But Murray was stationary; Truman was a moving target. It took some technological ingenuity but a solution was found: Rewiring enabled the sound technician to separate his recorder physically from the camera as long as he remained close enough that a wire connection was maintained. This permitted the camera team to maintain lip synch while recording the former president's comments.

The major problem was the camera. It was not easy for the camera operator to walk backward keeping his lens focused on his target and avoid jarring the delicate instrument. In order to keep his hands free to operate the controls, the film staff devised a rigging of leather straps and metal braces that distributed the camera's weight and permitted his hands to move freely. In an era of miniature camcorders the complexity of photographing a moving object while moving backward carrying an awkwardly configured camera may be difficult to comprehend, but this was 1953, and it worked. The former president's comments enlivened the evening news.

Later in the same year Don Hewitt's fertile imagination conceived of another daring stunt that failed to pay off as well. The new British queen, Elizabeth II, was scheduled to visit Bermuda on a brief flying trip. Arrival time at Bermuda's airport was approximately 5:00 P.M. New York time.

Hewitt checked with the British navy about the possibility that British naval aircraft might fly film from the arrival ceremony directly to New York so that it would arrive in time for the 7:30 news. There would be no time for sending the negative to the laboratory for processing, but Hewitt had an alternative plan. He knew a home movie enthusiast who had built a fast processing tank that could be set up in any room adjacent to the studio that had a source of running water. A few minutes, Hewitt was told, was all it would need to prepare the silent film to be rushed to the projector. He called to ask me to approve the gamble. I approved and offered to help.

The high-speed processor turned out to a wooden trough about four feet long, five or six inches deep and wide. Since it needed a running water supply it was set up in a ladies room adjacent to the telecine room where it would be projected. The prescribed chemical mix was poured into the trough and we waited for the arrival of the negative. Only seconds before the 7:30 deadline for going on the air a motorcycle courier rushed in with the film package. We removed the film from the can; I took one end, and another staff member took the other. We sloshed the film back and forth in the makeshift tank until we could see images emerging. We then signaled Hewitt, who in turn informed Edwards in the studio. Telecine operators racked it up on the projector. Hewitt gave Edwards the signal and he started the narration.

The film gave the impression that the queen's plane had landed in a rainstorm. It appeared to be a very wet day. The queen descended the ramp to a red carpet and held out her hand to shake hands with the Bermuda governor. Curiously it was the left hand she extended. The governor responded with his left hand. It was now clear what had happened. The apparent storm reflected the fact that the film had not been adequately dried, the left-handed handshake from the technician's inserting the film backwards. This mistake was never repeated.

The staff, however, continued to improvise. When, for example, the Soviet Union launched *Sputnik* in October 1957, CBS News was caught badly off balance. The fact that *Sputnik* was circling the earth and sending radio signals back was announced shortly before 11:00 P.M. on Friday, October 27. The news director, John Day, too politely asked the "Person to Person" producers, whose program was on the air from 10:30 to 11:00 P.M., to relinquish time to insert a bulletin. They refused, and at 11:00 P.M. network lines were automatically shut down. NBC and ABC remained on the air to furnish detailed coverage.

Hewitt was in early the next morning, Saturday, to help in the catch-up process. The most difficult problem he faced was explaining to viewers how an earth-circling satellite would look in the air and what kind of path it would follow. He sent out for a globe from a Rand McNally store and also sought a small electric motor and a coat hanger. With help from the technicians he attached a Ping-Pong ball to the end of the hanger and with the electric motor propelled the ball around the globe in a slow orbit. This was about as close a representation of *Sputnik* in orbit as could be devised and partially saved the day for CBS.

He was still thinking big a year later when President Eisenhower planned a trip to Italy, Turkey, and Afghanistan. Several days before the president's departure the phone in my office rang. It was Hewitt, telling me he had a plan to cover the trip. He proposed to charter a DC-4 cargo plane and install videotape recorders. He would cover the Rome stop by contracting with Italian television, which would feed its signal into the CBS tape recorders. European television, however, operated on a different set of standards. He would need a standards converter. The 625-line picture transmitted by Italian television had to be converted to 525 lines and the 50-cycle European electrical current converted to the 60-cycle American standard to be transmitted on American television. Using the elaborate conversion and processing machinery that had been assembled for the coronation five years earlier was out of the question. It had long since been discarded and components used for other purposes.

Hewitt, however, had a plan. One of the technicians working on news programming offered for a small fee to build a standards converter. I suggested he draw up a detailed budget but in the meantime continue planning under the assumption that we could find some source of funding.

The plane would precede the president's entourage into Italy. CBS technicians would set up to record the ceremonies there. Once the president was ready to leave Rome the technical crew would repack the plane and leapfrog over Turkey, proceeding immediately to Kabul, Afghanistan, to repeat the process. Turkey would be bypassed so that the equipment could be set up in Kabul before the president's plane arrived. Freelance cameramen would be relied on to furnish coverage from Ankara, Turkey.

Videotape reports would be shipped back to New York by commercial aircraft. To save time the signals conversion equipment was installed at New York's Idlewild Airport (later renamed Kennedy) so recorded material could be transmitted from there. Hewitt's promise that a videotape standards converter could be built in time and deliver adequate quality was fulfilled.

Everything seemed to be in order except for one problem. The cargo doors on the aircraft were too small to permit loading of the tape recorders. They had to be removed, the apertures enlarged, and new doors constructed and fixed in place. With the reconstruction completed the plane took off for Rome and its first program. The venture was a great success, so much so that the *CBS Annual Report*, issued the next spring, carried a large photograph of the chartered plane, about to take off, with a large black on white *CBS* stenciled on its fuselage. The accompanying text proudly boasted of the venture.[3]

Other innovations, perhaps less dramatic than the Ping-Pong ball *Sputnik* and homemade high-speed film processors, were constantly being proposed and many implemented. Optical sound was discarded in favor of a full conversion to magnetic stripe. Closer relationships were cultivated with European television broadcasters against the day when satellite transmissions would allow simultaneous coverage of major events on the other side of the Atlantic. And experiments were undertaken to develop expertise in the editing of videotape, which would eventually if not supplant motion picture film, at least supplement it.

7 •

Blacklisting and the Exploitation of Fear

Television news during most of the late 1940s was still too insignificant a target to attract the attention of a growing band of superpatriots who were firing salvos of outrage at a broad range of available targets. They directed their fire at government officials, freelance writers, and stage and motion picture actors and actresses. They normally accused targets with being "soft on communism" or "outright fellow travelers."

Before mid-1949 television simply was not important enough to attract anything but peripheral attention; by then, however, the number of homes equipped with receivers had grown to the point where it was too tempting a target to be overlooked. Accordingly the zealots broadened their scope to include television.

A trio of former FBI agents had discovered by 1947 that there could be a lucrative market for a newsletter that identified writers and performers in Hollywood or on Broadway as Communist sympathizers or former party members. They formed a publishing company, incorporated under the name American Business Consultants, and set out to publish a newsletter, *Counterattack, the Newsletter of Facts on Communism.*

As soon as it began to attract widespread attention, television offered a fertile area for exploitation. As it enlarged its entertainment program schedules it recruited on a "run of show" basis a broad array of freelance producers, directors, writers, actors, and actresses, many of whom were politically liberally inclined. Television companies were more vulnerable than the theater because they depended for their income on advertising support rather than box office receipts. Much of that advertising support came from manufacturers of a variety of staples including grocery products. Consequently, they and their advertising agencies were particularly suscep- tible to pressure.

Among the networks CBS was the most vulnerable. It had set out after the war to build and own its own programs rather than to function simply as an conduit for programs owned by advertising agencies or independent producers. This meant that it was acquiring a broad range of talent on its own payroll. Without detailed background files it was almost inevitable that some who were selected would come under the not always wholly impartial scrutiny of *Counterattack* and others seeking to "root out com- munists and communist sympathizers."

In late 1949 with set ownership climbing above the 3 million level, *Coun- terattack* and like-minded citizen groups began to identify personnel in broadcasting as Communists, Communist sympathizers, or fellow travelers. Attention was focused on the industry's most vulnerable flank, its adver- tising base. Advertisers were urged not to permit the employment of per- sons described as former party members or Communist sympathizers on programs on which their advertising appeared.

Counterattack's strategy was working. Advertisers and advertising agen- cies began to take note. The newsletter had experienced a miraculous growth in circulation over its bare two years of existence. By late 1949 it was on the desk of virtually every advertising agency executive and radio and television network official in the New York City area.

Advertisers and their agencies began to ask questions concerning the em- ployment of persons whose names were mentioned in *Counterattack*'s pages. The newsletter's reach was sufficiently broad that the appearance of one of its targets in the credits of a program on either television or radio frequently was the signal for a torrent of negative mail and telephone calls.

The nation had already been jarred by the Whittaker Chambers–Alger Hiss hearings in Congress that had been seen on television by the few set owners at the time. The sensational Rosenberg spy case was still reverber- ating in the news media. The motion picture industry was reeling from the notorious "Hollywood Ten." Actors and musicians who were identified by the self-styled "protectors of the nation's capitalist tradition" were finding it increasingly difficult to get assignments. All it took to bar them from employment was to charge, accurately or otherwise, that they may have been guilty at some time of "subversive activities." The zeal for ferreting out the "reds" was being given additional stimulus by charges being vented in the hearings of the Un-American Activities Committee of the House of Representatives under the chairmanship of J. Parnell Thomas of New Jer- sey. By late 1949 Thomas had gone to jail on a payroll padding charge, but the embers had been stoked and the flames were apparently burning out of control. In his *Report on Blacklisting, I-Movies* published by the Fund for the Republic in 1955, John Cogley observes, "Thomas was . . . reunited with members of the Hollywood Ten in prison."[1] The jailing of Thomas, however, failed to slow the zealots.

A climate had been created for angry charges and countercharges. The nation was prospering, but there was a substantial core of distrustful skeptics who were ready to accept charges without rational analysis. They were eager to believe evidence of a real danger that the nation might be subverted by a Communist-led conspiracy. The Soviet Union was pouring gasoline on the fire by its aggressive policies in Western Europe. The takeover of Czechoslovakia, a near triumph for communism in the 1948 elections in Italy, and the prospect that Communists might take control of the French government in 1949 elections poured on more fuel.

I had followed the hearings of the Dies committee, the Thomas committee, the Hiss-Chambers controversy, the Rosenberg case, and the Hollywood Ten, but they had all seemed quite remote and hardly worth getting excited about. There was an unreality about it all, a fictional quality. It had never occurred to me that I would at some time find myself in the middle of this unreal world. On my second day on the job in CBS New York in early January 1950, it became abundantly clear that everybody in broadcasting, I among them, was going to be affected in some way.

As I was preparing to leave for the day the telephone rang. It was Winnie Williams, Frank Stanton's secretary, informing that Dr. Stanton wanted to see me. When I entered his office he pulled a sheet of onionskin paper from a desk drawer, handed it to me, and cautioned me to carry the list with me and under no circumstances employ any of the persons on it on any of our programs. It was obvious from his manner that he did not want to talk any further, so I folded the list, placed it in a pocket, and left. I would have liked to ask, Is this absolutely firm or can there be exceptions? Is it really this serious? But it was clear that this was not a topic for public discussion or even private questions.

On returning to my office I examined the mysterious document. There was no identification of its source. There was, however, a cryptic line at the top in capital letters that suggested it was not a CBS document:

PROTEST THEIR PARTICIPATION IN PROGRAMS BY WRITING TO THE *MANUFACTURERS OF THE PRODUCT THEY ADVERTISE.*

The list of names was headed, "MOST UNDESIRABLE."[2] (I have retained a copy of this list, which is in my files under "Blacklisting.")

An explanatory opening paragraph read, "Because of their record of affiliation with communist fronts and causes the following radio, television and other personalities are rated 'most undesirable.' "

I counted later and found that there were 128 names on the list divided into nine categories: Producers and Moderators, Guest Stars, Actors, Music, Writers, Announcers, Commentators, Dancers, and Scenic Designers.

Under the Producers and Directors category there were at least three who had appeared on credits for CBS Public Affairs programs: Mitchell Grayson, Norman Corwin, and Robert Lewis Shayon. Shayon had been, in fact, the producer of the highly acclaimed "The Eagle's Brood," the first in a series of radio documentaries that had won many honors and considerable acclaim for the network. The documentary unit was one of the units I now supervised. Norman Corwin had written the highly acclaimed CBS salute to the end of the war, "On a Night of Triumph," broadcast on the night of VE Day to uniform praise of critics and listeners.

Among the writers listed were three who had played significant roles in a variety of CBS Public Affairs programs: Arnold Perl, Peter Lyon, and Millard Lampell. I only glanced at the lists of "guests stars" and "actors." It didn't appear likely then that we would be employing many actors and actresses for public affairs programs. Neither Shayon nor Corwin remained on the CBS payroll and the others had been hired only sporadically on a freelance basis for specific projects. There did not seem to be much to be concerned about.

A couple of months later I had a rude shock. A charitable organization requested our documentary unit to produce a program to be broadcast on CBS radio using a format comparable to those in the CBS documentary series. Costs would be paid by the organization but artistic control would remain with the documentary unit. Before accepting the offer it was necessary for me to report to the program plans board, requesting a scheduled broadcast time. I was asked what personnel we contemplated using on the program. The star, I replied, would be Fredi Washington, a highly respected black actress who had significant Broadway credits. I was firmly informed that we should find someone else. No reasons were given and the subject was dropped. There was no opportunity to question or to plead the case. On return to my office I checked the list. There, the last name under "guest stars," was Fredi Washington. It was a rude and unexpected introduction to blacklisting. Now it was real but still mysterious. It was there but not to be talked about. I could not even explain to my own staff why Fredi Washington could not be used in what promised to be a harmless program.

Needless to say I began to check the onionskin paper regularly thereafter before making recommendations to the plans board.[3]

Counterattack, the letter size four-page weekly, became must reading for virtually all senior staff members. There was little conversation about it. No one seemed willing to acknowledge its impact but targets of the newsletter less and less frequently showed up on program credits. It was reassuring that news and public affairs at CBS were clearly under less pressure than the entertainment program departments. And no CBS news or public affairs employees, as contrasted with freelance performers, writers, directors, and producers, were cited on the lists.

That, however, changed in midsummer 1950. In late June *Counterattack* published a 214-page paperback, *Red Channels*. The book did more than list names, it identified organizations, presumably Communist-oriented, to which the persons listed had made contributions or whose activities they had participated in. One CBS executive, Robert Heller, vice president for radio programs; one news correspondent, Howard K. Smith; and one part-time correspondent, Alexander Kendrick, were named along with organizations to which they had allegedly belonged or to which they were said to have contributed.

There was no sign, however, that senior management was going to react. Howard K. Smith continued as European bureau chief in London, Kendrick continued as a noncontract correspondent, occasionally broadcasting from Vienna, and Heller remained on staff as vice president for radio programs. The relative absence of heavy pressure on news and public affairs personnel suggested that senior corporate management was going to deal a little more lightly with news staff members and executives than with freelancers appearing in network programs.

One explanation for the apparent leniency appeared late in the year, the week before Christmas, when all employees were asked to sign a document delicately called a "questionnaire." It began with the usual "Are you now or have ever been a member?" and appended the attorney general's list of subversive organizations. There were three questions: The first asked about membership in the Communist party, the second about membership in fascist organizations, and the third about the respondent's present or past membership in any type of organization that threatened to overthrow the government of the United States.

The questionnaire was quickly dubbed by employees a "loyalty oath" but seemed to stimulate more uproar among civil rights groups outside the corporation than within. Some of the news department correspondents were furious, but Ed Murrow signed without protest and the excitement quickly subsided.

Between Christmas and New Year's Eve, though, I had a stunning shock. One morning I found a note on my desk, signed "Bob." It was obviously written by Bob Heller, the Radio Program vice president and former head of the Documentary Unit, who occupied the office next to mine. The handwritten note explained that he was sorry he had not been able to say good-bye, but that he had removed all his possessions from his office and would not be back. There was nothing further. It was particularly startling when I remembered that when I had left at approximately six o'clock the night before everything seemed to be in order. The note seemed so bizarre that I walked around the corner to Heller's office to check for myself. The office was empty, the desk clear. I assumed that his sudden departure was in some way connected with the citations in *Red Channels* or perhaps the CBS "loyalty oath," but no one was talking. A replacement program director moved into Heller's office and there seemed to be no break in continuity.

Pressures from *Counterattack* and similar superpatriotic organizations continued to build but the Public Affairs department seemed somehow immune. The Documentary Unit, which had originally seemed the most likely target, had escaped unscathed. Although documentary production was limited, the unit had created a highly successful panel talk show. It had been produced originally for radio but a television version later went on the air, its title, "We Take Your Word." What would appear to be a stuffy intellectual exercise in studying word origins was enlivened by the pairing of a noted academic with a highly refined sense of humor, Lyman Bryson of Columbia University, with a quick-witted and surprisingly erudite show business personality, Abe Burrows. Bryson and Burrows were the regulars; they had a rapport that gave the program a distinctive and compelling character. Critics noted that the combination of the erudite Columbia professor with the sharp sense of humor and the show business comedian armed with a surprising wealth of information made for a winning team.

Then the word came down that we should immediately discontinue the use of Burrows. Again there was no word as to why. Simply, "Discontinue using him." A quick glance at *Red Channels* furnished the apparent reason for the order. Burrows was cited as having been a member of four Hollywood organizations that American Business Consultants looked on as subversive. After Burrows left, the show limped on for several years but without the spark that had made it distinctive.

One area in which we expected no problems was religious programming. We were producing two half hours weekly. One was largely a discussion and talk show; the other used a ten-minute dramatic vignette to establish a problem that would be followed by discussion. The ten-minute dramas were written by some of the same talent who were producing scripts for the longer dramas that had choice nighttime commercial positions.

One of the more frequently assigned writers was Allan Sloane, who, among other assignments, had written the script for a full-length motion picture on Martin Luther commissioned by the very conservative Lutheran church, Missouri Synod—hardly a subversive organization. There were two seemingly relatively innocuous citations under Sloane's name in *Red Channels*.

In late October 1952, Daniel O'Shea, the CBS corporate vice president who had been assigned the unenviable task of serving as buffer of the witch hunting groups, called to tell me that a script Sloane had written for "Lamp Unto My Feet" on the coming Sunday, no matter how inconvenient it might be, should not be broadcast. A substitute script should be found to replace it. I protested but my protests were unavailing. O'Shea simply insisted that Sloane's script be abandoned. The writer called a number of times to urge that he be permitted to continue. My options were limited so I called the producer to inform her that a change had to be made. It was not long before Sloane again began calling, urging that I use his script. When I rejected his pleas he called again.

Sloane's requests were so insistent that I finally called O'Shea and asked to discuss the matter in his office. On my arrival O'Shea reached into a desk drawer and extracted a file. It indicated that *Sloane* was an assumed name and that under his real name he had in fact been involved in activities that undermined his pleas of innocence. The file completely undercut my position and shook my confidence in the defense of any of the accused, even though the memberships might have been quite innocent.[4]

The most dramatic encounter with charges of subversion occurred in midsummer 1954 days after I had been elected a CBS corporate vice president in charge of news and public affairs for both radio and television. Shortly after assuming the new position I had a call from O'Shea to go to his office. He opened the conversation by telling me that I would have to fire Winston Burdett, one of the most respected of the CBS News staff correspondents, who was then stationed in Washington, D.C. I wasn't being asked to ease him out; the order was "Fire him."

The request was made in such a matter-of-fact tone that it took time to react. I finally responded that I would comply if absolutely necessary but there were two conditions I insisted be met. O'Shea would have to reveal the evidence on which the discharge would be based and I would have to discuss the matter with Ed Murrow before taking any action. Unless I explained the decision to Murrow, I told him, Murrow would "tear the whole news division apart."

O'Shea asked whether I thought Burdett was worth saving. I answered in an enthusiastic affirmative, pointing out that he was surely one of the most effective correspondents on our roster. His departure would constitute a damaging blow to our whole News and Public Affairs department. O'Shea softened his position and said he would see what he could do. We left the matter there. From time to time in subsequent months he would tell me that he was still working on a plan to keep Burdett on the staff. I should be patient a little while longer.

I had no idea at the time that Burdett had replied yes to two questions on the questionnaire distributed nearly four years earlier, in December 1950: "Was he then or had he ever been a member of the Communist party USA or any Communist organization?" And whether he had ever been a member of any "organization, movement, group or combination of persons that advocated the overthrow [of] our constitutional form of government?" Paley, Stanton, Ream, and probably Murrow had certainly known about

Burdett's confession since December 1950 and nothing had been said. It is quite conceivable that other correspondents on the staff had been let in on the secret by Murrow, if by no one else. But I had heard not a single rumor.

Nearly a year later, in June 1955, O'Shea called to tell me that he thought he had things worked out with the Senate Internal Securities Committee chaired by Senator James Eastland of Mississippi. He did not give me the full account but did say that Burdett was going to tell a story that would shock many people and he was going to name names. His revelations would capture banner headlines in the press. He suggested that I talk soon to Burdett.

It appeared obvious that Burdett needed relief from his Washington assignment. Life there would be unlivable after he testified and New York would not be much better. Pressure from colleagues who would resent his testimony, particularly the naming of names, would clearly make him an outcast.

My first step was to check overseas correspondent assignments with the news director, John Day. Day reported that we needed a part-time vacation replacement in London as soon as we could get one onto the scene. Additionally Day and I had previously had serious discussions about changing the permanent Rome assignment, probably in early autumn. Burdett would be the ideal replacement in Rome. His wife was an Italian, whose grandfather had been mayor of Rome and had been, in the pre-Mussolini days, an outspoken opponent of Il Duce. Day, who apparently had not had so much as a hint of the upcoming testimony, agreed to the plan, so I called Burdett to suggest meeting.

I opened the conversation by telling him I knew about the testimony that he was to give before the Eastland committee and inquired how he would feel about being reassigned to London immediately with the Rome assignment probably to follow early in the autumn. He seemed relieved. I suggested that he start planning immediately for the move.

His testimony was even more startling than I had expected. He had been a Communist party member when he was a young reporter on the *Brooklyn Eagle* early in the war. During the Finnish stand against the Soviet military invasion he had traveled to Finland on a mission for the Soviet government. He had begun broadcasting for CBS in Norway rather than return to his old job on the *Brooklyn Eagle*. From Norway he moved to Bucharest, Belgrade, and Ankara, where he joined the CBS staff as a correspondent. By this time he had broken with the Communist party and the Soviet Union. It was evident from his testimony before the committee that the London assignment was a lifesaver. In his appearance before the committee he described situations and named names of colleagues who had participated with him in pro-Soviet activities or he knew to be involved.

Life in Washington, or New York for that matter, among the angry reporters who believed that implicating others was a serious breach of journalistic ethics would almost inevitably have been insufferable. He went to London on schedule, spent the summer there, and reported to Rome in early autumn. He remained as Rome bureau chief during the remainder of his career, covering North Africa and the Middle East in addition to southern Europe. His performance in this assignment was so superior that no thought was ever given to moving him elsewhere.[5]

The Burdett episode did not mark an end to the debilitating Red Scare but it was evident that it was running out of steam. The demise of Senator McCarthy after the Army-McCarthy hearings in 1954, which had followed the "See It Now" attack on the Wisconsin senator, defused much of the rancor and encouraged the general public to be a little less trusting of wild charges of subversion. But the momentum built over nearly a full decade subsided slowly.

Only one other memorable case directly involved the news division. The Public Affairs department of the division had been asked to revive a morning show to compete with NBC's "Today." One of the personalities considered as a permanent host was John Henry Faulk, the Texas-born raconteur, essayist, and comedian. Faulk had made his debut in New York as an essayist-monologist on the CBS Radio Network and had many friends at CBS. As his name came up for consideration for the morning show he was broadcasting his "Johnnie's Back Porch" regularly on radio station WCBS. He seemed a likely candidate to compete effectively in the early morning hour against the highly successful "Today."

Faulk was invited by the Public Affairs director, Irving Gitlin, to audition along with several others for the assignment although it was expected that he would ultimately win the position. As had happened before with other talent, a gentle but firm call came from O'Shea's office suggesting that we not audition Faulk. There was no point going through with the audition, it was clear, because we would not be able to offer him the position, even though he was our number one selection. There was no available weapon with which to fight an invisible enemy. The audition was never scheduled.

After the Faulk case the news division had little direct contact with the Red Scare movement. Other issues intervened and demanded full attention. The staff members and freelancers who had come under attack either were no longer working on CBS programs or had cleared themselves. No questions were ever raised about Howard K. Smith or Alexander Kendrick, both of whom had been listed in *Red Channels*.

In retrospect it is fascinating to recall the curious manner in which enforcement was achieved (or red-baiters appeased). Little was ever said out loud in the CBS offices or corridors; it was all very hush-hush. Reasons were never given for taking action unless they were insistently requested, as in the case of Allan Sloane. Even in the case of Winston Burdett I was never told why he was in trouble. I found out by reading the story in the newspapers.

John P. Cowden, longtime senior CBS executive in Sales Promotion, Advertising, and Public Relations, described to me the reason he was given for discontinuing contracting with the artist Ben Shahn to produce art for CBS promotion and advertising: "We think it would be better," he was told, "if you did not use him as an artist and identified with anything at CBS. There may be vestigial influences that creep into his renderings."[6]

8 •

Not So Strange Bedfellows:
Politics and Television

The fuel that propelled television news to an astonishing period of growth in the early 1950s was politics. The spark that ignited the fuel was coverage of the political conventions of 1952 and the election that followed. It was not only television that changed dramatically; the entire national political structure began an equally climactic transformation.

Television had been on the scene for the 1948 conventions, but that was only a warm-up, a trial run for the big game four years later. In 1948 there were 400,000 television receivers in the entire United States, in July 1952 approximately 18 million. In 1948 network lines extended as far south as Washington, D.C.; in 1952 they went all the way to Miami. In 1948 the westernmost terminus was Pittsburgh; in 1952, the Pacific Ocean.

Across the wide expanse from Pittsburgh to San Francisco, coaxial cables and microwave relays enabled television signals to reach vast areas that were dark in 1948. Live service was now available across the Gulf states to Texas, down the Mississippi and Missouri valleys to the Gulf, and through the Rocky Mountains to the mountain states and Pacific coast. Additional broadcasting stations, however, were few in number because the FCC freeze on granting licenses had not been lifted until the spring of 1952. One new licensee, though, was so eager to get on the air to cover the conventions in July that he, Hugh Terry at KLZ-TV in Denver, rigged up temporary facilities to let viewers see for themselves the big show in Chicago.

The author being interviewed by Mike Wallace and Buff Cobb in June 1952 regarding CBS coverage plans for the 1952 political conventions in Chicago. Photo courtesy of Sig Mickelson. Used by permission.

The political year opened with the primary in New Hampshire. Coverage there for television was not easy. It was not only the New England winter weather that created a major obstacle. There were no airports in the state accommodating commercial airline service. Roads were frequently snow-covered or icy. Same day pictorial coverage was out of the question; exposed film had to be shipped by train or bus to New York or delivered by private auto. Once in the city it had to be processed on the West Side of Manhattan and carried crosstown to the East Side for editing and transmitting. Political news on television was a sufficient novelty across the nation, however, that it stimulated an unprecedented degree of interest in the political campaign.

Chester Burger of CBS tells the story of his experience filming the campaign with a cameraman, Larry Racies, in Peterborough in northeastern New Hampshire one late afternoon and evening in February. Since there was no available means of shipping their film to New York except a train from White River Junction, Vermont, more than three hours away by icy and snowy mountain roads, they determined that they had to put their package aboard that train. It was scheduled to leave at three o'clock the next morning. When they had finished filming less than four hours before the train's scheduled departure they rushed on icy mountain roads to assure the story would make the 7:30 P.M. program the next day. They sped into the station just as the conductor was giving the final signal for departure, ran to hand him the package, and relaxed with the knowledge that a courier would meet the train at Grand Central in the morning. They could be sure then that it would be on the 7:30 news that night, less than twenty-four hours after the event they had covered.

The intensive coverage given the New Hampshire primary by both CBS and NBC contributed in large measure to a radical transformation of the process used by the political parties in nominating candidates for the presidency. New Hampshire was covered so intensively that it inspired envy across the entire country. Ironically, the sharpest impact of the coverage was felt not in New Hampshire but in the other forty-seven states in the Union. New Hampshire was one of the few states that had no television transmitters within its borders. There was a scattering of television homes in the portions of the state bordering on Massachusetts and Maine, but most of the population was out of range of the network news programs.

Jack Gould, the television critic of the *New York Times*, caught the significance in a column on March 12, 1952: "There was undoubtedly a very great effect on citizens hundreds of miles from New Hampshire." That Gould added is the new and unknown wrinkle in politics in 1952.[1]

It had generally been assumed that television would play a significant role as a vehicle for political commercials but few had anticipated that it might be a more powerful force in news coverage. "But the New Hampshire primary showed," Gould wrote in the March 16, 1952, edition, "that television's complementary role of the independent reporter may be of even greater significance."[2]

Gould noted that the "most rewarding and absorbing film 'shots' from New Hampshire were the informal and unprepared scenes which caught the human equation in the raw and told their own stories in terms of character and spontaneity." Television had broadcast candid scenes from the state showing Senator Robert Taft dourly shaking hands with workers outside factory gates; Senator Estes Kefauver, dog tired, shoes off, half lying and half sitting on a bed in a dingy hotel room carrying on a conversation with a television reporter; and Governor Earl Warren munching on a chicken leg while being harangued by a woman sitting beside him at the head table. It was something that viewers who were not members of the political inner circles had never before seen. And the pictures, thanks to the new AT&T relays, went out to the entire country.

Other states noted with envy the attention paid to New Hampshire and later Wisconsin, where the intimate coverage of New Hampshire was repeated. The lure of television exposure on a rapidly increasing number of television screens was a powerful motivation to state political leaders to find a method for duplicating the national publicity accruing to the states with early primaries. Uncommitted delegates to the national conventions became fewer and fewer in subsequent convention years as additional states shifted from state conventions and caucuses to primary elections to select their delegates, many of them to precommit the delegations they selected to specific candidates. As primaries grew in popularity and more and more delegates were precommitted, the contest element in the national convention was gradually extinguished.

In 1952, however, no one was quite sure what impact television would have. Executives in the industry assumed it would be big but how big they could only guess. Most political leaders knew vaguely that it would be important but had no basis for estimating how important it would really be.

The CBS News and Public Affairs departments were in some disarray in the summer of 1951 as the political year 1952 approached. Rumors were floating through halls at network headquarters that radio and television were to be split and function as separate operating units. But the future of news and public affairs was skipped over lightly in the rumors. The most likely speculation had Radio News absorbing the Radio Public Affairs unit and Television News joining with Television Public Affairs in the Television division.

Whatever the future might hold, the early evening news continued to experiment, innovate, and solidify its position. As the number of television homes in the nation rocketed from the little more than 3 million at the beginning of 1950 to 7 million plus in January 1951 and 10 million by midsummer, news ratings continued to grow in proportion to the increase in the number of households. There were some 5 million homes regularly watching the two network early evening news programs in 1950–51 and nearly 6 million in 1951–52.[3]

The preoccupation with news at CBS, however, did not emphasise television, but radio. There was relatively little contact between the two; television sometimes had limited access to members of the correspondent staff, but the primary focus of news management was on radio.

In early June 1951 I received a surprise request from Jack Van Volkenburg, the vice president and general sales manager for both radio and television. Van Volkenburg asked that I arrange to meet with representatives of the two national political parties to urge them to permit the television networks to solicit commercial sponsorship of convention coverage. It was an unusual request. It should logically have gone to the news director rather than the public affairs director. Van Volkenburg was concerned that coverage would be enormously costly in both out-of-pocket costs and losses of revenue due to preemptions of commercially sponsored programs that would have to be cleared out to make way for convention coverage. In 1948 that had not been a problem. There was not enough income from commercial sales to concern management. By mid-1951, however, sponsors were beginning to fill out nighttime schedules and expand into daytime as well. Preempting large blocks of time would cut sharply into income. Commercial sponsorship would not compensate for all lost revenues but would mitigate damage.

The CBS Television Network Research department estimated, in response to an appeal for data to present to the national committees, that the number of television homes within range of an over-the-air signal in the summer of 1952 would probably reach a minimum figure of 17.2 million and might be as high as 18 million. The department estimated, further, that as many as 55 million individuals might be watching convention programs at one time. The department prepared charts that indicated that the number of television homes would increase from 3.2 million on January 1, 1950, to 7.2 million on January 1, 1951, to 10 million plus on January 1, 1952, and 17.2 million by July 1.[4]

A national map showing that coaxial cables and microwave circuits capable of carrying a television signal would expand dramatically was prepared. In June 1951 service ended at Omaha on the west and Jacksonville on the south. Interconnections were projected to reach all but relatively lightly populated parts of the country by the summer of 1952.

Personnel and production costs for the two conventions were estimated to total about $500,000 and preemptions would cause loss of revenue estimated at between at $4 million and $5 million, a severe blow to a new industry.

Guy Gabrielson, chairman of the Republican National Committee, was the first person approached. The Republican convention would occur first.

The pattern established there would probably prevail with the Democrats. Gabrielson was amenable to a meeting so I packed up my charts and took off for Washington to meet with him and the National Committee publicity director, William Mylander.

Both responded favorably. They insisted that commercials not preempt significant portions of the convention nor be in bad taste. It was easy to give assurances on both points. They offered to take our proposal to the Democrats with the caveats they had enunciated. Within a few days we had favorable replies from both parties so hurdle number one had been surmounted. Television was in a position to break new ground.

By mid-July 1951 the official announcement came from the twentieth (corporate executive) floor at CBS that the separation of radio from television had been effected. Jack Van Volkenburg would be president of the Television Network. I would be director of News and Public Affairs, reporting to Hubbell Robinson, vice president for programs. It was now obvious why I had been selected to make the presentation to the national committees.

Little more could be done on political planning until reorganization of the department was complete. In the meantime the Japanese Peace Conference intervened to delay the process even further.

By mid-September the eight networks involved, four from television, ABC, CBS, DuMont, and NBC, and four from radio, ABC, CBS, Mutual, and NBC, met to organize a pool to deliver coverage from the convention site. It was certain it would take place in Chicago but the auditorium had not been selected. There were two venues under consideration, the Chicago Coliseum, an indoor sports arena, and the International Amphitheater at the Chicago Stockyards. The network pool decided to inspect both sites and be prepared to make recommendations to the national committees. CBS was to organize the pool. This would entail representing the networks before the national committees and making all arrangements for producing a pooled signal of official convention proceedings.

The site inspection trip resulted in a firm recommendation that the national committees select the International Amphitheater rather than the Coliseum. The Coliseum was a large shell of a building designed for basketball or hockey but had little auxiliary space, certainly not enough for broadcast operations. It was concluded that the Coliseum would simply not do; the Amphitheater, on the other hand, had ample auxiliary space for all media needs.

In mid-November we learned that the chairmen of the two parties and their principal aides were to meet in the offices of Werner Schroeder, a Chicago attorney and vice chairman of the Republican Arrangements Committee, the next day to make a final decision concerning the convention venue. This meant that it was imperative that I, as representative of the networks, be in Chicago the next day to state the network's case. Since weather in Chicago was threatening I called the weather bureau and was informed I could try to fly but it was likely I would wind up in Kansas City or Omaha. The Twentieth Century Limited on the New York Central was fully booked but the Broadway Limited on the Pennsylvania line had space so I headed for Penn Station. The train would get me to Chicago with minutes to spare before the meeting was to begin.

The trip was uneventful until I awakened in broad daylight. I looked outside and saw deep snow. A porter informed me that we were stalled temporarily in Lima, Ohio, and would be approximately three hours late into Chicago. Fortunately weather in Chicago had delayed the meeting's opening. The chief executive of the Stockyards company, William Wood Prince, I discovered, was testifying when I arrived at the Schroeder law offices. I was next with my bulky charts demonstrating that the Coliseum was totally inadequate for television purposes. On completion I headed back to the La Salle Street station to catch the Twentieth Century back to New York. The next morning in Hastings, New York, the switching point where conventional engines were exchanged for electric power, I bought a copy of the *New York Times*. On page 1 I found the story I was looking for. The committee had selected the Stockyards in preference to the Coliseum. Television had won a major victory.

Planning was proceeding but there was considerable concern about sponsorship at top CBS executive levels. We had permission from the two parties to make a sale, but there were no prospects in view and the product we wished to sell had no precedent. Furthermore, the limited number of television stations on the air complicated the problem of stitching together a network for a venture as long-running as a political convention.

Both the competing networks (ABC and NBC) possessed an advantage that was difficult to overcome. Each owned full complements of five television licenses in major markets. CBS owned only two stations outright and had a minority position in a third. It had owned WCBS-TV since it went on the air, had acquired a minority position in WTOP-TV in Washington in 1950, and in January 1951 had bought outright station KTSL in Los Angeles, which it promptly renamed KNXT. NBC owned its outlets in New York, Washington, Cleveland, Chicago, and Los Angeles; ABC, in New York, Detroit, Chicago, Los Angeles, and San Francisco. Ownership of stations in these major markets gave both networks a powerful base that CBS lacked. CBS boasted in 1951 of fifty-one interconnected affiliates,[5] but some of them owed primarily allegiance to NBC. In order to compete successfully it would be necessary to create an attractive prospectus and get it on the market early.

I was surprised one afternoon in early November when I returned from lunch to find Van Volkenburg sitting in my office with two men I did not recognize. He introduced them as John McKibbin, vice president for white goods (consumer products including television receivers) of the Westinghouse Electric Corporation, and Edgar Parrack, executive vice president of the Ketchum, McCleod and Grove Advertising Agency of Pittsburgh.

They asked me to describe our plans for covering the 1952 conventions. I told them in detail what I had in mind. We intended to cover the conventions as a major news story. Our plans called for keeping our viewers informed not only of what was happening on the convention floor but at any point in Chicago or elsewhere where news that would bear on the convention outcome was being made. Reporters would be deployed to all major venues and communications channels would be constructed so that a central control point would have access to all pertinent information and would be in position to sort it out and pass it on to viewers. Even more importantly our ringmaster in the central studio would have enough information to interpret arcane maneuvers on the rostrum or on the floor. He would, I boasted, be the best informed person in Chicago.

They asked questions. Although unprepared for a grilling I replied as specifically as possible. During the course of the conversation I discovered that NBC, their apparent first choice for the order, had been rather vague, so vague that they had decided to look elsewhere. We were asked to prepare a specific proposal and get it to Pittsburgh immediately. In a few days it was on its way, complete with a suggested schedule, program components, equipment requirements, personnel complement, and price.

I had made one serious error in outlining our coverage plans. We had assumed, on the basis of radio coverage of previous conventions, that we would carry only the highlights, including major speeches, debates on the credentials, and platform committee reports, nominating and seconding speeches for candidates, balloting and acceptance speeches. We assumed that this would consume about fifteen hours so we based our planning and pricing on a fifteen-hour schedule for each convention. This had been the broadcast pattern back to 1932.

A few days before Christmas a call came from Pittsburgh to Van Volkenburg's office asking that CBS Television representatives be available at the Duquesne Club in Pittsburgh on the morning of December 26. William Hylan, Television Network Sales department vice president, and I were designated to make the trip.

On a snowy late Christmas afternoon we made our way to New York's Pennsylvania Station to board the overnight Pittsburgher. On arrival we went immediately to the Duquesne Club, where we met the delegation from Westinghouse and the advertising agency.

The atmosphere was friendly but it was obviously a negotiating session. The first request from Westinghouse was for twenty hours of coverage rather than the fifteen we were projecting but for the price of fifteen. I was a little concerned whether we would be able to squeeze out twenty hours of exciting program material but assented to the request. Hylan called New York to clear the five free hours; New York agreed. Full election night coverage was included in the package. Next, Westinghouse, in addition to buying the convention-election schedule, asked for a series of eight one-hour nighttime programs between the conventions and the election as a "bridge" between the events. Since this was an unexpected bonus it offered no problems. It had been previously agreed that the CBS radio network would be included in the final package. Since there would obviously be no final decision that day, Hylan and I headed for the airport to fly back to New York.

During corporate management's Christmas party for senior staff only two days later, Van Volkenburg was called out of the room to take a telephone call. It was Pittsburgh. In a few minutes the television network president returned to the party and jubilantly announced that Westinghouse was placing a firm order along the lines we had discussed. A major hurdle had been crossed. Now we had to deliver.

Both NBC and ABC, as soon as they heard the news, mobilized all of their resources and succeeded within a few days in obtaining sponsorship from Philco and Admiral. It is probably noteworthy that all three sponsors were manufacturers of television receivers in addition to refrigerators, stoves, dishwashers, and assorted household wares, all products in short supply as a result of the postwar population boom and migration to the suburbs. The *New York Times* reported later that Westinghouse had paid CBS $3 million. Philco bought NBC coverage for $2.4 million and Admiral paid ABC $2 million.[6] Television had broken a long-standing barrier against commercial sponsorship of political events and carried radio along with it. The sums paid would have barely covered the cost of a thirty-second commercial at a Super Bowl in the late 1990s but a precedent for commercial sponsorship had been set.

DuMont had participated only halfheartedly in convention/election planning and within a few weeks asked CBS Television to feed the stations it owned in New York, Washington, D.C., and Pittsburgh. Furnishing service to the DuMont stations in New York and Washington would be costly in that it would dilute the CBS audience on its wholly owned station in New York and its partially owned station in Washington, but it desperately needed Pittsburgh, the home base of Westinghouse. Pittsburgh was a single-station market. Without it Westinghouse personnel would not see the CBS coverage. CBS reluctantly accepted the dilution of its New York and Washington audiences in favor of finding an outlet in Pittsburgh.

At a Republican arrangements committee meeting in San Francisco in early January I received a pleasant surprise. A major item of business was a report to the full committee by its vice chairman, Werner Schroeder, the Chicago lawyer in whose office it was decided to book the convention into the International Amphitheater rather than the Chicago Coliseum. In his presentation to the full committee, Schroeder used the same data I had used in arguing the case for the Amphitheater in his office two months earlier.

Even though it was apparently difficult for committee members to realize fully the role television would play, Schroeder's talk gave them a surprising array of data. What they did not fully understand is that television would, over time, radically transform the whole election process and turn the national convention from a decision-making business meeting into a giant party rally and pageant created primarily for the camera tube.

Two puzzling problems had to be solved by members of the television network pool. One stemmed from the inadequacy of the AT&T transmission circuits to serve all sections of the country equally. There, for example, was still only one circuit capable of carrying a television signal west from Omaha to the Pacific. This meant that only one program at a time could break through the Omaha bottleneck and proceed to the half of the landmass of the United States that lay west of the Missouri River. Similarly Louisiana, Texas, Oklahoma, and Kansas could only be reached by a single circuit that went down the Mississippi from St. Louis to New Orleans, turned west there to Houston, and from Houston northward to Austin, San Antonio, Dallas/Fort Worth, and cities in Kansas and Oklahoma. Atlanta was a terminus for the three southbound circuits leaving Florida, Alabama, and Mississippi with only one signal.

NBC's early aggressiveness in tying up primary affiliations in large markets posed another problem that was compounded by the FCC freeze on licensing. If it fully exercised its rights to priority program acceptance ABC and CBS would be shut out of such large markets as Buffalo, Indianapolis, St. Louis, Milwaukee, and Grand Rapids/Kalamazoo. NBC held the primary affiliations in each. It was obvious that the playing field was not level, but was there a solution?

A pool meeting grappled with the problem. An equitable division of the telephone company's single, channel circuits, if a formula could be devised, would solve one problem, but that would still leave the single-station market question. A simple answer would be to devise a standard or formula for dividing the convention into definable segments that could then be parceled out by lot. The first step was to define a program unit. Out of these deliberations came a phrase that was to dominate news stories and conversations about convention coverage for more than two decades: "gavel to gavel." A session was defined as a period extending from gavel to gavel, from the time the chairman officially opened it until he dropped the gavel to recess. The network drawing number one would have access to the AT&T lines and the single-station markets for the first session. Numbers two and three would follow in sequence through as many sessions as the convention required. A network would be permitted to program as much as it desired before and after the gavel, but between gavels the rules would be in force and a pool signal available.

The gavel to gavel decision would in the long run be, in a sense, a trap.

No one of the three networks in subsequent convention years dared to break the tradition of programming gavel to gavel until ABC finally decided in 1972 to cover only highlights. For two decades the three networks had adhered religiously to the formula even when much of the excitement had been drained from the events.

CBS Television News had another major problem to solve, an internal one. It had to select a member of its staff to play a central role in the coverage, to serve as an "anchorman." It needed a strong personality with background in political coverage to occupy a pivotal position. The person selected would have to be knowledgeable enough that all coverage could revolve around him and possess a strong enough personality to earn the full respect of the viewers. On the basis of his experience in 1948 and his nearly four years as the central figure in the network's early evening news program Douglas Edwards would appear to have been a logical selection. But as well as he had done in building the early evening news he did not seem strong enough to carry the full load. My choice, and only choice, was Walter Cronkite. He had demonstrated at the Japanese Peace Conference and in the eleven o'clock local news in Washington that he had the strength, the background, the will, and the audience respect to carry the substantial load. And he was an excellent reporter.

Hubbell Robinson, the television network vice president for programs, was doubtful. He argued that we should make every effort to free Bob Trout from his radio assignment. Trout, he reasoned, was already a big name. He was a superb ad libber and had been involved in political convention coverage since 1936. Using Trout would be playing it safe. Through several sessions I held out for Cronkite. My contention was that Trout was a master at creating word pictures but we already had the pictures. The cameras would deliver them. What we needed was interpretation of the picture on the screen. That was Cronkite's forte. Robinson finally yielded and Cronkite had the assignment. No thought was ever given to using Edward R. Murrow in that role. He seemed much better adapted to coming on screen from time to time, if we could free him up from radio assignments, to add background and perspective to our coverage. He and Eric Sevareid filled this role to everyone's satisfaction and Cronkite went on to become a television legend.

Shortly after Cronkite's selection was announced, reporters asked what he was going to do. I replied that he was going to be our anchorman. The term stuck and has since become one of the most overworked words in the broadcaster's lexicon.

One facet of commercial sponsorship concerned us; we were worried that abrupt switches from the convention rostrum to commercials for Westinghouse might cost us viewers who would resent the intrusion. We were hopeful that we could cut away only during pauses in the action, but it

1952 Convention in Chicago

was likely that such pauses might be infrequent. That meant seeking some method or device that would reassure viewers that when we did cut away they were missing nothing significant.

A CBS engineer, Paul Wittlig, who was experimenting with new electronic tools, had a possible answer. He had perfected a device he described as a "wedge-wipe" amplifier. As he explained it, when the convention was in session, we could insert Cronkite into a corner of the screen while the remainder of the convention hall was in full view. We could then gradually "wipe" Cronkite up to the full screen and as we were ready to go back to the rostrum, "wipe" him back to the corner and then out. This appeared to be a reasonable answer. No cut-away to commercials would be abrupt. The viewer would be able to see that there was a relative lull on the floor. Wittlig was asked to conceal his idea until we had introduced it at the conventions. Cronkite and the "wedge-wipe" became a trademark of CBS convention coverage.

The wedge-wipe amplifier was a valuable find but it was not the whole answer. Our technicians also devised a buzzer system, audible to the viewer as well as to the broadcast staff, that would signal an immediate switch from a commercial to the rostrum when unexpected action on the floor demanded that the commercial be interrupted. Our viewers were constantly reminded that the signal would be used whenever warranted. It was demonstrated a number of times to reinforce the promise.

There was one other sophisticated technological device that we desperately wanted, a small hand-held shortwave camera that would enable us to transmit close-up interviews from the floor and candid shots of delegates in action. The CBS general engineering staff made a thorough survey of manufacturers who might offer such a device but the effort was futile. Units were found that might deliver service under optimal conditions but were hardly worth the trouble. NBC did bring a "peepie creepie" to the floor with something less than outstanding success.

By mid-June all three networks were geared up and ready to launch the great adventure. Technicians were already on the scene installing the intricate structure of electronic circuits required to deliver the convention signal. By the end of the month program personnel would begin to arrive in the convention city for their first nationwide political extravaganza.

9 •

Television News Comes of Age

Television had never undertaken anything quite so massive as the two national political conventions scheduled for July 1952 in Chicago. Philadelphia in 1948 had been a useful practice session but this was the main event. When the gavel opening the 1952 Republican National Convention fell on July 7 some twelve hundred television writers, reporters, producers, directors, cameramen, sound technicians, lighting experts, and maintenance personnel had moved into the headquarters city from New York, Washington, D.C., and Los Angeles. Additional personnel were recruited from other parts of the country. It was clearly the largest cadre of television personnel and the most massive assemblage of television equipment ever mobilized at one site and the biggest news story television had ever covered.

There were seven pool cameras in the convention site, and each network was able to call on another twenty to twenty-five deployed on the periphery of the Amphitheater and at downtown hotels and in mobile units poised to move at short notice to any locale where significant news might be developing. Never before had so many television cameras been massed at one event.

Party leaders and convention planners were generally aware that television would add a dimension to convention coverage, but they had no experience that would enable them to foretell its impact. The Republicans, for example, balked when the pool requested at least two boxes in the Amphitheater side balconies for placement of television cameras. Their ar-

The author meeting with CBS program directors in Chicago prior to the opening of the Republican National Convention. Don Hewitt is third from the left and Frank Schaffner in the center rear. Photo courtesy of Sig Mickelson. Used by permission.

gument: that would deprive fifteen to twenty faithful Republicans of choice seats in the hall. They finally gave in but flatly refused to give the network pool permission to erect a camera stand in the center rear area of the main floor. Their reasoning was logical, if flawed. It would obstruct the view of persons sitting behind the stand. They could not, however, see that a few hundred in the hall would have an unobstructed view but millions in the television audience would be deprived of a head-on look at the speakers at the rostrum. As a result, there was never a head-on view, only three-quarter profile views from cameras in boxes in the side balconies. Arguments that the International Amphitheater would seat only approximately 12,000 whereas up to 50 million would see some parts of their convention on television had little impact.

It was equally evident in the program schedule that convention leaders had little genuine comprehension of what television might mean. The leaders recognized that it would open new opportunities to reach a vast public but were unable to reconcile that vision with traditional program schedules and time-honored practices. No effort was made to time convention highlights to coincide with peak television viewing hours. Morning newspaper deadlines were still more important. On the day, for example, on which General Eisenhower made his speech formally accepting the presidential nomination, the climax of the convention, the record shows that adjournment took place at 9:20 P.M. EDT. The acceptance speech had fallen within prime time, but barely. Peak viewing time was still ahead as the gavel fell adjourning the convention.

The leadership had listened to projections of the size of the potential audience but were apparently only vaguely aware of the excitement coverage might generate. Making concessions was painful; in the opening ceremonies, for example, the chair asked that all delegates, alternates, and visitors in the hall sit quietly while the lights were dimmed for the official convention picture. No thought was given to the fact that all of the proceedings, including the announcement of the picture taking, were watched by millions on their television screens. Dimming the lights, however, blanked out the television picture and gave the television directors an excuse to leave the hall and seek more exciting scenes elsewhere.

Procedures at both conventions were unchanged from those of previous years. There were the usual speeches from party leaders, honors given to party faithful, lengthy nominating speeches, and innumerable seconding speeches. There were no restrictions on another device that had held over from previous conventions, the polling of delegations. During the calling of the roll on a vote any member of the delegation called could ask that each member be polled. The chair would then, with the aid of the clerk, call out the name of each member of the delegation in question, including some entitled to only half votes so that each person with a ballot would be formally recorded. It was a great opportunity for a publicity-hungry delegate to be seen on television by his family and friends at home but a great waste of time and sheer boredom for millions of viewers.

Nor was any effort made to curb the seemingly interminable demonstrations for candidates. At the sound of the candidate's name at the end of a flowery and frequently much too long nominating speech, scores of demonstrators carrying signs, placards, whistles, drums, and musical instruments would push their way onto the floor and carry on a frenzied march through the aisles until they wilted from exhaustion. Demonstrators apparently assumed that the louder they shouted, sang, rattled their noisemakers, the longer they could avoid falling in the aisles with exhaustion, the more certain it was that their candidate would win. Television in subsequent years stopped this tradition dead in its tracks by showing pictures of the demonstrations forming up in the wings or outside the convention venue while the nominating speech was still in progress. Thereafter, "spontaneous" demonstrations seemed a little less spontaneous.

By 1956 both parties had recognized the power of television to make or break candidates or political parties. They resisted abandoning many entrenched but anachronous convention traditions, but in response to television, the old patterns gradually changed. Polling of delegations was outlawed. Restrictions were placed on the length of demonstrations and the number of seconding speeches. Programs were reworked to schedule show pieces in prime time. Delegates were asked, not always with favorable results, to maintain reasonable decorum on the convention floor. Gradually the process was reshaped to make better use of television time. Party leaders tried, however, with only minimal success to produce program features that they believed would compel the attention of television executives and attract television viewers

The Democrats in 1956 scheduled a motion picture film produced by Dore Schary and narrated by a young U.S. senator from Massachusetts, John F. Kennedy. CBS refused to project the film on the basis that the network was there to cover a business meeting and not a political party rally, but the other two networks dutifully racked up their film projectors and showed the program in its entirety.

The GOP thought it might introduce a little showmanship into its convention in San Francisco that same year by scheduling speeches by each member of President Eisenhower's cabinet. It was assumed that cabinet members would draw an audience. The ploy did not work. Just as Herbert Hoover, Jr., substituting for Secretary of State John Foster Dulles, who was out of the country on a diplomatic mission, began his report, the first of the series, television crews from all three networks stationed in San Francisco International Airport's control tower spotted a blip on the radar screen. The blip represented the president's incoming plane. It was flying over Travis Air Force Base, only a few minutes by air from San Francisco. All three networks kept their cameras focused on the radar screen, following the blip as it approached and the plane landed. They then picked up the president's motor caravan and followed it down Bayshore Drive to the St. Francis Hotel and held there while the president, about to be renominated, disembarked and disappeared into the lobby. Only then did they return to the Cow Palace as the last of the cabinet members was completing his remarks. By the conclusion of the convention it was obvious that both parties recognized the power of television and were trying somewhat awkwardly to cater to it.

In 1952, however, none of the party leadership was quite sure what impact television would have. The prognosis for exciting conventions was favorable. For the first time since 1928 there would be no incumbent in the running for the presidential nomination of either party. Dissatisfaction with the administration of President Truman had grown to the point that there was widespread demand for change. The apparent stalemate in the Korean War stimulated frustration. Red-baiting, charges by the "China Lobby" that the Truman administration had undermined Generalissimo Chiang Kai-shek, and sympathy for General Douglas MacArthur, who had been sacked by President Truman, all contributed to an angry mood among the electorate.

Senator Robert Taft of Ohio was the front-runner for the Republican nomination. The unanswered question as the campaign got under way in January was whether General Eisenhower, then the commanding general at NATO, could be induced to make the run. An influential group of moderate eastern Republicans including Governor Thomas Dewey of New York, who had been the losing GOP candidate in 1948; Senator Henry Cabot Lodge of Massachusetts; General Lucius Clay, who had commanded U.S. forces in Germany; Paul Hoffman, former administrator of the Marshall Plan; John Hay Whitney, publisher of the *New York Herald Tribune*; and Walter Thayer, an associate of Whitney's, determined to make the general the Republican candidate.

Contrary to the views of the overall party leadership they had confidence in the potential influence of television. Their strategy from the outset was based on exploiting television to upset the well-entrenched senator from Ohio, who had the support of old line Republicans and much of the party machinery. They were convinced that effective use of television could build sufficient public support to overcome the advantage Taft maintained among party regulars. Dewey had used television masterfully in winning election as governor of New York in 1950. He also had the support of two television-minded advertising agencies, Batten, Barton, Durstine and Osborn (BBDO) and Young and Rubicam (Y&R), a leader in production of television programs. The presidents of the two agencies, Ben Duffy of BBDO and Sig Larmon of Y&R, were both enthusiastic Eisenhower supporters and among the nation's most skilled users of television for advertising campaigns. Duffy and his staff had plotted Dewey's successful campaign for the governorship of New York in 1950.

The unanswered question during the winter and early spring related to General Eisenhower's intentions. Would the general resign his post as commander in chief of Supreme Headquarters Allied Powers in Europe (SHAPE) and come home to make a run for the presidency? There was no definitive answer from Paris; it was the great mystery that spring.

At this point CBS's Television News department had a lucky break. Radio news had been cold to television, almost to the point of being obstructive. News reporters on the CBS staff, except Douglas Edwards and Cronkite, were all carried on the Radio division payroll and were jealously guarded by Radio News management. David Schoenbrun, the bureau chief in Paris, however, decided to gamble on serving both masters.

As a member of an inner circle of American correspondents serving in the French capital, he was invited to a private lunch on March 20 with General Eisenhower at the home of Preston Grover, the Associated Press bureau chief in Paris. After the lunch Schoenbrun sent me a private eleven-page confidential memorandum describing Eisenhower's performance in graphic detail, including the fact that he had two light scotches before lunch and a glass of white wine with lunch.[1]

It was clear from the nature of the general's remarks that he had made up his mind to resign. He speculated aloud whether he should send his letter of resignation as commander of SHAPE to Secretary of Defense Robert Lovett or to President Truman. It was also clear that he was beginning to plan his return to the United States. He did not want to go home before the Oregon primary scheduled for May 15 and he thought anything after June 1 would be too late. He did not say explicitly that he intended to go for the nomination but it was evident that was his intention. He would formally announce his availability, probably in his hometown, Abilene, Kansas, early in June.[2]

Schoenbrun's record was reliable enough that CBS Television News could plan with some assurance that the general would be in the race. Furthermore it proved to be right on the mark. Not until several weeks later was it learned officially that Eisenhower planned to arrive in Washington, D.C., in late afternoon on Sunday, June 1. He would schedule his farewell to NATO at a press conference (his last meeting with the press while on active duty) for Tuesday morning, June 3, in Washington and fly to Kansas City that afternoon. On June 4 he would proceed to Abilene by train and speak in a city park that night. The next morning, June 5, he would hold a press conference in a motion picture theater in Abilene.[3]

The press conference immediately became a subject of controversy. There would be no radio and television coverage. The Eisenhower support group explained that television and radio could cover the speech the night before but that this would be a session for the print press.

CBS and NBC were both committed to spend the $80,000 AT&T would

It's important to point out that radio from the beginning had been a nemesis to television.

need to build a temporary microwave relay to carry the signal from Abilene to Omaha, where it would be linked into the trunk line to New York. CBS contracted with its Omaha affiliate to send a mobile unit and crew to Abilene to make the pickup; NBC contracted with its affiliate in Kansas City to provide a similar service. Both networks kept pressure on Eisenhower's people to open the press conference to television coverage, but the planning group was unyielding. On several occasions I pleaded unsuccessfully with Chairman Paley at CBS to use his influence or to agree that we might go ahead, but it was apparent he didn't think we should press the issue.

The June 4 speech, delivered in an open field in a driving rainstorm, if not a disaster, certainly did little to help the Eisenhower cause. The speaker, as he was pelted by raindrops, appeared uncomfortable with his script. It was something less than a solid base from which to start an uphill fight for the presidential nomination.

The next morning a miracle happened. As I was preparing to leave home for the commute to New York the telephone rang. It was Bill Paley. "Oh Sig," he said, "don't you think we ought to cover the press conference in Abilene this morning?" That was all the encouragement I needed. I immediately got Abilene on the phone. Paul Levitan, the producer of the CBS coverage, answered. I gave him the message and urged him to start immediately to move his heavy equipment into the theater. He was one step ahead of me. At the conclusion of the speech the night before he had issued orders to store the cameras, microphones, and control equipment in the theater lobby. All he had to do was move it inside. I requested that as soon as he had assembled his crew and started setting up in the theater he hunt up Robert Mullen, Eisenhower public relations director. He was to tell Mullen that his cameras and microphones were in place in the theater and would be removed only on orders from New York. He reached Mullen, who was on his way to pick up the general for the short walk to the theater. All Mullen could do was tell Levitan he would inform Eisenhower.

Mullen told me later that he was fearful that Eisenhower would be furious over the intrusion but the general's response, in effect, was that since the cameras are in place there is not much we can do.[4] The press conference turned out to be a rousing success. It was so successful, in fact, that one wonders whether members of the Eisenhower support team might have called Paley the night before and suggested surreptitiously that covering the press conference would help mitigate the damage done by the unfortunate rain-soaked speech in the park.

Within days it was clear that television news had won a major victory. Even *Editor and Publisher*, the voice of the newspaper industry, headlined a story regarding the CBS decision to force its way into the press conference, "Only White House Doors Will Stop TV Now." In the story under the headline, the publication's managing editor, Jerry Walker, wrote, "General Eisenhower's give-and-take with the reporters in the Abilene theater

Politics had found in its bedfellow in television. It is an example how tv could help politician cause. It has remained a staple in tv news.

on June 5 helped him more politically than his formal address the previous evening . . . and some politicians . . . are wondering now why there was any hesitancy about letting TV cameras in the hall."[5]

Jack Gould of the *New York Times* on June 15 was even more impressed by television's aggressive move. "For the first time . . . the video industry stood up for its rights as a new form of journalism. . . . And it won."[6]

The launching of the Eisenhower campaign solidified some support for the general but it was Senator Taft who had a clear lead in pledged delegates as the July 7 opening of the convention approached. An informal poll of delegates compiled two weeks earlier had shown that Taft was in the lead with 454 committed delegates to General Eisenhower's 390. The magic number for nomination was 604. The only other potential candidate believed to have a chance at the nomination was General Douglas MacArthur; some felt that many uncommitted delegates would hold out to see whether a ground swell for MacArthur would develop. There was an undercurrent of feeling that his oratory during the keynote speech on the opening night would so mesmerize the delegates that it would initiate a stampede to his support.

The likely key to winning the nomination lay in the decision that would have to be made by the credentials committee about thirty-eight delegates from Texas who were committed to Senator Taft but were being contested by the Eisenhower forces. If they could be snatched from the Taft column and moved to Eisenhower's, victory for the general, if not assured, was likely. It was the intention of Eisenhower supporters to fight the battle on television screens. Young, attractive, thoughtful, and articulate spokesmen were enlisted by the Eisenhower leadership to support the cause. They were selected to contrast with the older and more traditional politicians supporting Taft. The Eisenhower forces, however, were frustrated by the Taft camp's decision to close the committee sessions to the press and debate the issue behind closed doors.

Even though the sessions were closed it was soon evident that information could be contained within a closed room. A camera set up outside the meeting room was nearly as effective as one would have been inside the closed meeting. There was no problem following the debate behind the closed doors. A camera in the corridor was as attractive to Eisenhower delegates as a bowl of honey to a hill of ants. Eisenhower supporters attracted by the camera shuttled in and out of the committee meetings in a constant stream. It is likely that, even outside the room, information was nearly as complete as if television had had full access to the sessions.

By the third day CBS was even better informed. Network technical operations personnel slipped into the meeting room at night after the sessions had shut down and installed a private audio line that they bridged into the public address system. Cronkite was then able the next day to sit in a makeshift studio installed in a fifth-floor suite and overhear the proceedings. No one at the time questioned the ethics of the enterprise, but nothing similar has been undertaken since. By week's end there was still no decision from the credentials committee, which would not come until the committee reported out to the full convention on the following Tuesday.

CBS, meantime, had a serious internal problem. The Radio Writers Union, which had an exclusive contract to represent television news writers, declared a strike against CBS News effective July 5, the Saturday before the convention would open. That strike, coupled with the haughty attitude of the radio news leadership, from whom little or no help could be expected, made it evident that television might be badly hurt.

There were only two correspondents formally on the television staff, Cronkite and Edwards. For reporting from the field, writers and reporter contacts on the New York staff normally carried the load. The strike, however, took them out of circulation. To compete with the other networks, CBS recruited Bill Leonard (later president of the News division) from WCBS in New York, Grant Holcomb from KNXT in Los Angeles, and Jim Bormann from WCCO in Minneapolis and St. Paul. Schoenbrun, although under tight rein from radio, was helpful in keeping television informed of developments in the Eisenhower camp. Edwards was also available for reporting duties.

Another concern was the twenty-hour commitment to Westinghouse. It was decided to stockpile a couple of hours on the Saturday and Sunday before the official opening of the Republican convention. The publicity staffs of both the Taft and Eisenhower campaigns were so eager for any exposure they could get that it was easy to persuade them to organize minidemonstrations on Michigan Avenue and in the Conrad Hilton lobby. An hour on Saturday night furnished an opportunity to get one Westinghouse hour on the record and to serve as a dress rehearsal for the coverage to come. There was one memorable scene that television cameras caught in the Hilton hotel lobby during that hour. Senator George Bender of Ohio led a throng in the center of the room singing the Taft campaign song, based on the music to "I'm Looking Over a Four Leafed Clover." Cowbell ringing, banner and placard waving, and marching through the lobby gave viewers a taste of preconvention Chicago. The policy principle involved in informing the Taft and Eisenhower staffs that cameras and microphones would be in position for a live program was overlooked.

The outcome of the convention is a matter of history. The MacArthur keynote speech on Monday night that some experts predicted might start an unbeatable boom for the general bombed. The credentials committee issued its report at the Tuesday night session. It supported seating the Eisenhower delegates and was ratified by the convention as a whole. But Eisenhower still lacked a clear majority. Television caught the flavor of the frequently acrimonious debate and even moments of high comedy, including an uproarious episode involving members of the Puerto Rican delegation arguing in full view of the television audience concerning who had the right to cast an alternate vote on a critical credentials issue. Even the chair broke up in laughter as a judge with a heavy accent played a deadpan game with other members of the delegation and won his point, another small boost for the Eisenhower forces.

The original intention in planning broadcast coverage was to keep focused largely on the rostrum, but it quickly became evident that the story of the convention could not be told without talking with the delegates on the floor who were plotting strategy and by switching from time to time to the credentials and platform committees that continued to meet in hotels in the Chicago Loop.

The system devised to keep Cronkite, in the so-called anchor studio, "better informed" than anyone in Chicago lived up to its publicity. Some hurried changes, though, were needed to compensate for inadequacies in planning. It turned out that reports from members of the reporting staff working the convention floor were so critical to understanding the complicated political maneuvers that were under way that some method had to be found to show them on camera. Hewitt solved the problem by winning permission from the Radio News department to place a camera in the CBS radio booth above the rostrum. To enable the cameraman in the booth to search out and focus on a reporter and his interviewee Hewitt improvised a method. He sent a page out to buy flashlights for the floor reporters. When they had interviewees lined up they were to light their flashlights, point them toward the camera in the radio booth, and prepare to go on the air. The system worked and the three imported reporters were indefatigable.

The system devised for delivering information to Cronkite at his desk in the anchor studio also worked smoothly. When not broadcasting directly, floor reporters used private line telephones or their walkie-talkies to call editors sitting in the control room alongside Hewitt. The editors filtered calls, merged the information relayed from the floor reporters with wire service information, condensed the data, and kept reports flowing to two aides to Cronkite, who sat beside him and placed the bulletins on the desk in front of him.

The success of the system was attested to by two social science researchers, Kurt Lang and Gladys Engel Lang, in their analysis of the 1952 conventions:

> CBS sought to cover the convention as a news service would. Information was channeled through a central point where various reports were collected and, if used, their source was identified for the viewer. Throughout the long evening CBS never let its viewers forget the political implications of the many moves on the floor. It attempted to identify each maneuver . . . and to make some sense of what was being shown.[7]

There was one question of policy on which all three networks waffled. Whereas many of the speeches by Republicans of lesser importance were skipped over or carried only in part, the lengthy address of Senator Joseph McCarthy was carried in its entirety. No one dared challenge the wrath and the acid tongue of the Wisconsin senator. McCarthy had been on the offensive for two and a half years. Targets who stood up to him were being devastated by his vitriolic attacks. The easy way out was simply to let the pool signal run without cut-ins.

Innovation, impromptu maneuvers, spur of the moment decisions characterized the coverage. Hewitt discovered at the opening session that the graphic arts team from New York had not brought its type fonts. Without them there was no way to superimpose names and titles to identify speakers on the screen or delegates on the floor. Hewitt devised his own solution. While eating breakfast at the counter of a fast food restaurant near the headquarters hotel he noticed the menu board on the wall. It had movable letters that were set into position to spell out items on the menu. If the board could spell out "bacon and eggs" or "cakes and sausages," he reasoned, it would have no problem with "Gov. Dewey" or "Sen. Lodge." He arranged to buy the board and the letters that went with it. The problem was solved. Hewitt arrived at the convention site that morning, poorer by twenty-five dollars but with his menu board under his arm. As soon as it was set up in the studio it was ready to go.

The Democratic Convention, opening just eleven days after the Republicans finished, was, if anything, louder and more raucous, and its ultimate choice of a presidential candidate was more in doubt. Whereas there were only two genuine front-runners at the GOP meeting there were at least five with a reasonable chance to be the Democratic choice. The ultimate selection of the Republicans depended largely on a decision by its credentials committee, but the Democrats faced an equally formidable problem. They were badly split by the festering sore created by racial tensions in the South. Whereas the Republicans met for long hours, the Democrats met even longer. The twenty-hour guarantee to Westinghouse was met before the second day was over. One session at the Democratic meeting ran more than fourteen hours nonstop.

Reporting the credentials committee proceedings at the Republican meeting was, except for the attempt at closing the session to the press, a relatively straightforward process, simplified by the shuttle relay established by Eisenhower forces to keep media informed of proceedings behind closed doors. The machinations of the competing factions at the Democratic meeting were more complex. They reflected a continuation of the split that had led to the angry walkout from the convention floor in Philadelphia four years earlier and of the tensions that would ultimately lead to the erosion of the old Democratic stranglehold on the South. The rancor displayed on the floor reflected the turbulence within the southern delegations. Television had demonstrated that it could deal effectively with debates on the floor and rulings from the rostrum, but like an iceberg, the floor debate in this case represented only the one-seventh above the surface. To convey the underlying reasons for the tensions reporters would have to investigate the nature of the complex personal relationships within delegations and probe the deals being cut between delegates. The story could only partially be told by relying on speeches on the floor and rulings by the chair. Untangling the complicated threads was, in a sense, a final examination for television news before its graduation to full standing as a medium on a level with newspapers, newsmagazines, and radio.

The CBS staff on the floor, led by Bill Leonard, moved into the southern delegations with their shortwave radio units, their flashlights to get the attention of the cameraman in the radio booth, and their microphones and headsets for communications with Hewitt and the editors. They combed through the delegations, talked to both leaders and members, queried them on motivations and prospective actions, and kept relaying information to the editorial desk. They offered both live interviews and background on what turned out to be the most difficult issue the Democrats had to resolve. It was a new challenge to television news and one that ultimately proved its capability to report beyond the obvious as the camera sees it.

Senator Kefauver was the leader in committed delegates as the convention opened. He could deliver approximately half of the 604 votes required for nomination but he faced stiff opposition from Senators Richard Russell of Georgia, Robert Kerr of Oklahoma, G. Mennen Williams of Michigan, and Governor Averill Harriman of New York. A small group was working behind the scenes on behalf of Governor Adlai Stevenson of Illinois, but at this stage Stevenson was a long shot. He had no pledged delegates. His eloquent welcome to the delegates on behalf of the state of Illinois, however, stimulated a strong undercurrent of support.

The most dramatic moment of the CBS coverage was in a sense an accident but one that demonstrated a unique capability of television. One of the mysteries at the convention revolved around which candidate President Truman would endorse for the presidential nomination. The president was officially listed as a delegate from Missouri. Even though he was still in Washington, a polling of the delegation during the roll call of the states would probably smoke out his position. It was assumed that a poll would be called for and his alternate on the delegate roll would be requested to express his preference.

As the roll call moved toward Missouri, a remote camera at Washington National Airport caught the president in his open limousine on the apron approaching the White House plane, *The Independence*. A cut back to the convention floor showed that the alphabetical polling was approaching Thomas Gavin, the president's alternate. When Gavin's name was called he stood up, removed an envelope from his pocket, and extracted a note

CBS President Frank Stanton, the author, and research director Leon Rice in the election studio on election night 1952. Photo courtesy of Sig Mickelson. Used by permission.

signed by Truman authorizing him to cast his vote for Adlai Stevenson. As Gavin finished reading the note, the scene switched back to Washington to catch the president standing at the top of the ramp of the presidential plane waving his hat. A cut back to the convention showed the polling continuing.

The first ballot ended indecisively but Stevenson had become a major factor in the race. In two more ballots the Illinois governor had won the nomination. Television had demonstrated that it could not only ferret out a significant news story that relied more on intelligent reporting than on electronic wizardry, but add electronic legerdemain to the coverage of that story, thus giving it a dimension that print or radio could not.

Once Governor Stevenson and his choice for the vice presidential nomination, Senator John Sparkman of Alabama, had made their acceptance speeches, the cameras were turned off and the complex electronic switches, tubes, and amplifiers in the control room disassembled and packed up for return to network headquarters in New York.

Ratings had exceeded expectations. Some 60 million viewers had seen some part of the conventions, at least 55 million at one time.[8] Westinghouse, the sponsor that insisted on 20 hours of coverage at each convention, received a combined total of more than 130 hours at the two. Walter Cronkite was no longer an obscure Washington news broadcaster; he was almost as recognizable as the two candidates. The audience for the early evening news broadcasts on CBS and NBC that had totaled approximately 5.8 million homes in the 1951–52 television year by 1953–54 had almost doubled to more than 10.7 million.[9] Convention coverage was undoubtedly a critical factor in the phenomenal growth. Of even greater significance, however, was the fact that television news personnel had passed a critical test. They had held their own with the print press, not as an offshoot of show business but as bona fide members of the Fourth Estate. Representatives of the new medium had demonstrated that they had the competence to participate on an equal basis with the more established media.

The new status was recognized on July 13 by Jack Gould in the *New York Times*: "The spectacular medium of TV last week really won its spurs as an original and creative reporter willing to stand on its own feet and not be pushed around. As such it is a vital and welcome addition to the Fourth Estate."[10] After the Democratic Convention he wrote, "Many millions have gone through a unique and unprecedented educational experience (television coverage) that in one way or another will be reflected in the voting booth in November."[11]

Fourth Estate: newspaper, magazine, radio, television?

10 ·

The Great Airplane Race

By the beginning of 1953 American television viewers had been treated not only to daily news programs but to close-up views of an impressive array of events they could never before have seen without being present. They had been fascinated by live pictures of the Kefauver hearings, meetings of the UN Security Council, the Japanese Peace Conference, and the 1952 American political conventions and elections but nothing so glamorous, colorful, or tradition-steeped as the coronation of a British monarch.

On January 20, 1953, they would be able to watch the inauguration of President Dwight D. Eisenhower, but that would be a pretty drab event compared to a British coronation, with all its tradition, pomp, ceremony, medieval costumes, and royal splendor.

King George VI of England had died in February 1952. Princess Elizabeth became queen immediately on her father's death, but the formal coronation ceremony would not take place until an as yet undetermined date several months in the future.

The announcement that the formal ceremony would take place in June 1953 came during the 1952 political conventions in Chicago. Tension ran so high while the conventions were in progress that little thought was devoted to planning coronation coverage. The performance at the conventions, however, had exceeded everyone's expectations. In the euphoria that followed no assignment, including a coronation, seemed daunting.

Why not, for example, even though it seemed unreasonable, aim for same-day coverage in the United States? The odds against it were formidable. There was no way a television signal could be transported across the Atlantic by electronic means. The ceremony would have to be filmed and shipped. Satellite service was still at least a decade and a half away. A television signal's trajectory was limited to line of sight, a maximum of approximately seventy-five miles. Television had crossed the North American continent but only because signals were transported by microwave relays and coaxial cables. That system would hardly work across the North Atlantic. Microwave transmission depended on relay towers spaced approximately seventy-five miles apart and there were no coaxial cables under the Atlantic, nor would there be.

By midsummer 1952, a date for the event had been set, June 2, in Westminster Abbey in London. That would allow about six months' lead time after the American election to lay out a plan and mobilize whatever resources would be required for implementation.

The prospect of making a kinescope (a television recording) of the event was considered but offered serious if not insurmountable problems. British television was transmitted at a rate of 405 lines per frame, the U.S. signal at 525 lines, British standards set projector speed at 30 frames per second; the U.S., 24 frames. British electric power operated at a 50-cycle rate and U.S. at 60 cycles. The two systems were totally incompatible. But there seemed no alternative to kinescoping. Only by reaching an agreement with the BBC for access to its signal could an American company show scenes from within the abbey.

AT&T was scheduled to place a new transatlantic cable in service on January 15. Would it offer a possible solution? It would have bandwidth capable of carrying a telephone signal. Might it also be able to transmit television? William B. Lodge, vice president in charge of general engineering for CBS, quickly dampened that dream. The new cable, he said, was quite capable of transmitting the coronation film if the film were to be cut into separate frames, transmitted one frame at a time, and then reassembled at the New York cable head. At 30 frames per second this would mean that one minute of programming would consume 1,800 frames, an hour 108,000 frames, and three hours more than 300,000. At an absolute minimum of 10 seconds to transmit each frame the total time consumed in transmission of the entire ceremony would amount to 3 million seconds or nearly 35 days. Added to that would be time spent in cutting frame from frame at the British cable head and reassembling them in New York. That seemed a little excessive. It would save time to wait for a copy of the BBC telerecording and ship it across the Atlantic by slow freighter. Some more practical solution was required.

An exploratory trip to London seemed to be in order. I took off in mid-December to explore possible alternatives. Howard K. Smith, the CBS London bureau chief, had scheduled appointments with George Barnes, the director of the BBC Television Service, and Norman Collins, a former BBC program controller who had resigned to join a company planning the production of a high-quality telerecording (kinescoping) unit. Barnes assured us that BBC would give us permission to use the BBC television signal, but it was up to us to determine where and how to record it and how it might be transported to the United States.

Collins proposed a plan that seemed to meet the recording requirements. His company, High Definition Films, had designed a device that promised to deliver higher quality than the American kinescoping system, but it was not fully tested. It was a gamble that any units would be off the assembly line in time for the June 2 event, and there was no assurance that the system could make the necessary conversion from British standards to American. Further exploration was obviously necessary. The idea of using telerecording, though, was intriguing. If we could find a way to convert the British system to U.S. standards, same day coverage from within Westminster Abbey might be a possibility.

Employing British camera crews to film the event in a 35-mm format was an alternative, although it was unlikely that sound would be available. Film, except from the newsreel pool, would also miss the main event, the actual crowning of the queen. Pool film would not be available until days after the event. Whether or not we should decide on film, it seemed imperative that we apply immediately for camera positions along the route of march. I walked the full route to be able to select likely locations for which we might apply. I also went to Westminster Abbey to make a preliminary survey of what might be expected during the ceremony. Some innovative way of using the kinescoping process seemed to offer the only hope for full coverage delivered the same day. Bill Lodge was asked to find an answer.

In the meantime, delivering a program on a same day basis was no longer a dream. It had become a necessity. CBS Television was still suffering from its decision some years earlier to discourage many of its major market radio affiliates from applying for television licenses. They had been urged to await a favorable decision by the FCC on licensing the CBS color system. For a full three years the FCC freeze on granting licenses had blocked potential applicants from submitting applications. Consequently, NBC still had a preponderance of primary affiliates in a number of important markets. The CBS Television sales force found that in some cases it could interest an advertiser only if it could deliver a full network including some of those stations that had signed primary affiliation contracts with NBC. In marketing coronation coverage it wouldn't be enough to argue that CBS's would be the best. The only way to be sure of winning acceptance from stations that had a choice among networks would be to guarantee to be first. The prospect of investing so much capital on an unsponsored program without hope of any reasonable return did not inspire enthusiasm in CBS executive ranks. To protect its investment, CBS had to be first.

Some company executives held out for film. A representative of the Technical Operations department with film experience went to London to check further into 35-mm possibilities. He returned with assurances we could find a sufficient number of freelance cameramen to film the coronation parade, but the ceremony in Westminster Abbey was out. He also had commitments from a film laboratory that promised to process the exposed negative on a rush basis. On the basis of his report, a BOAC Stratocruiser, the largest passenger plane in transatlantic service, was chartered for a flight to the United States immediately after completion of the coronation ceremony. Seats in the cocktail lounge in the lower level of the plane would be removed to install film editing equipment. Logan Airport in Boston, an hour closer to London than New York, was chosen as the originating point for the program.

The five-hour time difference would give the film editors approximately fourteen hours from the conclusion of the ceremony at 1:00 P.M. London time (8:00 A.M. back on the East Coast) until 10:00 P.M., the projected air time, to assemble a program out of the mass of footage that camera crews would deliver. It would, however, be silent footage with no scenes inside the abbey.

Lodge, meanwhile, had been exploring other options. He had concluded that although there was no equipment on the market to kinescope the ceremony, it might be possible to design a unit that could record, make the necessary standards conversions, and process a kinescope rapidly enough to make the one o'clock flight. It would be a complicated problem. The prospective device would have to perform miracles. It would have to make the conversion from British to American standards, process the negative, and dry it so that it could be projected on a screen all within less than a minute.

Lodge assigned three of his engineers to do preliminary design work. General Precision Laboratories in New York agreed to accept the assignment to build a unit to their specifications. The unit, which had to be built within weeks, would record BBC's live picture at whatever point we selected, convert it to U.S. film standards, process it, dry it, and project it on a wall screen fifty to sixty seconds after the event. Sound would be recorded on a separate track. Film editors would take the processed and dried film from the projector, match it with the separately recorded sound track, cut it to a specified length, and prepare it for shipment while the event was still in progress. The concept was revolutionary.

Much of the editing would have to be done "in camera." The camera would be turned off during portions of the program not regarded as vital to the finished package. Decisions concerning segments to be cut would have to be made in advance. This process would save time by reducing the volume of film to be edited. The cuts had to be made judiciously so that commercials could be inserted without disturbing the flow of the ceremony.

Many details remained to be ironed out, but there was now a product the sales department could market with hope, if not full assurance, that CBS Television would be the first to transmit it to American stations. There

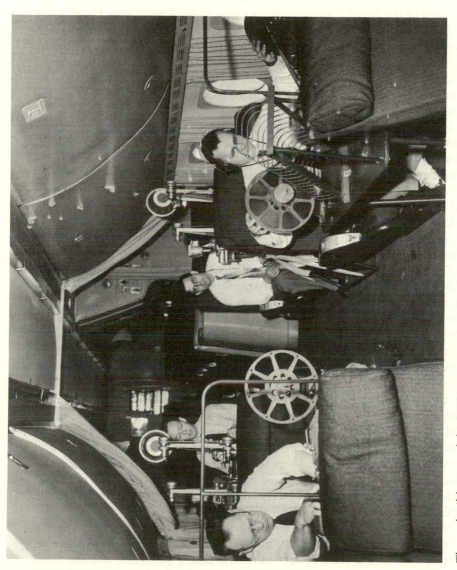

The cocktail lounge of the BOAC Stratocruiser Champion converted to a film editing room as the plane proceeded across the North Atlantic from London to Boston on coronation day 1953. Photo courtesy of Sig Mickelson. Used by permission.

was little word as to what NBC or ABC was doing. NBC's plans were well guarded and ABC seemed only mildly interested. Shortly after the program was offered for sale it was snapped up by an advertiser, with the understanding that it would be first on the air in the United States. The advertiser was the Willys-Overland motorcar company, makers of Overland, the "Queen of the Road." Some eyebrows should have been raised at "Queen of the Road," but none were. Once the sales order was signed, the network's Station Relations department went to work to build a station acceptance lineup that would give the advertiser the national market he desired. The big single-station markets, including Buffalo, Indianapolis, St. Louis, Milwaukee, Grand Rapids-Kalamazoo, and Norfolk, had to be given assurances that CBS would be first.

Space for installing the recording, processing, and editing equipment was rented in a partially abandoned building adjacent to a taxiway at London's Heathrow Airport for recording and at Logan Airport for projecting the program to the network. Plans were completed to ship the high-speed processing equipment, as soon as it had been assembled at General Precision Labs, to the London airport for installation. Lodge's three engineers bought tickets for the London trip to be on the scene to install the new hardware. It was estimated that even leaving in early April they would be barely finished by the June 2 deadline.

The BBC in combination with the Canadian Broadcasting Corporation (CBC) by mid-April had offered a solution to the problem of arranging quick transportation across the North Atlantic for early film packages. They had a commitment from the Royal Canadian Air Force to make a Canberra jet bomber available to carry CBC film to Montreal. The American networks were offered the opportunity to ship their film aboard the same flight. There would be a refueling stop at Goose Bay in Labrador. They could either off-load a package there or send it on to Montreal. As an alternative they had the option of taking the CBC feed from Montreal, thus eliminating the necessity of producing separate programs. Taking the CBC feed would be an inexpensive alternative; would have been a tempting prospect had we not already invested a substantial sum in the project and obtained a commercial sale. There was another compelling reason for going ahead on our own. A CBS-produced program would have its own character and its own talent and would be timed to fit a specific schedule. Use of the CBC feed was not given a second thought.

The second option seemed more realistic: accept the CBC offer to fly the program material to Goose Bay and find a way to get it from there to Boston. We would then project our own edited program, not the CBC uncut version. In order to capitalize on the CBC offer, however, we had to find a high-speed carrier to transport the cargo from Goose Bay to Boston. The chartered BOAC Stratocruiser would leave London shortly after 1:00 P.M. but would take up to fourteen hours to make the flight to Logan

Airport. That would be satisfactory for a program assembled out of 35-mm motion picture film but was not nearly as attractive a prospect as a late afternoon release carrying the actual crowning ceremony. What we now needed was an aircraft poised at Goose Bay for a run to Boston as soon as the RCAF plane unloaded its cargo.

Fortunately the network's Station Relations department had an answer. Jimmy Stewart, the Hollywood actor, owned one of the fastest aircraft in the nation, a souped-up World War II propeller-driven P-51 Mustang fighter. Its regular pilot, Joe DiBona, had won a number of races with the aircraft. Stewart, by a bit of good luck, owned a partial interest in a CBS affiliate in Galveston and Houston. He was asked to make his plane available for the run from Goose Bay to Boston. Both he and DiBona were enthusiastic. The combination of the RCAF Canberra and Jimmy Stewart's P-51 reinforced our optimism that we could make good on the commitment to be first. NBC might be able to find another speedy plane but not one with a record comparable to Jimmy Stewart's. Projection time from Boston before 5:00 P.M. EDT seemed a realistic possibility.

There was, however, one major hitch. At some point the film had to be edited. Some editing could be done in camera (by recording only those elements in the program that were virtually certain to be included in the final product), but there would still be a considerable volume of fine cutting to do. The sound track posed a separate but complex problem. Since it would be recorded separately it would have to be matched with the film, a time-consuming job. The fourteen-hour flight across the Atlantic on the Stratocruiser would have allowed ample time for matching sound and picture and for cutting the final program to fit within the hour allocated. There would be no time or space, however, for editing on either the Canberra or the P-51. The cockpit of the P-51 is so tiny that there was even some question about how many film cans could be accommodated.

Editing would have to be completed in the rented space at Heathrow Airport so that a completed package cut for transmission from Boston could be shipped out with the RCAF flight. Editing in camera would substantially reduce the volume to be cut, but that meant the ceremony would have to be studied in such detail that the recording gear could be shut down during those segments that were not essential to the finished product. Fortunately the 1937 coronation of the queen's father, George VI, had been recorded from beginning to end and distributed as a 78 rpm record album. Studying the album would provide clues about portions to cut. The *Times* of London's verbatim report of the 1936 ceremony was also helpful. Advance schedules for the 1953 event suggested that the program content would be similar if not identical. Both the record album and the special edition of the *Times* were quickly obtained for intense study.

Since the Stratocruiser had already been chartered there was no choice but to go forward with that alternative, partly to provide insurance in the event any calamity would befall the kinescope project and partly to be able to offer a second and quite different view at a different hour. The program would follow the procession from Buckingham Palace to Westminster Abbey and presumably capture all the color along the route.

Walter Cronkite was selected to narrate the 16-mm program scheduled for late afternoon release and Ed Murrow the 35-mm program now booked for 10:00 P.M. Murrow would broadcast as a member of the CBS Radio team along the parade route and then rush to the airport to catch the one o'clock flight. Don Hewitt would work with the film editors organizing material for the early program and board the chartered plane to produce the 10:00 P.M. version.

There was still no word from ABC concerning its plans. NBC had announced that it had chartered a DC-6 from Pan American Airways and that it would mount a major effort. BBC also reported that NBC had accepted the CBC offer of transatlantic passage for a program on the RCAF Canberra and was setting up a recording facility at an airport southwest of London.

With less than three weeks to go, the CBS and NBC Press Information departments began a publicity battle that was designed to squeeze out every possible advantage. The focus quickly narrowed to the race to be first. Both networks unleashed the power of their publicity machines to forecast impending victory, even though it might be by minutes or even seconds. The technical problems involved in coverage and the ceremony itself were overlooked in the frenzied effort to focus on the race.

As Walter Cronkite, Mrs. Cronkite, and I boarded the sleek new transatlantic steamer the *United States* for the five-day trip across the Atlantic we carried along with us the London *Times* special edition of twenty-six years earlier and a thick packet of coronation information distributed by the BBC and the British Ministry of Information.

On our second day in London the BBC hosted a reception for all visiting media. It was there that the blow struck. NBC, we learned, had obtained its own jet transportation. The NBC staff would ship its taped program on another Canberra jet bomber, this one built by English Electric for the Venezuelan Air Force. The manufacturer, we learned, was scheduled to turn the plane over to the Venezuelans on or about June 1. A British airplane ferrying company would ferry it to Caracas to deliver it to the Venezuelan Air Force. The ferrying company had agreed with NBC representatives to time the trip to coincide with the coronation, enabling them to transport the NBC film across the Atlantic, stopping in New York en route to the Venezuelan capital.

This would be a tough combination to beat. The margin of victory for NBC would not necessarily be substantial. It appeared that we had lost not only the race but also the commitment to our affiliates. The humiliation might be even worse.

Even though it was past midnight New York time I called the CBS Television president, Jack VanVolkenburg, to urge him to ask the Press Information department to tone down the airplane race frenzy. I told him I thought we would not be defeated by a wide margin but we had better be prepared to come in second. It was a dismal prospect, made even more so by the tumultuous press information campaign that had stressed the race, not the ingenuity involved in surmounting the odds against same day coverage.

Logistical problems to be encountered during the last twelve hours before Coronation Day were further irritations. At sunup on June 2 the entire area of London in any way involved in the coronation festivities would be sealed off to all but limited high-priority traffic. There would be no ingress or egress from what was described as the "box." Since most of the personnel involved in the CBS coverage were housed inside the box, that meant moving the night before to quarters outside the restricted area. Most of the CBS team would stay at the Old House in Windsor, a half hour taxi ride from Heathrow Airport.

An early start for the airport was necessary in order to clear customs and immigration before starting to record the program at 8:00 A.M. At 5:30 A.M. taxis were not easy to find in Windsor. One of ancient vintage finally showed. The driver was skeptical that he had enough petrol to make it to Heathrow but he might find a filling station en route. There was no apparent alternative so four of us with baggage jumped in. There were no filling stations open so we instructed the driver to keep going. Less than a mile from our destination the ancient taxi wheezed its last. The petrol tank was empty. The trip to the nearest airport entrance was not too far away to cover on foot except for the heavy load of baggage we were carrying. It seemed more sensible to instruct the driver to remain at the wheel while we pushed the cab the last three-fourths of a mile to our destination. Not a good omen to start a day when the odds were against us anyway.

The film editors took up their positions. Cronkite went to a desk at the back of the room that had been set up for his commentary. The recording and processing machinery would be manned by the engineers from the CBS General Engineering department who had designed the equipment and installed it, assisted by an engineer from General Precision Laboratories. It was ominous that they were all engineers and not operating technicians. The film editors and their equipment were on a slight rise above the main floor, where they could work apart from the bustle on the floor but could keep an eye on the screen that projected the film after its recording and processing.

The inexperience of the engineers as operating technicians quickly became apparent. We had decided to make our first cut approximately fifteen minutes into the ceremony. The pause would also furnish an opportunity to change reels in the film recorder/processor. One of the engineers trying to replace a reel froze. His fingers turned to rubber. He needed help to get the old reel off the sprocket and a fresh one installed. The job was finished barely in time to resume recording at a previously determined point in the ceremony.

The film editors, meanwhile, were swamped under the pressure of working with unfamiliar equipment and facing a more complicated assignment than they ever dealt with in New York. The processed film and accompanying sound track came in a flow so rapid it engulfed them. As the torrent increased in volume they got further and further behind. Matching sound to film was done only haphazardly and there was no effort to tie the whole program together in one continuous reel. Film cans were haphazardly marked and set aside for delivery to the Canberra. It was hoped they could be untangled and properly aligned in Boston before going on the air. Some were shipped without adequate instructions for reassembling.

Meanwhile the 35-mm film from the camera positions along the route of march was slow in arriving. An elaborate master plan employing motorcycle couriers had been designed to pick up exposed stock from cameramen at their positions along the route, rush it to the laboratory for processing, and deliver it, once processed, to the rented facility at Heathrow. Since the processing took some time it was not surprising that it was late morning before shipments started arriving. But then they began to arrive in torrents.

While the frenzied activity continued in the makeshift studio and recording room, the BOAC Stratocruiser, carrying the name plate "The Champion," was towed into position on the tarmac just a short walk from the recording and editing studio. Promptly at 12:30 P.M., the queen had been crowned, the recording equipment was shut down, film cans were labeled and prepared for shipment to the RCAF Canberra, and the 35-mm film shot along the route of the parade was moved to the waiting plane. By 12:55 the last member of the team mounted the steps into the aircraft. At 1:00 P.M. doors were closed and the plane was ready for takeoff.

The film editors, who had been working since eight o'clock that morning, only had time for a quick lunch before they took their positions at the moviolas in the downstairs lounge. The editing procedure was more complicated than had been contemplated. The editors had been accustomed to working with 16-mm reversal film cut largely with the use of hand cranked viewers and sound readers. They had very little experience with the more sensitive 35-mm film and the much more sophisticated moviolas. There was no script; it would have to be written after screening the film. Murrow was upset because there was neither natural sound nor recorded sound to back the footage. Hewitt was left with the unenviable task of trying to make something out of a disparate collection of disconnected film segments. He was supported by a group of harried film editors and a disgruntled narrator.

To compound the discomfort, Captain Anderson, the commanding officer of the aircraft, decided that head winds were likely to be so strong that we would have to land at Gander, Newfoundland, for refueling, thus reducing what little latitude we had for making the scheduled 10:00 P.M. program slot. Compounding the gloom was the knowledge that the Venezuelan Air Force jet was racing to North America with NBC's package aboard—and the possibility that NBC's Pan American DC-6 might make the crossing without a fuel stop.

Approximately four hours out of London the captain went back to the passenger cabin and suggested that we drink a champagne toast to the queen. Murrow, Hewitt, Lodge, and I joined in. A steward brought out a bottle of champagne, filled our glasses, and, standing in the center aisle, we lifted our glasses to the new British sovereign. While we were standing there, glasses in hand, a member of the crew handed me a cable that had been received in the cockpit. It was signed "Cronkite."

The cable read: "NBC Canberra returned London mechanical stop Pony Express Canberra No. 1 en route o.k. no return stop Pony Express 2 returned this load dispatched on relief Canberra."[1]

The cable needed no interpretation. NBC's Canberra had failed to make it across the Atlantic and was headed back to London. The RCAF Canberra with our film, and NBC's, would apparently make it to Goose Bay. An airplane race between Joe DiBona in Jimmy Stewart's P-51 and a pilot for NBC in another P-51 would decide which network would be first on the air in the United States with a commercial program. Actually, ABC would be several minutes ahead of us, but the program it carried would be CBC's uncut version, which it would pick up from CBC's origination point in Montreal. Further, since the BBC program would be time-sequential and uncut, the actual crowning would follow many minutes of preliminaries. It was a reasonable certainty that CBS would show the archbishop of Canterbury placing the crown on the queen's head before the CBC version reached that point. Furthermore, it would be a CBS-produced program, including the commercials from Overland. Prospects at this point looked good.

Prospects for the 10:00 P.M. program, however, were gloomy. Captain Anderson insisted on the Gander refueling stop. Information from the cockpit indicated that NBC's Pan American DC-6 was following a more southerly route and would make it to Boston without a stop. Refueling would add forty-five minutes to an hour to the flight time but it appeared that we would still land in Boston a few minutes before air time. It was obvious from a check on the film editors that they needed every minute. The Champion landed at Logan at approximately 9:40 P.M. EST. As it taxied across the airport to the temporary studio where the program would originate, the editors were still putting on finishing touches. They had barely finished as the passenger door opened.

The program itself was an anticlimax. Murrow was obviously unhappy at the absence of sound. Film kept breaking up in the projector, whether because of a problem with the projector or with the splices that had been inserted by an inexperienced editing crew we did not know. Joe DiBona, we learned, had won the airplane race by several minutes, but NBC had been on the air with a coronation program thirteen minutes ahead of us. When an NBC executive noted that the NBC pilot was running well behind DiBona he called ABC, offering to pay ABC's costs for importing the CBC program from Canada if NBC could share the ABC feed. ABC accepted the offer so both networks were on the air ahead of CBS but with the original uncut BBC program.

The day was not wholly a disaster but very little had gone right. The only bright spot was that only CBS had its own program, recorded with its own narration, edited by its own staff, sponsored by an advertiser, and on the air first with the highlight of the day, the actual coronation scene.

But was it worthwhile? Other than demonstrating that the infant medium of television could perform feats bordering on magic, should it have attempted a venture that apparently was beyond its capabilities and those of the communications technologies available to it?

The press thought not. The *New York Times* was bitterly negative. Jack Gould, the *Times* television critic, wrote in the edition of June 7, "The two American networks . . . moved in on the coronation with a depressing lack of understanding, judgment and common sense."[2] Gould criticized the "astonishing lack of discernment in the handling of commercials which tended to becloud some good editing." He was critical of the Willys-Overland commercial, which characterized an automobile as a queen. It was "simply inexcusable," he wrote. He was even more outspoken about an episode on NBC's "Today" program. "Utterly disgraceful was NBC video's interruption of the religious service on its morning program 'Today' in order to show a chimpanzee." He was equally critical of the publicity campaign that preceded the coronation programs. "Weeks before the coronation," he wrote, "the two networks engaged in a publicity war that steadily grew in intensity and coarse stupidity." To the credit of the networks, however, he noted, "Today marks the birth of international television."[3]

For all the mistakes, debatable taste, and opportunities bungled something may have been gained. Television moved another step forward. It was clearly a setback after the progress of the 1952 political year, but the many errors in execution, could probably be checked off to the growing-up process. The whole episode signaled what television would be able to do once it had videotape, electronic cameras, communications satellites, digitized video editing equipment, and experienced personnel.

The entire coronation venture may have been best symbolized by an experience of my own. On the second day out of New York on the USS *United States*, my birthday, Walter and Betsy Cronkite decorated a bottle of premium scotch with a bow and a card and had it placed on our dinner table. I took the bottle to my room unopened. On arrival in Southampton I packed it and took it along to London. In London I placed it, still unopened, on a chest of drawers. Bill Lodge, who shared the room with me, asked one night whether he might have a sip. I invited him do so but did not join him. Before leaving for the Old House in Windsor I repacked it, still untouched. From the Old House it went to London airport, to the BOAC Stratocruiser, and in Boston to the Parker House hotel. The next morning it went to South Station and onto a New Haven train for the trip to Bridgeport, Connecticut. In Bridgeport a porter set down the bag with the scotch on the cement walkway. I heard a crunching sound, looked down, and saw the bag surrounded by a large wet spot. When I arrived home it contained the remnants of a broken bottle and a mass of wet laundry. It seemed a fitting climax to a venture in which almost everything that could go wrong did.[4]

11 •

The Corporation Declares a Cease-Fire

As news operations at CBS Television returned to normal after a turbulent political year and the harrowing coronation experience two critical problems that had been in limbo required immediate attention. The network's News department still had not found a satisfactory solution to the vexing problem of coordinating narration, motion picture film, live action, and graphics in a fully integrated news report that reflected the full capabilities of television. It had concluded, however, that it would have to establish its own film gathering facilities to deliver a product with the imagination and creativity it was certain would be required.

A second problem was equally vexing. The network had failed to discover a workable pattern for sharing facilities and personnel with the radio network's larger, more experienced, and more adequately staffed news facility. The relationship between the two was disintegrating into a nasty family brawl dramatized by the close proximity required by coronation preparations. Tension had begun to develop as early as the Japanese Peace Conference and had been intensifying since. Prior to the 1952 conventions the newer medium was looked on as only a harmless nuisance. Now it was becoming a threat.

The embittered relationship with radio news, however, had to be set aside in favor of a more substantive problem; how best to illustrate information that would constitute the substance of its news reports, assuming that motion picture film adapted to television would be a key factor. Covering serious news graphically had been a prime concern since the pioneering days in the late 1940s but the goal was largely unrealized. It was assumed in the news room that reliance on outside film suppliers was unworkable and devising a method to create its own film product was essential. There had been no progress, only fruitless talk.

The tension with Radio News leadership was not helping solve the problem of pictorial content. It was an irritating distraction that had to be set aside while answers were found to the more basic question. Radio determined to maintain rigid control of the correspondent staff, who remained wholly on its payroll, and of the communication facilities required to coordinate its efforts. It was becoming increasingly clear that television would be served only after radio had satisfied its own needs. Since Television News had no reporters of its own it would have to depend on radio for occasional reporting assignments and for communications. It was assumed that a pictorial news service would not realize its full potential until it could fuse the reporting of a superior correspondent with imaginative video material. As a side issue television complained that it was being charged what it regarded as outrageous sums for the limited and begrudging service it received from the correspondent corps.

Easing tensions and setting up a more equitable pattern for sharing resources could only be accomplished by high-level corporate decisions, but the improving status of television's finances could help significantly in obtaining final approval. By 1953 television network income was beginning to increase dramatically and prospects for the future were perceptibly brightening. Newly licensed stations were beginning to complete construction and turn on their transmitters in increasing numbers after the lifting of the three-year FCC freeze. The number of interconnected stations on the CBS Television network grew from 66 to 113 during the 1953 calendar year.[1] Optimism concerning profit prospects was beginning to emerge after several years that had required continuing investment with little hope of return. Senior corporate officers now might look a little more sympathetically at a proposal to invest in improving film coverage.

Planning for producing news film in-house began while the election campaign of 1952 was still in progress. The first specific proposal to sever connections with Telenews and go it alone was contained in a memorandum from Mickelson to CBS Television president Jack Van Volkenburg and Vice Presidents Merle Jones and Spencer Harrison on October 27, 1952.[2] The memo proposed the establishment of a CBS news film organization adequate to furnish service to both the Television News department and, probably unrealistically, "See It Now." It was suggested that it might recover some of its costs by marketing a syndicated news film service to local stations. CBS Television Film Sales would handle marketing and sales.

Planning in London for the coronation of the British queen created an opening for examining prospects both in the United Kingdom and on the

Continent for creating an independent film service. It furnished an opportunity to meet with CBS bureau chiefs to take a reading on their recommendations and to seek the cooperation of Bill McClure, the European producer-cameraman of "See It Now."

McClure, who had signed on six months earlier with Fred Friendly as roving cameraman and producer in Europe, had worked on the Continent for several years for Pathé, at the time the most prestigious of the traditional newsreels. As a result he was acquainted with most of the camera personnel working in Europe for the American newsreels. He was also acquainted with many freelancers, some of whom he had employed on occasion to work with him. He had agreed during a New York visit several weeks earlier to discuss with me the possible shape of a CBS news film structure and had Fred Friendly's approval to assist as long as it did not interfere with his assigned duties.

In an all night session in a suite at the George V hotel in Paris the two of us worked out the details for an organization we believed would supply the service we needed. On the basis of McClure's wide-ranging experience we were able to suggest venues where we might base camera teams and to estimate costs. What we were projecting was an organization vastly more complicated and designed to deliver substantially more product than even the most productive newsreels and to aim primarily at hard news and interpretation rather than feature items. The reels had customarily produced one ten-minute release each week, two at most. We were aiming from the beginning to deliver raw material for at least a half hour of news daily with emphasis on fast-breaking important stories, not the soft features that were much of the content of the traditional newsreel. We had not the slightest doubt that the swiftly expanding television business would devour even more material in the future, thus imposing pressures that we could not then even contemplate.

The plan I took back to New York was to obtain raw material from three sources: our own soon to be employed camera crews, exchange agreements with television broadcasters or film production companies in major countries, and part-time personnel ("stringers") who would be paid retainers supplemented by fees for material ordered.

Permanent two-man crews were projected for London, Paris, Bonn, and Beirut with stringers in Berlin, Vienna, Rome, Copenhagen, Istanbul, and Tel Aviv. Exchange agreements would be sought for backup purposes in all major capitals, including London, where the BBC had already agreed to participate. National television systems would be our first choice for exchanges, but we could not hope for much at this stage. European television in 1953, except the BBC, was light years behind the United States.

McClure had personnel in mind for some of the slots we projected and promised to check out others during the performance of his "See It Now" duties.[3] Coverage of the Far East was omitted from this conversation except that it was agreed that there would have to be a bureau in Tokyo and a continued presence in Korea, at least until the end of the Korean War.

The projected budget for the European and Middle Eastern portions of a new news film operation was estimated to total approximately $650,000 exclusive of overhead costs and the additional outlay required to beef up the New York headquarters to a level consistent with requirements for managing the entire operation. To round out a fully international service, bureaus would have to be added in Washington, Chicago, and Los Angeles. The problem of the Far East coverage was deferred for later exploration. Careful analysis of the master plan encouraged us to believe that that the entire structure could be put in place for approximately $2 million annually. That was the amount we decided to request from the television network.

To offset some of the cost, plans were projected to create a news film unit that would deliver a syndicated service to television stations, now beginning to come on the air in increasing numbers. The content of station news might be primarily local, but news directors would need some national and international film coverage to round out their efforts. We were confident we could deliver a service superior to Telenews or the new UP-Fox alliance that promised to start marketing product in the spring. We had the dual advantages of close ties to our affiliated stations and reliance for marketing on an experienced film sales organization in the television network. It was also to our advantage that we were in the television business and presumably knew better than an outsider what kind of product television stations would want.

The project still, however, had to win the support of the television network. Prospects for a profitable year, the first ever for television, were favorable as the year opened, but the mood at the executive level remained cautious. The company was spending heavily to create entertainment programs that would win the ratings competition. A major investment in a worldwide film organization to support a broadcast activity that did not promise immediate profit was more difficult to sell. Since the late 1920s, however, CBS had operated under the theory that it might not always win the highest ratings for its entertainment programs but that winning prestige for news would ultimately pay off. Prospects for support from senior corporate management were optimistic; historically, corporate executives had taken great pride in the acclaimed news staff and desired to give it favorable exposure. Building an equally prestigious news film organization would clearly fit the corporate pattern.

A prolonged battle to win approval of the $2 million annual budget for the new enterprise began in late January. Haste was essential since the Telenews contract was to expire in mid-May. A short extension was unlikely. UP-Fox was frantic to sell its service, but CBS concluded that, in essence, it was only another Telenews. It might furnish superior service but it would offer no mechanism for coordinating ideas developed by a skilled reporter with pictures delivered by a camera.

A detailed budget was prepared. There were meetings with senior television network executives, one lasting all night, but still no decision. In mid-March corporate officers were brought into the picture. Dan O'Shea, the corporate vice president and former senior executive in the David O. Selznik organization, who had been the point man in the CBS effort to minimize damage from the blacklisting program, took his extensive Hollywood experience to the table. After listening to an exhaustive explanation of the news film plan, examining the projected budget, and participating in a detailed cross-examination, O'Shea closed the meeting with a short statement: "They say they can do it for $2 million. We should give them the chance."

The new venture was officially announced on April 8. The memo declared that CBS News and Public Affairs would be divided immediately into three equal units: News, Newsfilm, and Public Affairs.[4] Newsfilm would function as a supplier to the news department and would operate in close coordination with news management. Its assignment staff would work with the news director and program units.[5]

Time was short and immediate action was required. The organization to be created was named CBS Newsfilm. A former senior Pathé editor, Ned Buddy, accepted appointment as Newsfilm manager. The manager of broadcast operations for the Associated Press in Washington, Howard Kany, would be Washington bureau manager; Frank Donghi from the United Press picture service in Paris, foreign editor. Chester Burger, who had built the domestic stringer operation, became national assignment editor. John Cooper from International News Service would head syndication. As soon as Ned Buddy arrived he began to fill in the slots on the table of organization.

Immediate decisions on film stock were required. The reversal film that had been used since the news operation started in 1946 would have to be replaced, particularly if a syndication effort were to be undertaken. Only negative-positive film would yield the multiple prints required to satisfy syndication needs. Since the film stock was to be changed, it was time to seek higher quality than could be delivered by optical sound. Hewitt, among others, had been urging a switch from optical sound to a method in which the sound would be recorded on a magnetic stripe running along the edge of the raw stock. Making the change required adjustments in the laboratory. Using a negative-positive mode also meant that for the first time a useful film library could be built and maintained. It was even possible that library footage could be marketed.

All the while the May 15 deadline for going it alone was quickly approaching, and nothing had been done about activating a foreign service. Except for the December conversations with BBC and some informal talks with the French government television network no firm decisions had been made.

Friendly had promised to release McClure for a few days in mid-April to tour Europe with me interviewing and employing camera crews, signing commitments with stringers, and arranging exchange agreements with television and film services. In two weeks we covered seven countries: Denmark, Germany, Austria, Switzerland, Italy, France, and the United Kingdom. We employed full camera teams in London and Bonn and contract film correspondents in Berlin and Vienna. Contracts for providing service on order were signed with companies in Denmark and Italy and exchange agreements with BBC television and ORTF in France. Italian television was unavailable. The NBC correspondent in Rome had gotten word of our trip, hurried to Milan, and negotiated an exclusive contract prior to our arrival.

The London crew was ready to start immediately, the Bonn/Frankfurt team within a couple of weeks. The failure to find suitable personnel in Rome and Paris was a disappointment so we reluctantly decided to buy time by contracting temporarily with an Italian newsreel company, Incom, even though we were not optimistic about the choice. The company was so close to the Italian government it could be counted on to reflect only official points of view. It was at best a stopgap. We would keep on looking for a full-time employee. In Paris, prospects were even dimmer; French television, ORTF, was simply not ready to deliver a professional service. Fortunately, David Schoenbrun, the CBS correspondent on the scene, had on occasion employed freelance personnel who were passably acceptable and would probably be available for occasional assignments.

It was the beginning of a service but only the beginning. Equipment had to be purchased, raw film stock meeting the new standards shipped, and plans for traffic flow drafted. Communication links had to be developed and raw nerves among CBS radio personnel soothed. Trial runs in the film laboratory were necessary to assure reasonable quality. Setting up a system for controlling the flow of communications and film was a particularly knotty problem. A traffic department was organized and charged with the responsibility of getting exposed film to New York in the quickest possible way. Personnel had to be familiar with airline schedules. Propeller-driven planes then in use were slow. Commercial jet aircraft were still several years in the future. Range was limited so refueling stops were frequent. And flights, compared to those a decade later, were infrequent. Traffic personnel had the responsibility of seeing to it that film packages were shipped by the fastest possible routes and were able to make all the required transfers on the way, since direct flights were limited. Arrangements also had to be made for customs clearances. Meanwhile, the May 15 deadline for termination of the Telenews service was rapidly approaching.

Promptly on that date the new organization was on its own. The first few weeks were difficult. Quality levels were low. There was confusion in the traffic department. Film from remote points was late in arriving. Coordination with the laboratory was still awkward. Hewitt tore his hair trying to build high-quality programs with inferior raw material. The most discouraging blow came from CBS's chairman, Paley, who wrote and distributed a memo criticizing the quality of the independently produced product. The intense effort devoted to the coronation ceremony in London diverted attention for a short time, but the staff still had to face up to the fact that rapid improvement was essential. By midsummer wheels were beginning to mesh, quality was improving, and grumbling began to subside.

In late July a major blow struck. Ned Buddy, who had been counted on to lead the organization through this formative stage, suddenly died of a heart attack. Howard Kany, the director of the Washington bureau who had headed an effort by the Associated Press to enter the news film syndication field at an earlier date, was quickly moved to New York to replace Buddy. Elmer Lower was recruited from the United States High Commission for Germany in Bonn to replace Kany in Washington.

By the end of the summer the new organization was running adequately if not smoothly. The syndication service began on September 28 with KLZ-TV in Denver as its first customer. Televisa in Mexico followed shortly as the first international customer. There were still weaknesses that would ultimately have to be repaired. The relationship with Incom in Italy was at best a stopgap; Paris, too, was a problem. An active search was in progress in both capitals for capable camera operators who gave promise of being flexible enough to adapt their work to television requirements. Tokyo would have to be dealt with in time, but a freelance crew, under contract since late 1950 to cover the war in Korea, was a satisfactory solution until the war there ended.

The new venture quickly opened new wounds in relations between the radio and television news departments. It deepened a wound that had been festering almost from the day that they were split into separate units in mid-July 1951. Members of the Television News editorial staff, including writers, editors, and reporters, were still carried on the radio payroll, even though they were devoting full time to television. The depth of the animosity of radio news executives to television first surfaced during the Japanese Peace Conference. It was only a minor irritation but proved to be a forerunner of more serious altercations to come.

The political campaign of 1952 was covered by television with little dependence on radio. Reporter-contacts and writers went along with camera crews to cover some events, and others were covered by film only. At the conventions, television, except for enlisting Ed Murrow and Eric Sevareid from time to time to do analytical pieces, relied entirely on a makeshift reporting staff recruited from news departments of CBS-owned stations. The two departments operated as if they represented two entirely separate

companies. It probably did not ease the animosity that television performance attracted more favorable critical attention.

Television's early moves toward establishing its own film reporting unit
had deepened tension. There was already growing concern in the foreign
bureaus regarding occasional requests for help in filming news stories.
Word that television might create its own motion picture coverage unit
poured on kerosene. Pressures from "See It Now" had been considerable
and the fact that Fred Friendly did not conduct his relationships with a
velvet glove added to the resentment, but Ed Murrow was a revered member of the correspondent team and the opportunity to participate with him
in a highly successful venture helped ease the pain. Television news, however, was a different story. It lacked the prestige of "See It Now" and was
not an Ed Murrow venture. The five day a week television news program,
furthermore, had so far provided little opportunity for the type of serious
analytical pieces that characterized the contributions of the correspondents
to radio.

Both Howard K. Smith in London and David Schoenbrun in Paris had
been most cordial during my December 1952 trip. Both expressed concerns
about additional pressure that television would likely impose but neither
gave any sign of animosity. Smith was particularly vocal about the additional pressures the impending coronation would impose on his small staff
but that was a short-range problem. Schoenbrun indicated he could probably be appeased by addition of personnel and space.

By mid-March tensions had reached the point that some kind of solution
seemed to be imperative. Smith had complained acidly in a letter to the
Radio News director, Ted Church, that he was "totally unable to keep up
with his duties because of the tremendous increase in assignments in the
last couple of years." He added that "the upcoming CBS Television News
Film operation would be a completely unbearable addition."[6]

The Smith letter was sufficiently disturbing that Murrow, Friendly,
Church, and I met on Saturday afternoon March 28 to seek some solution.
Church offered to help reduce conflicts by setting up a new desk in the
Radio News department that would serve as a clearinghouse for all assignments involving overseas personnel. Since preparations for the coronation
constituted a major share of the increased work load, I offered to send a
representative from the television news staff to London to help for the next
few weeks. This would presumably ease some of the burden on Smith. It
was also agreed that all assignments transmitted to television camera crews
and stringers would be sent in duplicate to members of the foreign staff.
What we were proposing would only be a bandage on a deep wound but
it might mitigate the pressure at least temporarily.

There was nothing but cheerful cooperation during my trip with Mc-
Clure. It should have been obvious, however, that pressures on the correspondent staff would increase markedly with the addition of camera crews.

The flow of assignments, travel arrangements, and traffic messages through their offices would impose new strains. Fortunately, only London and Paris would be deeply involved, Rome to a lesser extent. "See It Now" pressures would continue, but Television News, as apart from the Murrow-Friendly program, was determined to hold its dependence on the foreign bureaus to the absolute minimum.

As soon as some degree of normality had resumed after the return from London, Television News personnel suggested solving the problem by separating completely from radio and building a totally independent organization. A memorandum from Mickelson to Van Volkenburg on June 19 described the proposed structure. It called for renting additional office space and employing secretaries or expediters in those capitals where either full film crews or contract cameramen had been employed. Significantly it was not proposed that any full-time correspondents be employed. Reporter-contacts, but not full correspondents, were suggested for London or Paris and possibly Tokyo. It was hoped, probably with excessive confidence, that the cameramen on the staff were equipped by experience and background to serve on many assignments without correspondent backup.

The charm of the proposal lay in the fact that the new organization could be established at considerably less cost than the monthly sum being paid to radio news for the begrudging service that it was delivering.[7] What the proposal missed was the intellectual leadership that experienced reporters could give the finished product. Without that leadership it would be difficult to discover formulas for fusing motion picture, sound, and ideas in such a way as to deliver a news report that included abstract ideas as well as reports on actual occurrences.

The plan to seek a divorce from radio was discussed with the television network president, VanVolkenburg, on Monday night June 15 but without any definitive answer. Corporate leadership was apparently unwilling at this time to support the recommended separation. As a result the skirmishing went on, with tempers smoldering on both sides and erupting from time to time in outbursts of rancor.

During August Television News prepared a detailed analysis of its recent relationship with Radio. It concluded that it was "spotty," satisfactory in some areas but disastrous in the Far East. A memorandum from Mickelson to Van Volkenburg cites the Television News staff as reporting that "in the Far East, disaster has almost struck on a number of occasions, and we have had nothing but turmoil, confusion, and bickering. . . . It is our considered opinion that a major news crisis at any of the points where we are dependent on CBS Radio personnel would leave us in a precarious if not impossible situation."[8]

The memo also quotes the foreign assignment editor Frank Donghi's complaint that in the Far East, "cooperation from CBS Radio has been untrustworthy, at some points verging on obstructionary." Donghi was most concerned about what he described as a "disastrous beating" suffered in early August when a freelancer substituting for CBS Radio personnel who were out on other assignments "manhandled instructions," placing critically important film relating to the end of the Korean War on the wrong plane. The problem, according to Donghi, stemmed from "a strong feeling in the Far Eastern theater that CBS Radio correspondents owe their primary allegiance to radio and serve television only after their radio duties have been completed and they have the time and the inclination to follow through."[9]

In a memorandum to Donghi, George Herman, the CBS bureau chief in Tokyo, specifically identifies the reason for his reluctance to serve television except when there is no conflict with radio, "One of our problems is the rivalry with CBS Radio to whom we at all times owe our primary allegiance. . . . In all cases where you want us to work for you and they want us to do something for them, we do it for them." Another problem cited was less a matter of loyalty to radio than of personal income. An earlier letter from Herman to Donghi, dated May 27 and cited in the same memo, called attention to the income factor. Appearances on radio paid fees. Working with television did not unless the correspondent's voice and likeness appeared on the screen, and that was infrequent. Television was less interested in on-the-spot commentary than in photographic coverage. If a correspondent had to choose between going along with a camera crew to add substance and depth to a television report for which there was no compensation and doing a ninety-second radio report for which he would be paid a fee, there was little doubt what his choice would be.

Skirmishing continued throughout the fall season with no definitive results. The television network moved to a number one position in national ratings. Profits increased by 41 percent over 1952 compared with 22 percent for the next best network. More dollars were invested by advertisers in CBS than in any other network.[10] With the acquisition of WBBM-TV in Chicago CBS Television owned outlets in the three largest markets in the nation and each dominated ratings in its own area. But the rancor between the Radio and Television News departments was permitted to continue. Resolving the dispute would depend on corporate action and corporate officers were still apparently unwilling to step into the fray.

The Television News staff had hoped to resolve some points of conflict when the foreign correspondents visited New York at year's end for the annual "Years of Crisis" program. All were invited to visit Television News headquarters, now fully installed on East Forty-fifth Street, but only Dick Hottelet showed up. All were invited to a meeting in my office but only three attended: Howard K. Smith, Alex Kendrick from Vienna, and Hottelet. Donghi remarked, "The results were most disappointing."[11]

Another attempt to reduce tension in the Far East resulted in the hiring of a cameraman/bureau manager, Wade Bingham. Bingham had served in

Tokyo and Korea for Telenews. He was a friend of Bob Pierpoint, who had succeeded George Herman as bureau manager. It was hoped that having a television employee on the scene would ease the pressure, but it only raised the level of tempers. Church from his New York office sent a cable to Pierpoint insisting that "everyone representing himself as a top man for CBS or as Bureau Manager for CBS Television was a fraud." He later sent a cable to Time Inc.'s Far Eastern bureau manager, Dwight Martin, in which he wrote: "Understand man named Bingham representing himself there as Bureau Manager Columbia Broadcasting System stop Any such identification in completely without authorization."[12] Bingham was devastated. He regarded it a personal attack on him. It also, he felt, jeopardized his relationships with his fellow correspondents in the Japanese capital.

The niggling arguments with radio personnel that had persisted almost from the date of the split between radio and television in midsummer 1951 had overshadowed Television News leaders' goal of creating a news report that combined all the best resources available through television technology. The long-term objective remained to produce a new form of news presentation using its resources to develop new understanding of complex topics in government, economics, science, and society. Not much progress could be made while squabbling continued.

A speech by Chairman Paley to the National Association of Broadcasters in late May 1954 served to refocus attention on larger objectives and simultaneously gave Television News executives new motivation to justify beefing up their service. It encouraged them to raise standards and to aim at more significant goals than simply winning ratings battles. But reaching those higher goals was stymied by the apparently endless skirmishing with radio. Corporate action was clearly required to put an end to the mindless competition. By June it appeared that the conflict would continue indefinitely with no apparent prospect of a quick resolution. Efforts to reach the goals the staff had set for itself would have to be achieved without radio cooperation.

In his speech Paley had challenged news personnel to raise their sights. "Issues have become extremely complicated," he wrote, "giving rise to intense emotion, a deep longing for answers, and hence demanding greater knowledge and, above all, understanding,"[13] exactly what Television News had been aiming for.

The speech, widely quoted and circulated generally through CBS offices, was the springboard for additional introspection within TV news. The result was the distribution of a detailed memorandum, "Basic Reasons for European News Expansion." The memo, dated June 7, cited the efforts of *Life* magazine seventeen years earlier to "pioneer still picture journalism." It argued that it was now time "to bring new intellectual life to the operation (Television News) and to discover new methods of translating the complex facts of political and economic life into easily understandable, colorful, intriguing pictures." It now appeared that television might have to go it alone.

Three years of tension between the two departments came to an abrupt end in mid-July 1954. The cease-fire was brought about by Chairman Paley and President Stanton. It was accomplished by uniting the warring news units into a single corporate department reporting directly to the president and chairman. The announcement ended the bickering that had permeated relations between departments for three years. The burden was now clearly fixed on the new department's leader to eliminate the squabbling and proceed to build an operation capable of harnessing the capabilities that had languished during the period of constant sniping. The television side was the ostensible winner. It now had direct access to the correspondent corps and the foreign bureaus. It had achieved parity in Washington. It was also significant that I was promoted to a corporate vice presidency as the director and general manager of the new department, clearing the way for the later creation of CBS News as an autonomous division.

The radical restructuring would obviously not result in immediate elimination of all frictions, but at the least it would enable a newly unified organization to go forward toward a unified set of objectives. The petty bickering over responsibility and authority would be eliminated. Perhaps the most significant benefit would be the release of personnel from the pressure of constantly defending themselves against attacks. Attention could once more be focused on discovering unique ways of using television to create a new methodology for delivering news to the public. And with direct access to corporate management it could expect quicker action on organizational needs.

12 •

Aftermath of the Cease-Fire

Merging the two news departments into a single corporate unit removed a significant roadblock from CBS efforts to create a news service designed for the television age; it cleared the way for better use of available resources, both human and technological, to produce unique programming. The merger had cleared the way to proceed but did not furnish a road map. That would have to be done by members of the enlarged staff.

One potentially damaging blow struck several weeks before the merger with dismaying force. One afternoon in late May Frank Stanton had called to ask that I go to his office at once. Sitting with him were General Sir Ian Jacob, the director general of the BBC, and Tahu Hole, the chief executive of BBC's news service. General Jacob had told Stanton that BBC was immediately canceling the news film exchange agreement that we had negotiated the previous year; Hole explained that the CBS service did not add enough to their input to justify continuation.

After their departure Stanton asked me to stay for a moment. He was curious how much the defection of the BBC might hurt and what we might be able to do to repair the damage. The BBC cancellation, I told him, would not affect us greatly; BBC's contribution to our daily report was minimal. The termination was, however, a damaging blow to our pride.

Among our weaknesses that may have affected our relations with the BBC, I told Stanton, were the lack of cooperation between the radio and television news staffs and television's lack of regular access to the CBS correspondent staff. Not much, I assumed, could be done about softening the radio leadership's attitude about service to television but it definitely adversely affected the substance in television reporting.

There was, however, I suggested, a possible alternative to the canceled alliance with the BBC. Reports from London indicated that the UK's Conservative government was likely to pass legislation creating a commercially supported competitive television service in the United Kingdom. It would inevitably need help organizing a news report and a reliable source of international news film. By preparing to move at the appropriate time we would stand a good chance, I thought, of being the logical candidate to furnish both. We agreed to keep an eye on developments and be prepared to act as soon as a discernible pattern emerged.

By midsummer 1954 the internal wrangling between the two CBS News departments had been terminated. In their place was a unified organization struggling with the numberless details involved in creating a new structure. Changes in news gathering and production methods in the television newsroom, however, were slow in coming.

Edward P. Morgan, the new director of news, was an able journalist but had little experience with television. His most valuable asset was his standing with the correspondents, critically important to creating a unified organization. He was an ideal choice to encourage them to apply their talents to television. What was needed immediately was guidance in making assignments and developing story ideas. The correspondents stationed in Europe could, if they would, make a substantial contribution. They represented the creme de la creme of the reporting staff but to this point had been more bystanders than participants. Their background and experience could be invaluable.

The improved climate was instantly apparent. An eagerness to participate in day to day coverage was evident. There was still irritation, however, at the volume of paperwork required to schedule a story, produce it, and arrange shipment back to New York. There was also controversy regarding decision making in the field. In radio the correspondent was clearly in charge; in television the lines of demarcation were less clear. There was a tendency among correspondents to resent a cameraman who gave orders even so elemental as where to stand for a short film take. Instructions from the assignment desk in New York raised hackles even more. They, the correspondents, were the experts in their geographical spheres; they resented orders from an inferior in New York assigning specific stories or describing possible approaches to take. They did not react kindly to being subordinate to an assignment editor they regarded as little better than a traffic clerk.

That left a question that had to be resolved: How could the experience of the correspondent, his background, his skills as a reporter, and his basic intelligence best be harnessed? How could he be integrated most effectively into the news gathering process? How could he contribute to raising television news output another step to ensure that it was at least on a level with the best newspapers, newsmagazines, and radio news broadcasts?

The correspondents proved to be remarkably cooperative even though they were moving into a field they had previously associated with the sorriest aspects of "show business." Ed Murrow's success with "See It Now" probably influenced a more sympathetic view. The remarkable growth of the medium from the handful of television homes in the nation at the beginning of 1950 to the more than 32 million in the 1954–55 year, a nearly ten to one growth in less than half a decade, could only have tempted them to stake out positions in so high-flying an industry. In 1950 there was doubt that television would ever be more than a novelty. By 1954 doubts had largely been erased; television was obviously here to stay.

A series of meetings on their home ground began to yield positive results. It quickly became evident that, except in unusual circumstances, a typical radio report would not be adequate for television. And there were vexing operational problems. Radio could be transmitted live by cable or shortwave with little time spent on production. Television had to be photographed, shipped by air, processed in a film laboratory, and edited before being inserted into a news broadcast. All the logistic details were time-consuming. The finished story could not reflect the same degree of immediacy.

The most useful device appeared to be an extension of Don Hewitt's two-projector system. The scheme was almost ideally adapted to the type of story the overseas correspondent would normally be called on to report: meetings of high government officials, summit meetings, foreign ministers' conferences, parliamentary sessions. Almost all of the working sessions traditionally took place behind closed doors out of sight and sound. The two-projector piece would enable correspondents to introduce the event on a sound camera outside the conference venue, include whatever press conference material or opening statements might be made available, and record any interviews that might be permitted. A silent camera could back up the narration by showing the venue, the comings and goings of major figures in the conference, and any other scenes that might add color to the broadcast. The film library, now beginning to take shape, could add background.

Creating a television news story that utilized all the best attributes of the medium would take imagination, editorial judgment, and planning, but it would enable the correspondent to demonstrate his capabilities in a comprehensive and pictorially attractive report. What would work overseas would likewise work on the domestic scene, particularly in Washington. By producing more reporting of this type the network news broadcast could move out of its rather awkward status as a cross between a newsreel and a radio report and start delivering a new variety of reporting more fully exploiting the assets of television.

The attraction of the two-projector technique was its capability for directly involving the correspondents, utilizing their considerable backgrounds and skills, and encouraging them to become full participants in creating a unique television news service. The inherent weakness of television news from the beginning was its inability to convey ideas, as contrasted with events. It was easy to convey information with a clear pictorial component, but too frequently the important news had limited picture possibilities. The two-projector technique offered a method of fusing the intelligence and background of the correspondent with the pictorial background. It would bring television about as close as it could get to delivering a news report with some genuine depth.

Conferences in Europe with correspondents and camera crews were a next essential step. Since the foreign bureaus had had only erratic and not wholly satisfactory relationships with television the time was ripe to welcome them into the newly integrated organization. Their contribution to television news output was certain to increase dramatically, and the two-projector technique would inevitably increase their participation in programming. A European trip would also provide an opening to look further into progress toward an independent television news service in the United Kingdom; reports from London suggested that the introduction of a new commercially supported service was inevitable.

Howard K. Smith arranged an appointment with Harry Alan Towers, a key participant in one of the groups applying for a franchise to participate in the new television venture. He selected Towers because he seemed most knowledgeable about the possible structure of the new independent system and was not shy about describing his role and that of other applicants.

Towers predicted that there would be four or five franchisees, each broadcasting to a separate geographical area. A separate corporation, supported by the franchise winners, Towers predicted, would furnish a complete news service to all franchisees. Sir Robert Fraser, designated to be the director of the Independent Television Authority, confirmed, in general, the Towers prediction.

This information clearly identified the target for a CBS effort to establish a United Kingdom tie, except for the specific identity of the potential winners of the franchises, who were yet to be selected. Once the selection process was completed, assuming Towers was right, the successful franchisees would be under pressure to speed the process of building their news service. This would be the signal for CBS to begin trying to sign an exclusive contract for worldwide film service. Winning this contest would be far more attractive than remaining as a limited partner with BBC.

Towers was right on the mark. September 1955 was set as the opening date for Independent Television News (ITN). Plans for implementation were well enough advanced by March to arrange a meeting in London with members of the newly designated ITN board to discuss specifics of a possible relationship. A dinner meeting at London's Garrick Club was scheduled for the night of April 13. The planned agenda called for negotiating specifics of a possible relationship. In order to answer any questions concerning our film production and shipping capabilities that might arise, I took along with me to the meeting Jack Bush, who had been appointed film production manager for the News and Public Affairs department.

Host for the meeting was Captain Tom Brownrigg (RN Retired) representing Associated Rediffusion, the winner of the franchise to serve the London market Monday through Friday. Harry Alan Towers was present, representing Associated Broadcasting Company Ltd., winner of the Saturday-Sunday franchise in London and Monday through Friday in Birmingham. The key attendee was Aidan Crawley, a former subcabinet minister and journalist, who had been appointed editor in chief of the yet-to-be-organized ITN.

There was some concern that we might face tough competition from the UP-Fox combine that was selling so aggressively in the United States. One of the principals in the Independent Television Network group with whom we were meeting, Gerald Sanger, had for some years been closely identified with Fox Movietone News. We were concerned that he might have an ongoing allegiance to his longtime employer. No opposition to an exclusive CBS-ITN relationship, however, surfaced, and by the end of the evening we seemed to have agreement in principle on a long-term relationship. Crawley and the designated production chief for the new ITN service, Philip Dorte, were assigned to meet with Bush and me the next day to draft a memorandum of agreement.

The contract drafting likewise went very well. The four of us borrowed a small office and a typewriter from the CBS London office. The document we finally completed was hardly an exchange agreement. ITN at the outset would have very little to offer so they were in effect buying a service from us; as they became established, the relationship would entail more of an exchange. One feature of the agreement provided that we would agree to train ITN personnel at our headquarters in New York. The agreement was signed before we left London. The BBC cancellation was no longer quite so painful.

There were still problems that had to be dealt with. A Beirut presence was established by sending out a junior correspondent from New York and employing a contract camera operator. A part-time correspondent was signed to a contract in Cairo and with him a cameraman on similar terms. Ed Morgan had resigned as director of news after only a four-month stay, preferring broadcasting to working as an executive. His successor, John Day, had been a managing editor of newspapers in Dayton, Louisville, and Jersey City and gave a new dimension to the News department, that of a senior news executive from print journalism.

It was only months before the newly built structure was fully tested. The

The signing of the agreement between CBS News and the new Independent Television News in London in April 1955. ITN editor Aidan Crawley is signing the document. Seated beside him is Philip Dorte, ITN's operations manager. Standing beside the author is Howard Kany, CBS Newsfilm manager. Photo courtesy of Sig Mickelson. Used by permission.

revised organization was barely in place when it was confronted by a series of potentially disastrous developments that eventually involved much of Europe and the Middle East. The first signs of an impending crisis appeared in Poland in late summer 1956. Unrest was growing at a rate that suggested a full-scale revolt was likely. Signs were ominous enough that Howard K. Smith was sent to Warsaw to keep an eye on developments. Smith had barely settled down in Poland when there were rumblings of an impending rebellion in Hungary against the stern Communist rule there. Ernest Leiser, who had been assigned to the post of bureau chief in Bonn a few months earlier, was sent on to Budapest against the possibility of a full-scale rebellion. He was followed shortly by Gerhard Schwartzkopf and his camera crew from Frankfurt.

While Eastern Europe was becoming increasingly restless Egypt's aggressive leader, Gamal Abdul Nasser, was making threatening moves that eventually led to his taking over the Suez Canal from the British and arousing the wrath of both the British and the French. Poland was beginning to calm down so Smith could return to London, where he could observe the growing Suez crisis. David Schoenbrun was tightly tied to Paris because of France's interest in the Suez Canal.

In October a full-scale uprising broke out in Hungary. Since Vienna was the most likely communication and shipping center for film from Hungary, it was imperative that a staff correspondent be stationed there for the duration of the crisis. Lou Cioffi, the second man in the Paris bureau, was sent. He had barely taken up his post when the British and French began moving troops to Cyprus for an invasion of the Suez area of Egypt. Cioffi, who had covered wars in the Far East including the French effort in Viet Nam, was the logical person to report from Cyprus. Winston Burdett went from Rome to replace him in Vienna. Burdett had barely taken up his post in Vienna when a war between the Arabs and the Israelis began. Since Israel had been part of his beat he was ordered to leave almost instantly for Tel Aviv. At this point there were no more correspondents available to dispatch to the scene. The problem was solved by taking Dan Karasik off the assignment desk in New York and sending him immediately to Vienna.

As soon as fighting flared up in and around Israel, Ed Murrow headed for the battlefront and sent regular reports back to his radio program and to "See It Now." Coverage from Jordan and Syria was desultory because those two countries impeded any effort to report from front lines and even made reporting from capital cities difficult. Reporting from the Egyptian front, however, was vastly better. Frank Kearns, the recently appointed contract correspondent in Cairo, sent back detailed reports from Sinai. As a by-product of the skill, organization, and courage of the Israeli army and pressures exerted on the British and French by the U.S. president, Eisenhower, it was only days before peace was restored. The newly rebuilt CBS News organization had passed its supreme test. It had survived the series of crises and demonstrated a cohesion and decisiveness that would have been out of the question only a few months earlier. Of even greater significance, antagonism toward television had disappeared. The test imposed by an international crisis had apparently sealed the merger of radio and television.

If the multiple crises had erupted a little more than two years earlier, television's coverage would have been shorthanded and superficial. Even six months earlier it would have been handcuffed by its dependence on radio. Radio assignments would have taken precedence and television would have had to pick up what crumbs were left. Frictions between the two would have encumbered whatever coverage television received. Television would not have been in position to air its integrated packages utilizing film to illustrate and back up oral reports. The two years of integration had produced two years of dramatic progress.

Staff and management problems that had impeded progress seemed effectively solved by the 1954 merger. However, two vexing questions remained unanswered. The first related to the inadequacy of much of the technical equipment available to television; the second, to the more baffling problem of discovering a method for covering news with little pictorial content. The two-projector technique was only a partial solution; too many stories did not lend themselves to that treatment. An alert assignment desk and mobile camera crews were capable of covering events that had visual components, but production of reports on new tax legislation, diplomatic negotiations, or economic trends did not lend itself to pictorial reports. Coverage depended on imagination, editorial judgment, and competence to fuse words with pictures. Imagination in conceiving of methods to convey ideas was the key.

The technological problem was easier to identify but equally difficult to solve. The 16-mm cameras available for television news filming were simply not adequate for professional use; a switch to 35-mm would solve the quality problem but would sharply restrict flexibility and dramatically increase cost. The 35-mm units were several times heavier and bulkier to carry and used film at a ninety-feet-a-minute rate, in contrast with the thirty-six feet for 16-mm. Both raw stock and laboratory costs would be substantially higher. Friendly could insist on 35-mm for "See It Now" since his program was released only once a week and operated on a much higher budget. A daily news program required the far greater flexibility offered by 16-mm and the cost savings resulting from reduced volume of film stock and processing time.

The Newsfilm Production department drew up specifications for what it believed would be a superior 16-mm camera product, but finding a manufacturer to undertake the project was frustrating. Even though newsreels were dying, manufacturers were still so wedded to delivering high-quality 35-mm units they saw no future in 16-mm. It was well into the 1960s before an American manufacturer offered to produce a unit to CBS specifications, but by that time electronic cameras were beginning to be considered a realistic possibility for the future.

The problem of inferior sound had been solved in early 1955, when all sound cameras and processing units at the laboratory were converted to magnetic striping. Don Hewitt described the move in an interview in 1996 as "the single most important technological development" of the period in which he directed the "CBS Evening News."[1]

Discovering a process for conveying ideas as opposed to actions on the television screen was the most difficult problem. Imagination would be required to illustrate abstract news developments, but it was the intention to enlist the creative skills of the entire staff to find the answers. The added intellectual dimension furnished by the correspondents was the critically important new element. The two-projector technique helped in many cases, but it could if overused become obvious, even trite. Crude animation was tried but was excessively costly and time-consuming. In recruiting new personnel for staff positions efforts were made to enlist experienced journalists from a variety of media—newspapers, newsmagazines, wire services, picture magazines, still picture services, and radio news—in the hope that each recruit could make some contribution to enriching the television news report. Gjon Mili, one of *Life* magazine's veteran photographers, met with staff members a number of times seeking any possible clues that might derive from his many years of experience at *Life*.

The search was not wholly futile. Some experiments yielded pay dirt but by and large the hunt had to go on. It was unlikely that any single magic formula would surface. Imagination was the key ingredient, imagination applied to each news item that was essentially idea-based rather than pictorial.

One technological item that would eventually relieve some of the pressure surfaced in April 1956. There had been a vague hope for several years that some genius would discover a process for making a practical videotape recording and playback unit, comparable to the audiotape units that had appeared on the market late in the 1940s. In April 1956 CBS General Engineering arranged for a demonstration of the first viable videotape unit at its affiliates' annual meeting in Chicago. It was an instant hit but the unit shown was a demonstration model. Production units would not be available for about a year. When it ultimately arrived videotape would provide a flexibility and speed that could never be achieved with film, but at this stage tape could only be used for recording. No available camera could record on tape.

Progress since the midsummer 1954 merger had been substantial. An integrated organization was now diligently trying to coordinate words, ideas, and graphic arts to create a genuine television news report, but there was still a long road ahead.

13 •

Spare the Rod but Don't Spoil the Picture

Clamor from critics for the inclusion of some educational broadcasts in television schedules began almost as soon as the medium started to reach mass audiences. It was easy to demand "educational programs" but much harder to define the term in the context of what commercial television could and should do.

By mid-1950 foundations, parent-teacher organizations and teacher groups had begun an unrelenting campaign for what they labeled "educational television." The television networks were not ready to respond. In early 1950 they were just beginning to lengthen their broadcast schedules to add some daytime hours. They recognized an obligation to broadcast some programs in the "public interest," and, in fact, were producing some. How educational programming would fit into this spectrum was unclear. Also questionable was what commercial television's role should be: No one knew what would constitute "educational television."

No one at this point had very effectively defined either the term or the product desired. Was it classroom instruction? Or general cultural programming? In 1950 the question had not even been asked. Almost two decades years later, in 1967, a Carnegie Corporation research team in the first definitive report on the relationship between education and television broadcasting[1] separated programming of an educational nature into two categories: public television and instructional television. Public television embraced a wide range of cultural and scientific areas; instructional television was limited to the classroom, either actual or simulated. In 1950 it was all lumped together as "education."

There did not seem to be a role for a network in instructional programming. It was most effective when programmed for broad mass audiences, not narrow segments. Furthermore, educational standards and curricula varied from region to region. The local commercial station or eventually the local educational station once it was built seemed the more logical outlet for narrowly classroom education. It seemed much more sensible to use the network's strengths to provide cultural enrichment, a service for both adults and school age children. It was assumed that when the FCC was ready to publish its new allocation tables, providing frequencies for additional stations, it would reserve spectrum space for a full complement of public "educational" licensees.

The staff of CBS Public Affairs began looking into a possible role for a television network in midsummer 1950. Discussions started with the assumption that the most useful educational service a network could supply would enrich rather than instruct. One approach considered involved translating applied research in major universities into programs that would not only be useful to viewers but entertaining. Scientific research might be the easiest to pictorialize but there would be room for a wide range of topics that would meet the test of service to the public.

Since Columbia University was nearby and boasted a number of major research facilities, it was approached concerning its possible interest in participating.[2] University executives were interested but negotiations conducted over more than a year failed to yield enough raw material to justify a full series at Columbia. There was an adequate volume of abstract research in progress but not enough applied research with its wealth of pictorial opportunities.

Cornell University was tried next. Negotiations there proceeded well enough that a decision was made to produce a short trial film. It turned out to be unsatisfactory but the idea was not totally abandoned. Shortly after the conclusion of the political conventions in 1952 an experienced producer, Roy Lockwood, was sent on a tour of a number of midwestern universities to determine whether a series could be built by working with a variety of major institutions rather than one or two. The state-supported land grant institutions of the Middle West and West seemed likely sources of program material because of their emphasis on applied research projects. It was hoped that a series of twenty-six programs might be produced by selecting the most interesting projects with the best pictorial potential.

Lockwood returned after approximately a month to report that the project was indeed feasible and could be undertaken immediately. The Program Plans Board approved the project at a mid-December 1952 meeting and production machinery was set in motion immediately after Christmas.

Although it had taken some eighteen months to develop the proposal, get it approved, and put it into production, another thirty months passed before it was ready to take its place on the television network schedule. Lockwood, an experienced film producer, was still dedicated to using a film technique. His proposal called for a fully scripted program with off-camera narration, motion picture–style. Television could be more informal and produce more inexpensively. Viewer identification with the topic could be established by making the narrator an on-camera inquiring reporter. The interaction between narrator and university researchers would add warmth and vitality to the program, humanizing the university personnel and their projects. And the production process could move more swiftly and at lower cost by using live spontaneous interviews, thus avoiding the tedious and expensive process of matching picture and sound tracks and adding off-camera narration.

Unfortunately there was no Fred Friendly to whip the program into shape to make it a television project rather than a motion picture film documentary. There was, however, an alternate choice available. Irving Gitlin, after completing a radio assignment, was given full production responsibility. He junked some of the work that had been completed and began anew to make it pure television. Instead of off-camera narration he used a reporter-interviewer-narrator in the field to carry the load on camera. There were interviews with professors, film clips showing research in progress, and on-camera conversations tying the program elements together.

When the series finally was ready for the air in September 1954 it had been enthusiastically endorsed by the presidents of the universities that cooperated in the project, twenty-six of the most prestigious institutions from coast to coast. In a memo to the program staff Gitlin had described the technique used in production as unique to television:

> We propose to dispense entirely with re-enacted situations and carefully written dialogue placed in the mouths of non-actors. In their place we are seeking an actuality quality, through the use of reporter-writers . . . who either bring about the events depicted themselves or skillfully prod the protagonists into speaking of them; but so truthfully and unselfconsciously that it is almost as though we were with the reporter at the time.[3]

Gitlin had discovered that the television screen required an intimacy that was foreign to the large motion picture screen. Off-camera narration worked in the motion picture theater. In the home, though, conversation with a human being on screen, he insisted, was more effective than the disembodied voice of the narrator. It gave the viewer a guide and friend to react to. Steve Fleischman, the producer who succeeded him when Gitlin moved on in July 1954 to become director of public affairs for the newly combined corporate department of news and public affairs, had also studied the reactions of television viewers. On being assigned the project he followed the Gitlin prescription to the letter.

Jack Gould, the television critic of the *New York Times*, caught the spirit of the program when he wrote, "It ("The Search") illustrates most hearteningly that 'educational television' need not be set apart in academic isolation but can hold its own on merit as a rewarding and exciting experience in viewing."[4] What Gould did not say was that "The Search" was one more piece of evidence that television was creating a new form of documentary, of which it was a prime example.

Starting later than "The Search" but reaching the air a year earlier was another bold effort to fill an education niche in the program schedule. The American Museum of Natural History in New York was one of the nation's greatest repositories of cultural and anthropological information and research, a rich source of background material for a broadly educational television series.

Alexander White, the chairman of the museum's board of directors, approached CBS during the frantic period preceding the 1952 political conventions with the proposal that CBS and the museum jointly produce a television series. The museum had assets that CBS eyed covetously: colorful exhibits, a film library, and a staff of articulate and respected specialists on a host of topics, including the noted anthropologist Margaret Mead. Since CBS had more on its hands than it could deal with, at least until after the election, it placed the museum project on the back burner until early 1953.

Before the election year was over, however, a producer had been appointed. Perry (Skee) Wolff, an experienced producer-director from WBBM in Chicago, a CBS-owned radio station, had been signed on in spring 1952 to function as an extra hand at the political conventions and in election coverage, after which he would be assigned the museum project.

Starting in mid-December Wolff spent most of his time at the museum acquainting himself with the facilities and personnel. By early January he had suggested an approach: producing the program live from the museum. Program components would include interviews with curators, live pictures of exhibits and artifacts, and film clips or still photographs from the museum's film library. The plan Wolff recommended was designed for television. It would eliminate the costly and time-consuming process of filming sequences, processing the film, and mixing sound, music, and effects tracks and a narration track before matching them with the picture track. It would involve some element of gamble but the financial savings would be phenomenal and the savings in time comparable. Moreover, it would take advantage of television's flexibility. It would enable a small production staff to produce a one-hour program each week. His objective would be to use the resources available to create an art form that was unique to television. Charles Collingwood was selected as program host and guide. Radio News released him from competing assignments. With that the essential elements were in place for going into production.

Wolff still needed, however, an associate producer, one who had some background in science and was skilled in communicating complex ideas understandably. He had one such person in mind, a friend on the reportorial staff of the *Chicago Sun Times* who specialized in science reporting. He invited Robert G. Northshield to New York for a weekend. Northshield, known to all his friends as Shad, was uneasy about leaving a steady and interesting job in Chicago to gamble on a future in as uncertain a field as television, particularly in as competitive a city as New York. He asked to talk to me about the future. Since he would only be available on a Sunday, I suggested that he and Skee drive out to my home in Westport, Connecticut, and we'd talk there. They drove the fifty-plus miles in a driving rainstorm on a chilly March afternoon. I could not give any assurances concerning the future but I could say that television was an exciting business with prospects that promised to exceed our most extravagant dreams. Its growth was just beginning. Taking the assignment would be a gamble but the stakes were so high he should have no reluctance to make the move. Before returning to Chicago he decided to take the risk. Anyone who has watched the progress of television over the years has noted the name Shad Northshield in production credits at both CBS and NBC. His most notable achievement may have been creating "Sunday Morning" with Charles Kuralt.

During its lengthy run "Adventure" presented programs on ornithology with the director of the museum's ornithology program, on astronomy with the director of the Hayden Planetarium, on anthropology with Margaret Mead, who also showed portions of her film *Dance and Trance in Bali* and even went out to the Bronx Zoo to escort two children through the Children's Zoo.

"Adventure" was not instructional television but it could be described as "enrichment" or as a cultural supplement to classroom education that was also appealing to adults. It demonstrated that television had the capability of serving a broad educational purpose even though it avoided involving itself in the narrower function of purely instructional programming. Its producers were discovering various ways of using the flexibility of the television camera and its telecine projection equipment to produce vastly greater volume in only a fraction of the time that it used to take film documentarians to accomplish the same objectives with film and to do it with less cost and more flexibility, intimacy, and direct contact with its viewers.

Another foray into broadly educational television, this devotion to U.S. participation in the Second World War, was stimulated by a visit in early 1953 of three U.S. Air Force Brigadier Generals, Elwood (Pete) Quesada,

Brooke Allen, and Sory Smith. They explained that they had access to a library full of Air Force training films that had been employed during the war. The Air Force, they added, had also had in storage many thousands of feet of combat film that could be made available for a series relating to the history of the war.

NBC had scored a considerable success by cooperating with the Navy on a similar project, "Victory at Sea." This raised a question: Should CBS run the risk of being charged with plagiarizing an idea by following so soon with a similar series, or would there be obvious differences that distinguished the two? A rather tentative decision was made to take the risk hoping that the series would be sufficiently dissimilar.

Once having convinced CBS to proceed the three brigadiers dropped out and were succeeded by a Strategic Air Forces colonel, Dal Bailey, who would continue as liaison. Prospects for producing a colorful and dramatic series serving as a useful addition to histories of the war were bright, but the task of bringing the diverse elements together promised to be immense. Since the series would be based entirely on library footage, the format employed by "The Search" and "Adventure," mixing live narration and interviews with film clips would be out of the question. The project would involve searching through film libraries and selecting footage from the millions of feet, all requiring screening and editing into tight sequences. An early release date was most unlikely.

Alfred Butterfield, who had been a Pathé newsreel editor and operated his own film production company, Information Productions, was selected as producer. There were millions of feet to screen and hundreds of pages of official history to read and assimilate before considering a specific format.

The project dragged on and on with little evidence of progress. When the new News and Public Affairs corporate department was created in 1954 by combining the News and Public Affairs departments of the Radio and Television networks, supervision of the project was turned over to Irving Gitlin, newly named director of Public Affairs. Gitlin for some time took an active interest in the project himself but finally decided to remove Butterfield and move Skee Wolff over from "Adventure" to complete it.

By late 1956 it was gradually taking shape. Norman della Joio was commissioned to write a musical score and Alfredo Antonini, conductor of the CBS orchestra, assigned to work with della Joio to prepare the score and conduct the studio orchestra. The finished project turned out to be a moving and dramatic history of the decisive war in the air. There were pictures of airplanes in combat but the emphasis was on the broad strokes of the war, economic and political developments as well as purely military details.

Perhaps the most important contribution made by "Air Power" was the pattern it created for the series that followed it; "The Twentieth Century," narrated by Walter Cronkite, became a staple on the CBS television network for several years and an invaluable background source for students of history.

It had taken a good part of the decade of the fifties but CBS had proved to its own satisfaction that intelligent and imaginative use of the medium could deliver broadly educational programming, attractive to its viewers, in substantial volume. In the meantime, educational stations came on the air in increasing numbers and a nationwide program supplier, National Educational Television, forerunner to the Public Broadcasting Service, began to service public stations.

14 •

Combat in the Corporate Stratosphere

Conflict between Edward R. Murrow, the strongest personality on the CBS news broadcast team, and the company's equally strong-willed chairman, William S. Paley, was inevitable. Murrow was self-confident—some might say arrogant—intolerant of sophistry, a champion of the rights of the underdog, and contemptuous of casuistry. Paley was proud of the accomplishments of the network that he had founded in the late 1920s and dedicated to the theory that delivering a superior news service would win public support. Maintaining objectivity in content, he believed, should be mandatory in its news product. Here Murrow, the champion of the less privileged, clashed with Paley, the exponent of information without opinion.

Conflict between the two was foreordained. Murrow believed broadcasting to be derelict in its duty to the public unless it exposed charlatans, supported the dispossessed, and decried injustice. He believed passionately that broadcasting had an obligation to redress obvious wrongs. Paley was conscious of the restraints imposed by the licensing of the broadcasting industry. He had been schooled in news by a former executive at the *New York Times*, Edward Klauber, who eventually became a CBS executive vice president. Klauber believed a news service should be objective. Contrary to the flamboyant news broadcasters in the early to mid-1930s, to whom delivering the news was more closely related to a vaudeville act than a service to the public, Klauber believed broadcast news was an essential element in keeping the public informed and as such a sacred trust. He was backed up by the first CBS news director, Paul White, who demanded a news service free of the reporter's opinion.

Parallels with newspapers were clearly not valid. Broadcasters were licensed. Newspapers were not. Nor was a comparison with a wire service or a syndication service accurate; the press agencies and syndication services distributed copy by teletype or mail, giving local editors ample time to edit or reject copy they found objectionable. Broadcasting delivered it directly to the transmitter. The local manager or editor was stuck with the network's editorial selection. Paley regarded permitting the network to vent personal opinions unfair to the local licensee, who had an obligation under FCC constraints to control the output on the facility licensed to him.

An eventual collision between Murrow and Paley was as inevitable as a major earthquake on an unstable fault line. In their approach to news policy they resembled two restless tectonic plates within the CBS organization: one represented by the chairman, who had long insisted on objectivity; the other, by the star news broadcaster, who believed passionately that broadcasting had an obligation to redress obvious wrongs. During the age of radio's dominance it was possible to contain tensions. Radio never struck the public with the intense force of television. In the age of television the impact was sharper.

The first potential clash between the two resolute wills was threatened in September 1950. A dispatch from Murrow in Korea for use on radio, not television, triggered the potential collision; television would come later. In his cable Murrow unsparingly criticized the United States leadership's (read General MacArthur's) conduct of the war there. Editors in the CBS newsroom, concerned about a possible policy violation, consulted senior management and killed the dispatch. Murrow on his return argued briefly with the chairman and smoldered for weeks but there was no open break.[1] An eventual clash, however, was inevitable. There was very little give in either personality; both were strong willed and disinclined to compromise. The two restless tectonic plates were constantly in motion and frequently nearing the clash that would send shock waves throughout the organization. The censoring of Murrow's cable from Korea registered only a minor blip on CBS's Richter scale but gave fair warning that a stronger shock was yet to come. A more violent reaction was probably mitigated by the fact that the dispatch was designed only for radio, a medium in which tensions never quite rose to the level of television. Radio, delivering only the one dimension of sound, never seemed to strike the public with the brutal force of television.

Of equal significance, though, may be the fact that CBS before the advent of television was a relatively small company. It had not yet begun to command rapt attention from Wall Street. Its net sales in 1949 had amounted to only a little more than $82 million; by 1953 they had nearly tripled to $237 million and were rising rapidly; by 1960 they had passed $460 million. Stock prices had moved up so rapidly with the advent of television that shares were split on a three for one basis in 1953.[2,3] As the company's income skyrocketed, interest in its stock followed suit. Investors began to follow the company's fortunes and make their attitudes known through their Wall Street brokers. Wall Street representatives on the company's board of directors had to be listened to and their voices were sometimes critical, particularly of items in the news that might be interpreted as "liberal." It was no longer the chairman's company to deal with as he would. Stockholders had to be taken into account. This was also the era of blacklisting and McCarthyism. Public sensitivities were raw and quickly inflamed. Critics were quick to speak out.

It was in this hypersensitive climate that Ed Murrow and Fred Friendly discovered the formula that would lift "See It Now" from successful program to smash hit. On October 29, 1953, shortly before the second anniversary of the program's debut, they varied their normal pattern, which presented two stories in each half hour; on that night they devoted the full half hour to one story, "The Case against Milo Radulovitch, A0589839."

Murrow had discovered a brief clipping from the *Detroit News* on Lieutenant Radulovitch in "See It Now" 's extensive newspaper file. He was sufficiently intrigued to urge Friendly to send a reporter, Joe Wershba, to Dexter, Michigan, the lieutenant's home, to check out the story, and Wershba found it exciting. On his recommendation Murrow's favorite cameraman, Charlie Mack, was requested to go immediately to Dexter to work with him in filming the story.

What Wershba learned and Mack filmed gave the "See It Now" team the raw material, some five hours of it, for the most striking program to date. Milo Radulovitch was a reserve Air Force lieutenant studying meteorology at the University of Michigan. He had been asked by the Air Force to resign his commission on the grounds that he was "associating with his father and sister," both of whom the Air Force charged with "harboring radical beliefs." He refused, whereupon the Air Force convened a hearing board that ordered his separation as a "security risk."

It was a story made to order for a dramatic exposé. The lieutenant was attractive and articulate. His father, a Serbian immigrant who had worked as a laborer in coal mines and at an auto plant, made an eloquent plea that his son not be penalized for associating with members of his family. People of the Dexter community came to the lieutenant's defense and his attorney was particularly eloquent in pleading his case before the camera.

Friendly and Murrow then made two decisions that would thenceforth affect relationships between Murrow and Paley. They decided that they would conclude with a strong, precise, and straightforward statement from Murrow, an "editorial." They also decided to let the story run for the full half hour, in contrast to the normal pattern. The reaction was uniformly favorable, enthusiastically so. Praise was heaped on the producers by press and public. Alcoa did not object. The Air Force finally backed down. "See It Now" had made the difference.[4]

From the point of view of the "See It Now" staff, however, the most significant result was that the program had discovered a formula that would catapult it to far more fame than the team had ever hoped. Murrow had said in his opening statement on the program's first release, "This is an old team trying to learn a new trade." After the Radulovitch program Friendly pointed out that it had taken two years to discover the missing ingredients in their drive to master the new trade. The missing ingredients, according to Friendly, were "conviction, controversy and a point of view."[5] Future programs would reflect that discovery. With a discreet nod to CBS policy and the Paley strictures against editorializing, Friendly added, "Ed and I argued that we weren't going to use our microphones and cameras as a monopolized pulpit from which to preach but that when there was a news story that dramatized the problem of guilt by association we might be able to make our point legitimately."[6]

There was no evidence on the seismic gauges measuring the twentieth floor's reaction that suggested that a major crunch was imminent, but almost certainly there was some uneasiness. This was the first occasion on which "See It Now" (SIN) had clearly stirred emotions and directly or indirectly taken a point of view. As such it was a clear indicator, in terms of long-standing CBS policy, that the relationship between Murrow and Paley would not always be serene. And it foreshadowed the ultimate break that would bring down SIN and lead eventually to Murrow's departure.

It was only a month before Murrow and Friendly once more involved themselves in a cause. The American Civil Liberties Union had rented the Indianapolis War Memorial building for an organizational meeting. The American Legion and a right-wing organization, the Minutemen, protested on the grounds that the facility should not be leased to a "left-wing" organization. The protest encouraged the auditorium's managers to cancel the lease agreement.

The program was a hard-hitting condemnation of the auditorium management and enhanced the program's reputation as a supporter of liberal causes, this at a time when McCarthyism and blacklisting were at their highest peak of support, but there was no specifically identifiable editorial. As after "Radulovitch," gauges registered no appreciable reaction from the twentieth floor.

A major test of "See It Now" 's freedom to take strong editorial positions, however, was in the making. The staff had begun to assemble a record on Senator McCarthy. Any coverage of the senator would involve risks; any slight mistakes might be fatal. In any event the staff could expect a counterattack, which could be nasty. Staff members had to be certain that their own records were absolutely clear. Any factual errors or any weakness in logic, or any conclusions without clear backing, while the senator was at the crest of his popularity, could backfire and severely damage staff members or even CBS. The senator was not above using the tactics against "See It Now," the program staff, or the entire CBS organization that he had used against others who had stood in his way.

The performance as it went on the air reflected the talents of the "See It Now" team at its best. It succeeded in hanging the senator on his own testimony. The selection of evidence was devastating; it carefully built a case that seemed irrefutable. And, surely contrary to CBS policy, Murrow in an extreme close-up, looking directly into the camera, concluded with a condemnatory statement that could hardly be defined as objective. "This is no time for men who oppose Senator McCarthy's methods," he argued, "to keep silent." A few moments later he added, "The actions of the Junior Senator from Wisconsin have caused alarm and dismay among our allies abroad and have given considerable comfort to our enemies." No matter how accurate these sentences may have been and no matter how much they needed saying, they could hardly be described as being objective within the CBS definition of that term. Equal time was offered to the senator within the text of the program to reply—he did so four weeks later—but that hardly altered the fact that the program violated the policy on objectivity that had been on the books at CBS almost from the network's beginning.

Critical response was wildly favorable. The program apparently released an emotional wave that had been bottled up since the beginning of the blacklisting epidemic in the late 1940s. It was evident that large segments of the public had been waiting for some person or institution to question the tactics of the blacklisters in general and the Wisconsin senator in particular. "See It Now" had penetrated the forbidden land for them and demonstrated that someone had the courage to attack despite the risk of vicious counterattack.

There was no response, however, from the twentieth floor. The internal seismometer registered no unusual activity. CBS Television had politely refused to advertise the program in advance, but that was not considered unusual. Newspaper critics were almost uniformly ecstatic in their praise. The senator used his half hour a month later in an amateurish production that, if anything, undercut his position further. From beginning to end McCarthy's performance contrasted vigorously with the consummate professionalism of the Friendly-Murrow team. There was evidence that many citizens who had been cowed by the tactics of the Wisconsin senator were waiting for some daring leader to land the first blow. After the blow was struck they were ready to join the fight. Within a little more than a year a Senate committee finally sealed the senator's fate; he was finished as a major force in American political life. Blacklisting went on for some years, but its fangs had been removed and the wave that had been so powerful in the early 1950s gradually subsided.

During the week after the McCarthy show I boarded the Twentieth Century Limited one evening for the overnight trip to Chicago. As I entered the dining car for dinner I saw, sitting alone, one of the longtime members of the CBS board of directors. Joe Iglehart had an office on Wall Street, controlled either directly or indirectly a substantial block of CBS stock, and had the ear of the chairman. He motioned to me to join him at his table. Iglehart opened the conversation by asking me whether I agreed that the McCarthy show was guilty of editorializing. I had to answer in the affirmative. He asked, "Wasn't it a violation of CBS policy?" I had to agree. There was no suggestion that I should have enforced the antieditorializing policy; the target was clearly Murrow. Iglehart had been a director during the years that Murrow had been on the board and had surely been party to discussions of news policy. There were no suggestions during the long dinner conversation that any specific action was likely, but I couldn't forget the dinner, the subject matter, or Iglehart's uneasiness with the tenor of the program.

The reaction from the chairman came within a little more than two months. He had been selected by the National Association of Broadcasters (NAB) as the winner of its Distinguished Service Award to be conferred at its Chicago convention during the last week in May. It was customary for the award winner, after the ceremony, to address the assembled broadcast executives.

There were no hints circulating in the CBS building concerning the prospective contents of the chairman's speech. It was assumed, though, that it would be a strong statement of CBS policy. The assumption was accurate. The topic was news policy and the theme was the necessity for the broadcaster to be dedicated to objectivity. It spelled out in detail the restrictions that should be applied and defined "objectivity."

It was obvious to even the most obtuse observer that Murrow and "See It Now" were obvious targets. The opening remarks, however, were focused on regular news broadcasts. The chairman expressed his deep concern that CBS news broadcasters avoid any expression of opinion. "In news programs," he said, "there is to be no opinion or slanting. The news reporting must be straight and objective." He went on, "In news analysis there is to be elucidation, illumination and explanation of the facts and situations, but without bias or editorialization." He conceded that "100 per cent objectivity might not always be possible," but the "important factor is that the news broadcaster must have the will and intent to be objective." That phrase, "the will and intent to be objective," became the gauge used by editors thereafter to judge the objectivity of copy.

Although he was referring at this point to news and not documentaries he must certainly have considered the concluding statement in the McCarthy "See It Now" program editorialization.

He then went on to what seems to be a direct reference to "See It Now." "In other types of information programs," he told the broadcast executives, "such as the feature or the documentary, produced by us, the expression of opinion might properly take place. When it does take place"—and here he seems to be aiming directly at "See It Now"—"it should be by the decision of the management or through the delegation of authority to a member of the staff producing that particular program." It was obvious that Murrow had no such "delegation of authority" in the McCarthy program.

Later he read a paragraph that was destined eventually to lead to an irreparable break with Murrow. "When opinion is expressed in any type of information program, excluding news or news analysis where opinion is not allowed, opportunity for reply is given to the person representing the opposite viewpoint." In a little more than a year this seemingly innocuous sentence would lead to an angry response and several months later to a profound rupture in relations between the two.

The companywide distribution of reprints of the NAB address and emphasis attached to it demonstrated that the chairman felt deeply about the contents and intended to enforce the policy rigorously. The first major step was the merger of the two news and public affairs departments, radio and television, into a single corporate department. Paramount among the instructions given me as the vice president in charge was an admonition to enforce rigidly the regulations requiring objectivity as laid down in the NAB speech, the "Road to Responsibility."

Shortly after the merger announcement Stanton urged that I have a study made of representative samples of CBS news broadcasts to determine the extent of editorializing that might be evident from an examination of the scripts. He suggested that the sample be made up of scripts from three regularly broadcast series: Alan Jackson's radio program carried five nights a week at 6:00 P.M. EST, the Murrow fifteen-minute radio program at 7:45 P.M., and the 7:30 P.M. Douglas Edwards television news.

We assigned the project to the School of Journalism at the University of Wisconsin. It took more than a year before a definitive report came in. It was exhaustive and detailed but failed to uncover any egregious violations of policy. Murrow's hard news section was perhaps surprisingly freer of overstepping the prescribed boundaries than the other two, but his analysis segment, which made up approximately one-third of his regular evening performance, flirted more frequently with the proscribed area. Generally, the research staff concluded, "Nothing we have seen in these scripts suggests anything but the highest will and intent to be objective on the part of all three broadcasters." They did, however, note "the skills that Murrow has displayed in avoiding the outright expression of his own opinion. Yet his opinions are surely there. . . . He will shape an analysis that will add up to a devastating defeat for the 'forces of evil.' "[7]

"See It Now" continued to deal forthrightly with controversial topics but incited no response from the twentieth floor. There was evidence, though, that Alcoa was getting restless. It finally gave notice of cancellation effective July 7, 1955. It was easy to assume that the company was getting tired of standing up to complaints regarding controversial subject matter; Fred Friendly, however, had another theory. He was convinced that the scheduling of the "$64,000 Question" in the immediately preceding half hour made the period occupied by "See It Now" too valuable to assign to a news-related program. An entertainment program would reach a vastly larger audience and return a considerably greater profit to the network.

"See It Now" was given an hour rather than a half hour but its frequency was reduced to approximately once a month. Seven one-hour programs were scheduled during the remainder of the 1955–56 season. One of them, a relatively innocuous treatment of farm issues in Iowa, touched a raw nerve in relationships between Murrow and the chairman. The Secretary of Agriculture, Ezra Taft Benson, felt that the program unfairly represented the administration's agricultural policies and the Republican National Committee requested time to reply. Friendly asked me whether I thought that the request would be granted. I replied, "Not a chance." But I was wrong. In Paley's "Road to Responsibility" speech to the NAB in May 1954 he had said, "When opinion is expressed in any type of information program . . . opportunity for reply is given to the person representing an opposite viewpoint." There is some question whether opinion was expressed but the Republican National Committee was given a half hour. Murrow grumbled but kept his temper under control.

The inevitable shock registering high on CBS's Richter scale came two years later in circumstances that could not have been predicted. "See It Now," now relegated to Sunday afternoon, scheduled the program "Statehood for Alaska and Hawaii." Although the content seemed quite mild there were elements of controversy in the program. Some members of Congress, for example, were concerned that "Communists," notably Harry Bridges of the Seaman's Union, would be given undue power once Hawaii became a state. There were also concerns about enlarging the Senate with four additional members, thus mildly diluting the power of the current ninety-six members. But generally the program was somewhat less than explosively controversial. A rather obscure congressman from Lackawanna, New York, John Pillion, however, felt that he had been wronged and requested time to reply.

There seemed little reason for granting the request. The decision would be made by a newly constituted editorial board composed of the corporate chairman and president, a staff vice president dealing with legal and policy matters, the presidents of three broadcasting divisions, and the president of the News division. The chairman usually sat at the head of the table and I at the foot. As the executive whose policies and procedures were up for consideration I normally would set the agenda and lead the discussion. Congressman Pillion's request for time was the first item on the docket. I recommended that we not grant the request. The chairman was adamant that we do so, I argued that there was nothing in the program that justified offering time to reply. The chairman held firmly to his position. He finally closed the argument by instructing me to go to the Murrow-Friendly offices and inform them that Congressman Pillion would be given the time he had requested.

It was well after 8:00 P.M. when I reached the "See It Now" offices. Murrow had finished his 7:45 P.M. radio program and the two were sitting in Friendly's office awaiting my arrival. I told them without embellishment that Congressman Pillion would get his time. I explained that I had argued the case for what seemed an interminable time but the chairman would not budge.

Friendly started to argue but quickly realized it was futile. Murrow sat stony faced without uttering a word. He soon stood up and walked out, still with no comment. It became apparent shortly later that the special relationship between the chairman and the star of the news staff was finished. The tectonic plates had clashed. That one short sentence in Paley's May 1954 speech, "When opinion is expressed in any type of information program . . . opportunity for reply is given to the person with whom issue has been taken," was the grounds for granting the request. It could be argued that there was little opinion expressed in the Alaska-Hawaii program, but the decision had been taken. There was no backing down.

"See It Now" for all intents and purposes was finished. It had had a spectacularly successful seven-year run. Information programming on television for years would be measured against it. Murrow and Friendly and their highly skilled team had created a new genre of television programming, one that would be almost impossible to duplicate without the intellectual and mechanical skills that were so skillfully recruited and molded into the "See It Now" team.

I had gone to the editorial meeting expecting some flexibility from the chairman. The issue, though somewhat controversial, was hardly the most hotly debated problem on the national agenda. And Congressman Pillion hardly seemed the logical spokesman for those opposing the grant of statehood. There was obviously a motive that transcended the case of Alaska and Hawaii and the request of the congressman. It had to be assumed that the grant of the free time was, in reality, a reflection of the chairman's irritation with many of what he regarded as transgressions of the objectivity policy. An accumulation of resentments dating back at least to "The Case against Milo Radulovitch, A0549830" certainly as far as the Senator McCarthy program, was clearly involved. As Paley had said to Murrow and Friendly in a meeting in his office shortly after the Pillion affair, "I don't want the constant stomach ache every time you do a controversial report."[8]

When the shows in the final editing stage had been shown, the run would be over. In July 1958 death came to the most acclaimed news-related series ever broadcast on network television. By September 1958 it was formally declared dead.

There was still no visible reaction from Murrow. It was evident from his demeanor that he had been grumbling. Friends were aware of his unhappiness but there was no public demonstration of his pique. It, however, was soon to be put on public display.

The Radio and Television News Directors Association (RTNDA) had invited Murrow to address their annual convention in Chicago in October. Murrow surprised the RTNDA leadership by accepting. The association was a twelve-year-old organization that was still struggling for prestige and recognition. Station managers had been slow in many cases to recognize the importance of news in their daily schedules and support for the association lagged. Murrow had appeared at an RTNDA convention in 1949 when it was still known as the National Association of Radio News Directors, but he had limited his remarks then to introducing the playing of his record album, *I Can Hear It Now*, which had just been released. This time, it was assumed, he would have something to say and, judging by his mood after the Pillion controversy, it might be explosive.

There was naturally curiosity at CBS headquarters concerning his text but security was tight around the Murrow office. I asked his assistant, Kay Campbell, whether I might see a copy of his manuscript. She assured me I would get one promptly.

The editorial board was scheduled to meet on the same day that Murrow was speaking in Chicago. As I was preparing to leave my office to attend the meeting Ms. Campbell gave me my copy of the manuscript. I glanced at it quickly, saw that it contained dynamite, put it into a folder, and rang for the elevator. Murrow by this time was in the air on his way to Chicago.

On arrival at the board room I put the manuscript on the table for members to read. The opening of the meeting was delayed while each took time to scan it. It was obvious that the chairman was disturbed. The lines on his face were taut. There was no question the speech was a slap in his face. It was calculated to cater to the self-glorification of directors, but the approach was so brutal that it would surely reopen festering wounds on the executive floor. The board members gathered around the table were clearly stunned by the biting tone of the message, by the fury of its attack on television programming, and by the contempt shown for broadcast management.

One paragraph in particular caught everyone's attention:

> The top management of the networks, with a few notable exceptions, has been trained in advertising, research, or show business. But by the nature of the corporate structure, they also make the final and crucial decisions having to do with news and public affairs. Frequently they have neither the time nor the competence to do this.

These lines didn't strike only at the chairman. Frank Stanton had been trained in research, the presidents of the three broadcasting divisions in advertising. But Chairman Paley was obviously the central target. He was the man in charge. He had set the tone for the network and the stations it owned.

Murrow was scathing in condemning program schedules: "If there are any historians about fifty or a hundred years from now, and there should be preserved the kinescopes of all three networks, they will find there . . . evidence of decadence, escapism and insulation from the realities of the world in which we live."

There was also an apocalyptic tone. "This nation is in mortal danger," he said. "Surely we shall pay for using this most powerful instrument of communications to insulate the citizenry from the hard and demanding realities which are to be faced if we are to survive. I mean the word 'survive' literally."

The news directors in the audience cheered wildly. Here was one of their heroes giving them new courage to stand up to management. It fed egos that had long suffered from what they considered inferior status in their stations. Their most prestigious annual award was shortly later named for the hero of the 1958 convention. The speech gave new self-respect to news directors. It stimulated pride in their work. It instilled new confidence.

But the news directors failed to see the other side of the performance, the direct attack on the management of CBS and particularly on the chairman of the board. They failed to see that a clear target was the executive who had made news the cornerstone of its effort to win the number one position in broadcasting, the executive who had created the opportunity for Murrow to achieve the rare prestige he had won. It obviously marked a rupture in a relationship that had persisted from the late 1930s. It was difficult to see how it might ever be patched up; the tone was too strident. With the completion of the speech the split between Murrow and Paley was irreconcilable. Murrow would still participate in widely acclaimed documentary programs, notably "Biography of a Missile" and "The Harvest of Shame," and continue his 7:45 P.M. radio program, but the magic of the earlier relationship was gone. The gulf was too wide, the tensions too intense. It was almost inevitable that Murrow would ultimately leave. That would happen in January 1961, when he was invited by the newly elected president, John F. Kennedy, to accept an appointment as director of the United States Information Agency.

15 •

The Changing of the Guard

Until the middle 1950s there was no question in the CBS organization concerning the identity of the ultimate authority on news. It was the company's chairman, William S. Paley. Under his personal direction in 1933 the fledgling broadcast network had audaciously challenged the entrenched newspaper and wire services by organizing a worldwide news gathering and broadcasting organization. He was brashly invading an area newspaper publishers considered their private reserve.

The bold move so annoyed the editors and publishers of printed news organs that it was only months before concerted pressures exerted by the publishers caused CBS to knuckle under. CBS and the other networks agreed to the demand of the publishers to broadcast only news passed on to broadcasters by the Press-Radio Bureau, which was established for the purpose by the wire services. Broadcasters were permitted a maximum of two five-minute news broadcasts each day.

Only the networks, however, had agreed to the restrictions. In less than a year the cumbersome system broke down under pressure from stations not affiliated with the major networks. By 1936 the United Press had started selling a service to radio. Months later the Associated Press entered the market. By then the field was clear for the networks to resume. CBS began a slower, less aggressive effort to build a news organization, a process that was accelerated as the world moved inexorably toward the 1939 outbreak of war.

As tensions swiftly built in Europe, CBS, led by Edward R. Murrow in London, began broadcasting shortwave radio reports from various European capitals. It was Paley himself who, according to his own account, personally asked the news director, Paul White, to gamble on a bold innovation, a world news roundup. As he tells it, he was at home ill during the height of the Austrian crisis in 1938, anxiously awaiting any morsel of information he could get from any of the correspondents broadcasting for CBS from Europe. He called Paul White, the CBS news director, to suggest that several news reports from European capitals be packaged together in one fifteen-minute period. Rather than return to New York between each report, London, for example, might cue Paris and Paris cue Berlin. Technicians argued it could not be done, but Paley insisted, and they agreed to try. It worked and the format has been used ever since.[1]

While Paley was overseas as an officer on General Eisenhower's staff, the CBS vice president, Paul Kesten, was nominally in charge of all network broadcasting including news. News at the Columbia-owned stations, however, came under the purview of Frank Stanton, then vice president. On Paley's return the mantle for network news programming was returned to him. As vice president in charge of News and Public Affairs in 1946 and 1947, Murrow reported directly to the chairman.

With the growth of television, however, the business became much larger and more complex. It was Stanton to whom I reported when I was appointed director of Public Affairs in January 1950. It was Stanton who watched over the department's budget and personnel decisions, but it was Paley who was still making the critical decisions concerning the content and form of news. It was he who also insisted on objectivity and on fairness and balance in all news and news-related programming.

His final grand gesture as the clear and last court of resort on news at CBS was his Chicago speech to the National Association of Broadcasters on May 25, 1954, the occasion on which he laid down his stern set of rules for objectivity in news and documentary programs. After the speech he did not retire entirely from the scene. His presence was still very evident; he still presided over editorial board meetings and kept a watchful eye on breeches of objectivity standards on regular news broadcasts.

The creation of the combined radio and television News and Public Affairs corporate department in July 1954 reinforced Stanton's position as the administrative leader, if not the final arbiter of policy problems. It was he, however, in an overt demonstration of his rising status in the news spectrum, who personally broadcast the first editorial that CBS had ever programmed. Stanton in a half hour broadcast on the full network on August 25, 1954, "asked viewers and listeners to support the principle that radio and television should have the same privileges as other branches of the press to cover Congressional hearings."[2] The entire project carefully conformed to the Paley guidelines as enunciated in the Chicago speech. It was clearly specified that he spoke on behalf of CBS, not as a private citizen. CBS affiliates had been informed in advance of the stand he was going to take, thus giving them the right to refuse the program if they disagreed or preferred not to be committed. It was notable, though, primarily because it was the company president, not the chairman, who was appearing on behalf of the corporation.

Stanton was the ultimate authority on news and public affairs budgets, personnel problems except selection of senior executives, and generally, with the approval of the program plans board, proposals for scheduling new programs. He was the principal point of contact on news and public affairs administrative issues, but whenever there was a policy question it was normally referred to the chairman of the board.

A significant event in 1957 effectively clarified Stanton's new role as the full heir to the Paley mantle. The story had been building for almost two years. In June 1955 on the occasion of the celebration of the tenth anniversary of the founding of the United Nations in San Francisco, CBS's "Face the Nation" had won a major victory. It had scheduled a half-hour program with the Soviet Union's foreign minister, Viacheslov Molotov, who would be in San Francisco attending the ceremonies.

The acceptance of the invitation by the Russian foreign minister was the result of a long-term campaign to win the confidence of the Soviet Embassy in Washington. The objective was to obtain an appearance by a high-level Kremlin official on "Face the Nation." The CBS director of Public Affairs in Washington, Theodore F. Koop, and the "Face the Nation" producer, Ted Ayers, had been nurturing a relationship with personnel at the Soviet Embassy for some time. Their ultimate intention was to induce a prominent Soviet official to appear on the program. They had established a particularly warm relationship with the member of the embassy staff assigned to public relations, a Soviet foreign affairs officer named Zinchuk. Zinchuk had promised that at the right moment he would deliver a Soviet official measuring up to their hopes. Acceptance of the invitation by Viacheslav Molotov, the Soviet foreign minister, was the product of their long campaign.

Koop and Ayers were jubilant at their coup. They flew to San Francisco on Monday June 20, the opening date of the UN anniversary week, to see that everything was in order for Molotov's appearance, which was to be recorded on Friday June 24. They thought they had adequately spelled out to Zinchuk that the program would be wholly unrehearsed. On arrival in San Francisco, however, they learned that the Soviet delegation insisted on seeing the questions in advance and editing them, perhaps even adding some of their own. Koop and Ayers replied that the program would have to be spontaneous and unrehearsed. Nothing more was heard from the Soviets. They tried every possible avenue to establish contact but there was no response.

By Tuesday afternoon CBS appeared to be deeply enmeshed in an international diplomatic crisis. I booked passage to San Francisco for Wednesday morning to be on the scene in the event of a major public relations cataclysm. In the meantime, there was not only no word from the Soviets, but no contact. Anticipating the possibility that we would hear no more from the Soviet delegation but unwilling to abandon hope we prepared a press release specifying that we had withdrawn the invitation to the foreign minister. It was timed for release at 6:00 P.M. Pacific Coast Time on Thursday, June 23, the day before the scheduled recording session. Unless we heard from the Soviets prior to the deadline we would release it then. At 6:00 P.M. we had heard nothing so I gave the order for the release.

The story hit the front pages across the country. Withdrawing an invitation to the Soviet foreign minister was a shock even in the United States, where broadcasters had normally been too timid to take bold steps in international relations.

We heard nothing more from any Soviet official for many weeks, but Zinchuk apparently did not forget the commitment he had made. Nearly two years later he asked whether they would still be interested in interviewing a leading Soviet government official. They replied in the affirmative, whereupon Zinchuk informed them that he thought he could now produce one who would meet their expectations. They accepted even though they were not sure of their guest's position in the Soviet hierarchy. Zinchuk assured them it would be at a high level.

Koop called me one day in early May 1957 with a pleasant surprise. He told me that he and Ayers had a commitment from the Russian Embassy that the Soviet chairman, Nikita Khrushchev, would be available for a free and unrehearsed film interview in the Kremlin in late May. We would have to send a crew to Moscow to produce the program. The Soviet government would provide a film crew, but the production would be managed by CBS. The chairman would answer questions with no strings attached.

I took the proposal to the next television Plans Board meeting and in addition to requesting approval for the venture suggested that we extend the program to a full hour rather than the half hour normally allotted in view of the fact that our guest would be the head of a major state. The proposal was approved and the program was scheduled for Sunday afternoon May 31. No objections to giving the time to the Soviet leader were publicly voiced even though the blacklisting era had not totally faded from the scene.

It was determined that Koop and Ayers would go to Moscow to handle production. Stuart Novins, the regular moderator, would go along to fulfill his customary role and Dan Schorr, the CBS correspondent in the Soviet capital, would be one of the interviewers. The other would be selected from the American press corps on the scene.

A few days before Koop, Ayers, and Novins left for Moscow, Koop and I went to the White House to pay a visit to Jim Hagerty, President Eisenhower's press secretary. Hagerty invited us to lunch with him in the White

House officer's dining room. There we told him of our plans and informed him that Koop would be leaving in a couple of days for the flight to the Soviet capital. There was no negative reaction. Hagerty suggested that as soon as Koop and his traveling partners arrived in Moscow they check in with the United States Embassy, but there were no further caveats.

The program was a smashing success. The Soviet leader was in rare form. Schorr and B. J. Cutler, the Moscow bureau chief for the *New York Herald Tribune*, were an articulate and knowledgeable interview team, and press response exceeded all expectations. On Monday morning, the day after the broadcast, the account of the program captured front page space and dominated headlines in major newspapers across the country. It seemed to be a major coup. Negative notes, if there were any, were lost in the flood of positive reactions.

On my arrival at the office on that Monday there was a call from Frank Stanton to go immediately to the board room. He had also invited Dick Salant, his policy adviser and general assistant; Irving Gitlin, director of public affairs in the News and Public Affairs department, under whose supervision the program fell; and John Day, director of news.

Stanton expressed alarm at the reaction in some government circles in Washington. He did not reveal his sources of information nor the depth of feeling except to say that it came from a high level. He was fearful that some retaliatory action would seriously jeopardize the network's status or the licenses of the CBS-owned stations. He was vague about the basis on which retaliatory action might be contemplated, whether it might involve punitive legislation or penalties imposed on the CBS-owned stations—or simply a dressing down by a government official. We never did find out but subsequently were told that Secretary of State John Foster Dulles was visibly upset and had complained to associates, presumably including the president.

Most of the day was spent in fruitless discussion. No decisions were reached and in late afternoon the session was recessed for the day. The stalemate continued the next day. In midmorning. however, the door opened and a senior partner in the Earl Newsome public relations firm, Bill Lydgate, walked in. Stanton had been trying for some time to interest Newsome in taking on the CBS account. This seemed to be a trial assignment for both adviser and potential client.

Lydgate's opening comment was, in paraphrase, "You fellows are way ahead of the game. Why the long faces? Why not do everything you can to exploit your advantage?"

The mood changed instantly. Stanton was apparently willing to accept the optimistic opinion of outside counsel that he had resisted accepting from internal sources. Lydgate urged us to move aggressively; take advantage, he urged, of the uniformly favorable response to the Soviet leader's appearance. From building defenses we turned to plans to exploit the "Face the Nation" coup. We decided to order full-page ads for Wednesday morning's editions of the *New York Times*, the *New York Herald Tribune*, the *Washington Post*, and the *Chicago Tribune*. Since President Eisenhower had scheduled a press conference for the next morning, it was assumed that one way or another the ads would be brought to the president's attention before he appeared before the press. The copy would be drafted with the objective of winning broad public support, thus softening any criticism the president might intend to voice. A request went out immediately to the Promotion department to order the space. We began at once to prepare a rough draft of copy that could then be refined by the department's copy writers.

A call went out to Charles von Fremd, the CBS White House correspondent. Von Fremd was requested to draft a question that he would ask the president and to arrange with Hagerty to be called on by the president. Our hope was that his question would elicit a reply from the president supporting our argument that the public profited from seeing and hearing the Soviet leader in an unrehearsed interview.

The ads ran the next morning as scheduled. Von Fremd asked his question. It was somewhat garbled and the president's reply did us little good but, at the least, no further damage was done. But Newsome was not finished. At a subsequent meeting in the agency's offices, with Newsome himself participating, we began to probe other possibilities for exploiting our position. Ted Koop was at this time serving as president of the National Press Club in Washington. The club frequently scheduled luncheon meetings at which major figures in the news would make brief speeches and stand for questions from the reporters in the audience. Frequently participants filled a rather large auditorium and the volume of press coverage was considerable. We proposed that Stanton be invited to speak and use the CBS defense of its rights in the Khrushchev case as a prime example of a licensed industry's standing up to government pressure.

A Stanton appearance before the club was scheduled for July 2. A speech was carefully drafted by Stanton himself with the aid of Dick Salant. The performance was a smash success. Stanton was a master at response to this type of interrogation. He fielded every question that came his way thoughtfully and reasonably with supporting evidence. Press coverage was everything we had expected. The Khrushchev interview was no longer a potential motivation for punitive action against CBS but rather an opportunity to exploit a campaign for extension of rights of free speech to broadcasters. And, notably, this was Stanton's campaign. He was the spokesman, not only for CBS but for the broadcasting industry. Paley, historically the dominant figure in CBS News matters, was in no way directly involved. It was Stanton's show.

Since the campaign had gained surprising momentum on its own, the Newsome group suggested that we keep it rolling and seek other opportunities to exploit our advantage. Three years earlier the Radio Television News Directors Association, embracing news directors of radio and television stations across the country and in Canada, had instituted a national award for exemplary service to broadcast news. It was named for the former CBS news director, Paul White. Ted Koop was the association's immediate past president and by virtue of his position chairman of the selection committee for the 1957 winner. Assuming Koop could win support of his committee, I offered to call him and urge that he use his prestige as immediate past president to name Stanton as the winner of the award. The CBS president's vigorous defense of the right of broadcasters to operate under the same freedoms as prevailed for the printed press would be the justification. Koop, needless to say, was quite willing to support the Stanton candidacy.

I went to Stanton to tell him I thought I could get him the award if he would promise to attend the annual convention in Miami Beach in November and speak at the convention dinner. He told me he would think about it and get back to me. Several times I approached him with the same question. Each time he wanted more time.

As time passed Koop needed an answer quickly. If Stanton were not available his committee would have to find an alternative. Within approximately two weeks of the Miami Beach meeting I told Stanton that if he intended to turn down the offer it was essential that I tell Koop immediately so that his committee would have time to select a winner.

At this point he confessed that he had been reluctant to accept the award because news at CBS had historically been the chairman's (Paley's) area. He was not sure whether he should intrude and, in effect, upstage his superior officer, who had been the longtime supporter, protector, and defender of CBS News. I was about to leave to tell Koop that I had failed when he stopped me and said that he would accept but wanted me to help him with his speech. Needless to say I had Koop on the phone within minutes to tell him that he had his man and that it could be announced as soon as his committee ratified the choice.

That episode, from my point of view, constituted the definitive step in the changing of the guard. Stanton had become the de facto spokesman for news at CBS, replacing the man who had built and defended the news operation for two and a half decades. The award would be, at least to me, the symbolic recognition of a new order. The passing of the baton was not, however, a clean and instantaneous break from the past. Paley did not fade from the scene completely. He continued as chairman of the editorial board and as a constant critic of the expression of personal opinion on the air. He continued as a vigorous defender of objectivity. He still wanted to see potentially controversial documentaries before they were scheduled for release to the network. He wanted to know about and pass judgment on appointments of senior staff in the news division. When Eric Sevareid became restive under restrictive editorship of his news commentaries, it was Paley he wanted to see to complain, and it was Paley who told him there was no alternative. There would be no expression of personal opinion on CBS programs.

The principal change that followed Stanton's acceptance of the RTNDA award was that by that move he had become the public spokesman for news and news-related programs, a role that he would exploit to an increasing degree in subsequent years, once even to the extent of offering to go to jail for defying Congress.

Stanton continued to demonstrate his newly increased influence on the news area. After the Soviet Union's launch of *Sputnik*, he encouraged the News department to undertake an intensive study of the status of America's capacity to compete. He arranged for a group of news executives and senior producers and correspondents to meet with Herman Kahn, the fast speaking head of the Hudson Institute and a student of Soviet and American military technology, as the first step in preparing to produce a definitive documentary on the topic. He further suggested that once the program had been researched and written it conclude with an editorial reflecting the position of CBS.

The result was "Where We Stand," produced by Les Midgeley and including many of the correspondents on the CBS staff. The concluding editorial, read by correspondent Howard K. Smith, pointedly declared, in careful conformance with the CBS policy as laid down by Chairman Paley in his Chicago speech in 1954, that it reflected the views of CBS, not of any single individual.

The gradual evolution of CBS News and Public Affairs from corporate department in 1954 to full autonomous division status by 1959 was overseen by the corporate president. The designation CBS News as the divisional title was also Stanton's recommendation, as was the title for "CBS Reports," which was, in effect, successor to "See It Now." By the end of the fifties the dominant figure in news and public affairs was no longer Chairman Paley. It was President Stanton.

Filling the "See It Now" Void: The Birth of "CBS Reports"

One of the obstacles undermining CBS's effort to promote a broad-based news and information program schedule had been the focus of attention on "See It Now." Since the birth of the Murrow-Friendly venture in November 1951 it had commanded the lion's share of critical attention and consequently diluted public recognition of the remainder of the CBS news and public affairs output. After its demise in 1957 the spotlight shifted to a broader range of programming. There was still, however, a lingering suspicion that, unless the regular news operation quickly filled the void, the advantage might be quickly dissipated.

After "See It Now" ended William S. Paley had no more cause for the "stomachaches" that he had told Ed Murrow were occasioned by his programs. There was no single replacement, however, on the CBS schedule that could capture the same degree of public attention, or generate the same volume of controversy. Both the News and Public Affairs departments had plans, but those plans were some distance from fruition and there was little optimism that they could generate the same degree of excitement. It would be pretty difficult to replicate Friendly and Murrow.

"See It Now" staff remained intact to produce a new series, "Small World." It was important and useful but hardly stirred up intense emotional response; compared to "See It Now" it was flat. It used imaginative applications of available technology to simulate face to face debate among world leaders, who were usually oceans apart physically. But a debate between a prominent member of the British Parliament and a United States cabinet member, no matter how ingenious the production and how live and spontaneous it appeared, did not generate the passion that flowed from a hard-hitting documentary on race problems or even statehood for Alaska and Hawaii.

Both the News and Public Affairs departments of what was rapidly being converted into a full-fledged autonomous division of CBS Incorporated were moving to fill the void. They were making progress toward developing the talented units required to create noteworthy product. And there were resources to draw from. The News department was discovering that its camera crews were frequently delivering much more high-quality film than could be accommodated in the fifteen-minute regular news broadcasts. Some of it was siphoned off into long-form reports used on a Sunday evening half hour news broadcast, but even that exposure failed to make full use of the material delivered, nor the talent of the film crews. Raw material was available, or could be made available, for more detailed treatment of a great variety of significant news. It was 16-mm film, not the superior 35-mm that Fred Friendly had insisted on for "See It Now." But it was frequently more spontaneous since it had captured news events as they were taking place, not carefully produced reconstructions, as were frequently used on "See It Now."

An opportunity to test the hypothesis developed as early as the summer of 1955. The governments of the West German Republic and the Soviet Union jointly announced that their respective political leaders, Chancellor Konrad Adenauer of West Germany and Nikita Khrushchev of the Soviet Union, would meet in Moscow in October. Richard C. Hottelet, the CBS News correspondent in Bonn, promptly applied for and received credentials to accompany the German leader on his visit to what had been enemy territory. He cabled the assignment desk in New York that it might be possible to obtain credentials for a camera crew.

This was the type of news story that would test the News department's capability to break out of the straight news mold and prove it could deliver extended coverage of major events. It was obvious that a face to face meeting between the leaders of two nations that had so recently been bitter enemies would generate public interest. Eleven years had passed since the Soviet armies had smashed into Berlin, occupied all of East Germany, and at one point in the late 1940s even tried to starve out West Berlin. A meeting of the two leaders would mark a historical milestone. Hottelet was given the go-ahead to apply for credentials for his camera crew, and not long afterward the credentials came through.

The television network's program plans board approved the scheduling of a thirty-minute program for Sunday night October 16 and a prospectus for the program went immediately to the network's Sales department. Marketing of a "news special" would break new ground. Television had not previously experimented with detailed long-form film coverage so soon after a major event. Fortunately, there was a potential sponsor in the wings, The Prudential Life Insurance Company. Prudential's agency, Reach McClinton, had been looking for a nonentertainment product for the insurance company. The agency concluded that a filmed report of the historic meeting might generate the kind of favorable response they were seeking. Prudential's management was squeamish about being so closely identified with an event on Soviet soil, particularly one in which the Communist dictator was one of the principal players, but eventually took the gamble and risked the wrath of the red-baiters.

Film came in from Moscow in good order. The cameraman, Gerhard Schwartzkopf, and the sound man, Geron Anderle, delivered more coverage and of higher quality than could have been expected. The producer, Les Midgeley, and his capable staff were able to deliver a product that exceeded even their expectations.

The program was deemed an unalloyed success by both critics and the advertising agency. The sponsor was pleased and a relationship was established that would yield rich dividends in subsequent years. Within a year Prudential had signed on for full sponsorship of "The Twentieth Century," an open-ended series of half hour historical programs designed to recreate major events by using historical film gleaned from newsreel and documentary film libraries.

Public Affairs, while the News department was gearing up for productions comparable to those of the Adenauer visit program, simultaneously made a dramatic entry into the production of single-topic one-shot documentaries. Working closely with the American Mental Health Association and the American Psychiatric Association the producer, Al Wasserman, set out to demonstrate pictorially in a real life situation recently developed procedures for dealing with schizophrenia. He arranged, within his program budget, to subsidize the treatment of several seriously ill patients. One was ultimately selected as the subject to be filmed during the entire treatment process.

Week after week for approximately a year, Wasserman and his film crew photographed every step of the treatment. Fortunately for the program the treatment resulted in a happy conclusion. Although not completely cured the patient was sufficiently improved to resume a normal life. The footage was assembled into a moving ninety-minute documentary, titled "Out of Darkness." It was quickly snapped up by a commercial sponsor and won a host of awards. It was cut to sixty minutes and was given two more full network exposures. The Public Affairs department, which had built a reputation by producing several acclaimed series, had now staked out a position as successful producer of single-episode programs dealing with issues of public concern.

Public Affairs producers were continuing to expand their horizons. They were discovering that they could deliver a product with a directness that had not been possible in the motion picture theater or auditorium. They were maximizing the advantages offered by the small screen and the intimacy of the viewing environment.

The News department, meanwhile, continued to hone its talent for creating long-form news programming. As the film staff increased in size and competence camera crews were becoming increasingly restive if their product was not fully utilized. Members of the correspondent staff who had scoffed at television as warmed over show business were becoming intrigued by the opportunities to expand their own careers. Hottelet's triumph with the Adenauer visit to Moscow proved that a correspondent–camera team could attack serious problems of public interest in a new and rewarding format. Suggestions began to come in from the field to the central news desk, and most major events were sized up not only for their relevance to the regular news broadcasts and for syndication but also for their potential to furnish raw material, including long background reports and interviews and features for "news specials."

The Hungarian revolution and the Egyptian-Israeli war in October and November 1956 were of such a scope as major news events that they could hardly be covered adequately in the standard fifteen-minute news broadcasts. And there were both sufficient public interest and adequate resources to deliver extended coverage. Several specials were produced and scheduled in November and December, but the story had not been fully told nor all the raw material converted to illustrate its elements.

Three half hour programs broadcast in early January 1957 demonstrated the capabilities of the news staff to exploit this new capability. It furnished an opening to use surplus camera footage for clarifying some of the murky issues that lurked in the background. News crews had remained in the Middle East after the conclusion of the brief and devastating war on the Israeli borders. Their objectives were to gauge the temper and attitudes of the people and their leaders, probe the underlying cause of the tensions, and assess prospects for the future.

One program, "The Arab Tide," dealt with the resurgence of the Arab peoples and their rising nationalism. A second, "Jordan, Key to the Middle East," called attention to the anomalous position of a nation that was created out of the war of 1939–45 with no background as a nation, not even a homogeneous population, but was destined by geography to live next door to a fast strengthening Israel. The third, "Kuwait: Middle East Oil Prize," foreshadowed a Middle Eastern war that would break out some three decades later and would directly involve the United States. Gulf Oil offered to sponsor the series, but the network surprisingly refused the order; the grounds: Gulf had a major commercial interest in Kuwait and was subject to conflict of interest charges. It is ironic that Gulf soon thereafter

Gerhard Schwartzkopf (far right), CBS News cameraman in Germany, being congratulated by Senator John F. Kennedy on winning an Overseas Press Club award for his film coverage of the Hungarian Revolution in 1956. Photo courtesy of Sig Mickelson. Used by permission.

turned to NBC and signed a contract for a running series of what became known as "instant news specials."

By the time that "See It Now" was given its death sentence in midsummer 1958 both the News and Public Affairs departments were establishing records as producers of thirty-minute and one-hour programs that elaborated on the news and probed its background. They had investigated such topics at racketeering, the turbulent life of Jimmy Hoffa and the Teamsters Union, the challenge to the United States position in the Far East posed by the Quemoy and Matsu tensions, the sinking of the transatlantic steamer *Andrea Doria*, and a host of other stories. One major effort stimulated by the Soviet Union's astonishing *Sputnik* space flight called on the full resources of the News department.

The objective was to produce a program that gave a detailed assessment of the relative military strengths and weaknesses of the United States and the Soviet Union, "Where We Stand." At its conclusion CBS tested its policy on editorializing. Howard K. Smith read a brief editorial reflecting the network's position. The process followed to the letter the policy laid down by Chairman Paley some four years earlier in his Chicago speech.

Before "See It Now" had its last rites in 1958 it was clear that there was an opening for a program dealing with major issues in a colorful way but without the controversy that "See It Now" had engendered. Both the News and Public Affairs departments had the talent and the experience to fill the gap and fill it in such a way that there would not be a continuation of the tension that led to "See It Now" 's downfall.

Working together, Irving Gitlin, the director of Public Affairs, and John Day, the director of News, prepared a plan for alternating between the two departments in producing a series of monthly sixty-minute programs. A budget was drawn up calling for an expenditure of $85,000 net for each sixty-minute production in a twelve-program series. It could thus be offered to sponsors for $100,000 gross per program. With the budget and a preliminary prospectus in hand I went to see Stanton to recommend that the television network Sales department test sponsor interest. As was frequently the case Stanton was noncommittal.

Several weeks later, in late March 1959, on a late Sunday afternoon the telephone in my home in Connecticut rang. It was Frank Stanton. He was curious whether we still wanted to sell the documentary series we had talked about. He told me that if I could be in Philadelphia at eight o'clock the next morning to meet with Charles Percy, the chairman of the board of Bell and Howell, and Peter G. Peterson, its president, he thought we might be able to sell a half interest in the series. Once half the series had been sold he was confident that we could find a buyer for the other half. Even though traveling from the Connecticut suburbs to Philadelphia in time for an eight o'clock meeting would not be easy I assured him I would be there and would have Robert Lang, the News division's sales liaison, with me.

Promptly at the appointed hour Lang and I were in the Bell and Howell suite at the Sheraton Hotel. It was a relatively easy sale. It was apparent that Stanton had discussed the project in some detail and that all that was needed was the additional detail that Lang and I could supply. Shortly after lunchtime we had the order and returned to New York.

Percy had made clear that he would in no way exercise any control over program content. His interest, he assured us, was in the commercials, a promise he made good on once the program was on the air. It was only a short time before Goodrich had committed to the other half. It was now time to consider more seriously the content of the program and the assignment of responsibilities for production. One aspect was certain. The title of the series would have to include the letters CBS; Stanton had been adamant on that point. This would be no "See It Now." The credit would not go solely to a producer or star; it would go to the corporation that created and sustained it.

Once full sponsorship was assured Stanton asked that I meet with him to discuss specific plans. As had been the case nine years earlier in discussing the future of radio documentaries, the first question asked was "Who is going to produce?" My original plan was to alternate between News and Public Affairs departments and to assign responsibility to Irving Gitlin for public affairs programs and to John Day for the news product. Stanton, however, insisted that we needed one strong personality at the helm for all programs in the series. The logical choice, of course, was Fred Friendly.

I was reluctant to push very hard for Friendly, assuming that it would be almost impossible to separate the Murrow-Friendly team and that we might very well be recreating "See It Now" under a new title. I assumed that Paley would be less than enchanted at seeing the Murrow-Friendly, team reunited and that Stanton could hardly achieve his objective of making this a CBS product if the duo dominated production. But it was clear that the project needed central direction with the kind of flair that Friendly would give it. The issue to be resolved, stated simply, was how Friendly could be persuaded to accept the responsibility without turning the project into a revival of "See It Now."

Friendly's first response to the invitation to accept the responsibility was predictable. It was clear that he was flattered at being offered the assignment and was enthusiastic about the prospect, but it was equally clear that he was unwilling to commit himself fully without assurances that Murrow would play a significant role. Friendly quickly clarified his position regarding Murrow's participation, stating it unequivocally in a memo he sent me shortly after our first meeting: "A clear definition of what will be expected of him [Murrow] and therefore Friendly and the unit [former "See It Now" unit now producing "Small World"] is a clear and present part of the problem."[1]

In a memo to the files dated June 16, 1959, I explained why I was disturbed at the sentence. "Actually I believe I have explained quite completely to Fred," I wrote, "what will be expected of him . . . as an executive producer he would be expected to make use of the resources of CBS News wherever they may be. In other words he might draw on the special unit of the News department for some production, on various units of the Public Affairs department for others and on his own 'Small World' unit for a reasonable share of the volume." It was obvious from his cool reaction that he was less than enchanted with the prospect of working with unfamiliar production teams and without Murrow's direct participation.

The issue was a sensitive one. It was my clear understanding with Stanton, and presumably with Paley, that the program series would be a showcase for the entire News division, the News department, the Public Affairs department, and the old "See It Now" unit, now referred to as the "Small World" unit. The negotiation was difficult because Friendly clearly felt more confident working with Murrow and quite obviously was desirous of regaining some of the luster of the now defunct program series. The dilemma was confounded by the fact that the sponsors had been assured that a variety of CBS News correspondents would be used. Bell and Howell even specified in its order letter that Howard K. Smith have some role in each program. The order had not yet been accepted, but the clause indicated its understanding that the series would not be a reconstituted "See It Now."

As of early June 1959 with the fall season rapidly approaching some action had to be taken, but prospects for a quick solution to the producer problem seemed remote. It was clear that Friendly was the logical choice, but the unhappy experience the corporation had had with the Friendly-Murrow team still rankled. It might have been reconciled were it not for the Chicago speech to RTNDA, which could be interpreted as a direct slap at Chairman Paley. Murrow had also spoken disparagingly of Stanton on too many occasions not to be noticed.

In my role as the principal negotiator I could not see Stanton and Paley agreeing to permitting Murrow and Friendly to share the responsibility for production of the new series, but that is what Friendly seemed to be insisting on. In a memorandum addressed to me on June 15 he made his position clear: "But none of these problems are solved by Friendly simply being selected as Executive Producer of the series," he wrote.[2] He was positioning himself, obviously, I thought, to insist that he and Murrow work as a team. Although Murrow's participation was possible, reconstituting the old Murrow-Friendly team was unlikely. One sentence in Friendly's memorandum, though, seemed abundantly clear on this point:

"Murrow could be depended on to carry much of the load."[3] This, I thought, was the eventuality that we were trying to avoid. The projected series was, I assumed, to be a CBS production, not a Murrow-Friendly enterprise.

The talks with Friendly left me uneasy, as reflected in a memo to the files dated June 18: "My negotiations with Fred are directly tied into an attempt by Friendly to use these conversations as bargaining power to re-establish a position for Murrow."[4] I had no personal objections to his apparent objective, but I assumed that the Paley-Murrow relationship had deteriorated to the point where a revived "See It Now" under any title was out of the question.

It was clear that the impasse could be broken only in a summit meeting. It was decided that the four individuals most directly involved would meet in Frank Stanton's office at 10:00 P.M. on Wednesday, July 8. The intention was to come away from the meeting with a flexible pattern that would not unduly restrict the Friendly-Murrow team but would showcase other members of the CBS News staff and serve as a showpiece for the entire CBS organization.

The mood at the meeting was far warmer than I had anticipated. In my memo of understanding distributed to the other participants on July 17, more than a week later, there was very little evidence of contentiousness.[5] It was anticipated that the big hurdle to be surmounted would be a demand by Friendly that Murrow be a principal in many or all of the programs. The memorandum of understanding reflects only that Murrow would participate in those programs produced by the "Small World" unit and that "Mr. Friendly would consult with him frequently, if not in fact, 'constantly.' " There was tacit agreement that the series would be a "CBS Production" and that exposure would be given to other members of the news staff. Friendly was to consider appropriate titles for the series with the understanding that "CBS" would be included in any title finally selected. Stanton promised full corporate support for the series and described it as the "Playhouse 90" of informational programs.

My fears that reviving the old Murrow-Friendly team would only renew tensions with corporate management and between Murrow and Paley proved groundless. The title selected made no reference to "See It Now"; it was simply "CBS Reports." Murrow appeared on one of the two programs broadcast during the autumn of 1959. Of the first ten programs broadcast during the 1960 calendar year he was the reporter on four, Howard K. Smith on four, Eric Sevareid on one, and Bill Leonard on one. Friendly was as good as his word. The programs dealt with controversial topics and did not shun potentially disturbing evidence but did avoid taking controversial positions that might have lain the corporation open to reasonable demands for "equal time." Stanton had accomplished his purpose.

The program, bearing the CBS label and showcasing CBS News talent, was a hit with critics and media alike and defused some of the grumbling in Congress that had been stimulated by the quiz scandals.

Murrow had started a twelve-month sabbatical on July 1, 1959, so he was not available for as much consultation and support as Friendly had once predicted. Even though he spent much of his sabbatical traveling, he remained in reasonably close touch with Friendly and continued to do "Small World."

The period of tranquillity, however, was short-lived. An entirely different problem provoked a nasty row with senior management that nearly resulted in an irreparable break. The notorious quiz scandal that had implicated both NBC and CBS broke during early autumn 1959. The network needed some tangible evidence that it was determined to keep its programming scrupulously honest and absolutely devoid of hanky panky. In an effort to mitigate damage Stanton composed a set of rules to apply to all programming including news. The rules would demand almost total honesty; there could be, for example, no interviews on the air that had been prepared or rehearsed, or, if there had been preparation or rehearsal, that fact would have to be revealed. It was a purity code that news personnel could enthusiastically subscribe to but not always scrupulously follow. There was some grumbling in the news room that the code was too rigid but generally it was accepted.[6]

In order to open up another channel to enlist public support for the honesty policy CBS Public Relations vice president Kidder Meade, who had joined CBS from the Newsome organization, sought a venue in which the corporate president could enlist public support and further publicize the newly written code. He decided that the annual convention of the National Association of Radio and Television News Directors scheduled to meet in New Orleans from Tuesday, October 13, through Saturday, October 17, would be ideal. It would presumably furnish an opportunity for Stanton to get a national hearing for the new purity code.

Convention planners were delighted with the prospect of Stanton's second appearance; he had won the Paul White Award and had spoken to their Miami convention only two years earlier. But Meade wanted more than an invitation to speak; he wanted an award to add further prestige to the appearance. It took a bit of arm twisting, but the association officials came through. They created a new Distinguished Service to Broadcast News Award and made Stanton the first recipient.

The speech accomplished Meade's purpose. It went out on the national wires and received substantial play in both newspapers and broadcast news reports. Jack Gould of the *New York Times*, however, was interested in further clarification of some of Stanton's remarks and caught up with the CBS president by telephone in Texas on October 19. Gould's lead sentence after the interview read, "Canned applause and laughter, 'spontaneous' interview shows that are actually rehearsed and other deceits that are common to television are to be weeded out of the schedule of the Columbia Broadcasting System."[7] Reaction might have been sharply limited had not Stanton, queried further by Gould, cited "Person to Person" as one of the programs guilty of violating his strictures. He explained, according to Gould, that " 'Person to Person' endeavored to create the illusion that it was spontaneous. In actuality, guests have known in advance the questions that would be asked." It wasn't much of a revelation; anyone with any understanding of television production would have realized that no program as complex as "Person to Person" could have been produced without intensive preparation. But it set off a storm.

This speech and the subsequent Gould column irritated Ed Murrow, who was in London at the time, so deeply that he issued a blast at Stanton that reverberated around CBS headquarters for days. Murrow had good reason to be upset. His most popular television program was not the much acclaimed "See It Now" but rather the popular celebrity interview program "Person to Person." "Person to Person" involved so much intricate staging and timing that under no circumstances could it have been aired without intensive rehearsal. Stanton's new regulations hit Murrow where it hurt him most.

I was in Burlington, Vermont, speaking to a Chamber of Commerce dinner on the Friday night that Murrow exploded in London. Early the next morning I went with the Burlington television station manager to a duck blind at the northern tip of Lake Champlain. As we returned to his pickup truck after a fruitless morning waiting for ducks that never showed up, the shortwave radio that he used to keep in touch with the station when he was out of telephone range was noisily insisting that he call his office. Since there were no phones within miles we had an hour's drive before finding a pay phone. The call was not for him; it was for me. Frank Stanton had been trying frantically to reach me.

I immediately called Stanton's office. On his arrival at the office that morning he had intercepted an intemperate and vitriolic cable from Murrow addressed to me. It blasted CBS for amateurism, for adopting of positions that were wholly unrealistic, and for lack of understanding of how programs were produced.

There was not much I could do from a telephone booth in the Green Mountains of Vermont. He thought I should attend a meeting of the CBS Televison Affiliates Executive Committee starting in Monterey, California, on Sunday afternoon. I was quite willing to do so but there were two difficult problems. Transportation could probably be arranged but what I would say to the affiliates was more complicated. I had not been involved in the New Orleans speech, nor had I identified "Person to Person" as a transgressor. He finally decided that the Monterey trip was not necessary.

It was clear that Murrow was furious. He had been goaded by the two

"Person to Person" producers, Jesse Zousmer and John Aaron, but was quite capable of reacting vigorously on his own. It appeared that all of the delicate negotiations of June and July regarding "CBS Reports" and the Murrow position in its production were now in serious jeopardy. It was even questionable whether the new rift could be patched over, or whether Murrow would even remain with CBS.

By the time I had returned to the office on Monday morning, a senior partner in CBS's outside law firm, Ralph Colin of Rosenman, Goldmark, Colin and Kaye, who also served as Paley's personal attorney, was dispatched to London to encourage Murrow to apologize for his outburst. The effort was futile. Colin came back empty-handed and Murrow carried on as if nothing had happened. Eight months of his twelve-month sabbatical remained; that might serve as a cooling off period but it was clear that the uneasy relationship could not go on forever.[8]

For CBS, however, it was significant that the News division, which had long since given up any pretense of controlling the "See It Now" unit, was now infinitely stronger. It was in a position to absorb the new "CBS Reports" production machine and contribute substantially to it. The new series started with enthusiastic response to its "Biography of a Missile," even though the missile exploded before reaching orbit, and followed it with the "Population Explosion," a study of population problems in India. After a rocky start a new series was under way and CBS, not the Murrow-Friendly team, was receiving the public plaudits.

The Happy Couple: Pigskin and TV Picture Tube

Lives of millions of Americans were dramatically altered in the autumn of 1956 by a bold move undertaken by CBS Sports. Ever since the television networks had begun to program Sunday afternoons, schedules had been devoted largely to what broadcasters generally referred to as "programs in the public interest" but television critics commonly derided as the "Sunday afternoon ghetto."

Professional sports had been a major factor in spurring television's rapid growth since in the late 1940s primitive receivers first appeared in living rooms and bars. Baseball and boxing were early starters; they were relatively easy to cover and for the most part were confined to major cities where television facilities, interconnections to the limited networks, and a growing audience were available.

Football was more complicated. Most of the public interest was focused on traditional college rivalries. Professional teams were building fan support but at a less intense level than the college game. Broadcasters focused little on the schedules of the pros. Building an attractive college schedule, however, was not easy for the immature industry. Many college games with the greatest fan interest were played in stadiums where pick-up costs would be astronomical or interconnections were either unavailable or nonexistent and set counts were low. There were still so few receivers in use that the prospect of absorbing the cost of picking up games was unattractive.

The professional game, although it had a following in the early 1950s, attracted relatively little public attention, at least compared to intercollegiate football or major league baseball. Most of its franchises, though, were in major cities, easy to reach with microwave or coaxial cable, and with growing numbers of television homes. Pro football, was a sleeping giant. All it needed was television exposure to convert it into a national craze. Supported by a unified national contract in 1956, it quickly established itself on a par with baseball as the national pastime. By the end of the decade it dominated Sunday afternoon programming and made names like Vince Lombardi, Frank Gifford, Jim Brown, Paul Hornung, and Bart Starr as prominent as those of movie stars. There was even some question whether baseball had been supplanted by professional football as the national pastime.

The professional teams had begun building television exposure on a limited basis before 1956. Each team in the league had organized its own regional network, varying in 1955 from the four stations carrying Green Bay games to the thirty-eight carrying the Washington Redskins. Ratings were satisfactory but the game failed to spark national interest comparable to that of college football or Major League baseball. It was apparent that it needed a unified national promotional campaign to reach that level.

Its quick ascent to status as a national craze came about almost by accident. Sunday afternoon in the early 1950s did not appear to be a very attractive time for building audience interest. The programs available on the networks were a melange of talk and discussion programs, education and culture. It was public service–oriented. It looked good on license renewal applications and was comparatively cheap. Spending limited funds on Sunday afternoons did not pose much of a risk because the time was considered commercially unattractive and well adapted to building goodwill.

All that changed, however, in fall 1956, when CBS Television dropped its Sunday afternoon public service emphasis in favor of a twelve-week schedule of professional football. The decision not only changed Sunday afternoons in the autumn for millions of set owners but converted sports programming into a big business. For thirty-eight years, from 1956 through 1993, it had seemed that CBS, the National Professional Football League, and Sunday afternoons in the autumn were interlocked, that they were made for each other.

But all good things come to an end. The upstart Fox Network announced in 1993 that it had stolen away the big prize, full rights to all NFL Sunday games starting with the 1994 season. CBS after thirty-seven years of a comfortable monopoly had unceremoniously been ousted from its presumably unassailable position. NBC, starting years later than CBS, with the somewhat less attractive American Football Conference, retained its AFL schedule.

In pure profit and loss terms professional football was never a big money earner for the network. Time charges were barely enough to cover costs. Shortly rights fees began to grow so astronomically that advertising sales revenues could cover only a part of the cost. Football did, however, deliver prestige and loyalty from affiliated stations and enthusiastic followings for advertisers. Though the games themselves did not yield much profit to the networks, the pre- and postgame shows did. For the affiliated stations it was a much more favorable story. Not only did they get programming that drew audiences undreamed of while they were broadcasting public service schedules, but they could sell spots at selected breaks during playing time and both before and after the game. Interest ran so high that they began to cater to the interests of a high-buying-power audience, particularly men, whom advertisers were especially interested in reaching. The stations had something to brag about in their home communities and the station managers in their country clubs and Rotary Club meetings.

Anyone acquainted with CBS's reputation as an innovative programmer might have assumed that professional football came to CBS as a result of vision, careful planning, skillful negotiation, and a gambler's instinct. In fact, it was not the result of carefully drawn strategic planning and slipped in almost by accident.

For the fall season of 1955 Irving Gitlin, the head of the CBS Public Affairs unit, and his staff had hopes for a two-hour block of Sunday afternoon informational programs. Sunday afternoon seemed the most appropriate time to schedule them. There was little competition for the time and chances of enticing advertiser support for any type of program that would draw commercially attractive ratings seemed limited. Sunday afternoon at this stage was considered a time that would attract little sponsor interest. Press reviews for the Gitlin schedule, what there were, were generally favorable. Few senior CBS executives paid much attention until they began examining data reflecting the number of affiliated stations carrying the programs.

In mid-October I seriously injured my back and found myself in the Harkness Pavilion of Columbia-Presbyterian Hospital for traction and assorted therapies. The injury was not so serious, however, that I could not attend to normal office routine, provided the problems came to me. Gitlin visited the hospital one day early in my stay to reveal some sad news concerning his prized Sunday afternoon schedule. He had just received a critical memo from President Frank Stanton calling attention to devastating information regarding the numbers of stations that were carrying the programs.

Starting with the opening of the professional season in early September even the most attractive of the programs was carried by only 26 stations of the entire affiliate list of some 200. Acceptances had plummeted as soon as football started. "Adventure," which had been shown in 78 stations in July, was down to 26 by October 10 and 23 by October 17. "Let's Take a Trip" fell from 85 stations to 18. The most attractive of the four programs, "Face the Nation," dropped from 85 stations to 23.[1] Only 12 stations carried all four programs. It was a disaster.

It was easy to pinpoint the problem: NFL football. Ad hoc regional networks had been created for the duration of the football season and were siphoning off CBS affiliates as well as independents and affiliates of the other networks. CBS's Washington affiliate, WTOP-TV, had gone a step further. It had built a regional network that carried the Washington Redskins south to Virginia, the Carolinas, Georgia, and Florida. A Chicago-based network carried the Chicago Bears and Cardinals down the Mississippi Valley to Louisiana and across the plains to Texas, Kansas, and Oklahoma. A San Francisco Forty Niners/Los Angeles Rams network covered the Pacific coast. Smaller regional networks had been created to carry the games of the New York Giants, Baltimore Colts, Philadelphia Eagles, Pittsburgh Steelers, Detroit Lions, and Cleveland Browns. Even little Green Bay had a limited network of its own. It was to these regional networks that CBS stations had gone. A total of twenty-three southern and southeastern CBS affiliates, for example, were listed among the thirty-six stations carrying the Redskins games.

As we checked the discouraging data I remembered a conversation I had had more than a year earlier with one Texas E. Schramm, then publicity director for the Los Angeles Rams. Schramm outlined a plan tying all these mininetworks together into one single CBS package. It could be accomplished, he explained, through negotiations with the NFL commissioner, Bert Bell. Under his plan CBS would negotiate for exclusive rights to the entire league and all its games. Once we were able to get Bell's support, Schramm predicted, we could take over the mininetworks. Each would have built-in sponsors, mostly local brewers, who would likely switch their accounts to CBS if the network were to take over the rights. An agreement with Bell's office, Schramm insisted, would enable CBS to acquire all the local contracts, permitting its affiliates to replace the nonaffiliates who had been included in the ad hoc networks.

I told Schramm that I was intrigued but CBS policy pretty well tied us into using Sunday afternoon for public service programming. Since the commitment to that schedule seemed firm I was skeptical that I could persuade management to make so radical a change. There was no way of foretelling then how severely professional football would erode the program acceptance base for the Sunday public affairs programs in little more than a year.

Trying to attract the interest of senior CBS management in high cost major sports events had also been frustrating. Sports at CBS had been something of an orphan. There was nothing in the record to indicate that there was more than a casual interest in sports broadcasts unless they were established high-visibility national events, particularly those scheduled during marginal time periods, with rights obtained at minimal risk. Management's prime objective had obviously been to build a solid network and a dominant entertainment program schedule; at this point professional football did not fit the established pattern. It was also hard to visualize Paley and Stanton as rabid sports fans. Saturday afternoon baseball, coming as it did in 1952 with built-in sponsorship, was welcomed. There was little other commercial interest in the time. Prospects for Sunday afternoon football, though, were not bright; if there were a change, however, I told Schramm, I would get in touch.

The sadly disappointing results of Gitlin's efforts to build a Sunday afternoon audience suggested that it was time to give in and swim with the tide. I asked Elmer Lower, then my second in command and later president of ABC News, to get in touch with Schramm to see whether his idea still seemed possibile. Schramm was optimistic.

The off-chance that we might carry professional football on twelve Sunday afternoons added new urgency to the matter of finding a new sports director. It would be folly to undertake anything as complex as a twelve-week, six-game-per week schedule of professional football or even to try to negotiate for rights to carry it without competent leadership. The spot had been left open since the creation of the corporate News and Public Affairs department two years earlier. Even if NFL football did not materialize, an able executive with management, planning, and negotiating skills would be essential in the expectation that management attitude toward sports would change.

We desperately needed someone with prestige and familiarity with sports and sports leaders for the endless job of negotiating rights agreements and struggling with inevitable personnel problems. We would need producers, directors, play by play and color broadcasters, camera crews, and mobile facilities to be deployed to the stadiums. A wizard at juggling heterogeneous elements would be required to oversee production of six games every Sunday afternoon for twelve weeks with a maze of complex overlapping circuitry and scores of commercials that had to be integrated. Perhaps what was required most was a style, a character, something to distinguish CBS from traditional sports broadcasting. It would be a monumental assignment that required adequate leadership, and it had to be done rapidly.

One prospect was the relatively young general manager of the Colorado Springs Blue Sox, a farm team of the Chicago White Sox. The prospect, Bill MacPhail, was a son of the legendary Larry MacPhail and a brother of Lee MacPhail, an executive with the New York Yankees. We hired him on the spot. In a few days he had resigned from the White Sox organization and moved to New York.

The next step was to determine whether the pro football package might actually be available. Schramm's optimism was well founded. Lower and MacPhail found Bell enthusiastically receptive to a proposal to the extent that he suggested procedures for bringing the intricate package to fruition.

By taking soundings from the commissioner and a number of owners of clubs they discovered that a complete schedule of six games each Sunday for the twelve Sundays of the season would probably require a little more than $1 million in rights fees, a pittance in subsequent years but a formidable gamble then.[2]

Key to winning corporate support would be William F. Hylan, the vice president for sales of the CBS Television Network. The sales force under his direction would have to assume the responsibility for marketing the complex schedule.

One hazard surfaced immediately. Home games were to be blacked out. This was a particularly devastating prospect with respect to Chicago, then the second largest television market in the United States and the site of one of the three CBS-owned stations. Bell was adamant that no signal could be broadcast from a transmitter within seventy-five miles of a game site. Chicago had two clubs, the Bears and the Cardinals, and one of the two would be playing in Chicago each Sunday during the season. This meant no football for Chicago and no football income for CBS-owned WBBM-TV.

The contract with the NFL would require that all games away from home, even though they were blacked out locally, would have to be transmitted back to the network of the visiting team. This would impose a backbreaking burden on both personnel and physical facilities. AT&T had barely enough television circuits to serve the intricate spider web that the schedule would require. In the 1990s, using satellites and fiber-optic lines, it would be a cinch; in the 1950s it involved an almost superhuman task. To add to the problem, mobile units to serve as control centers in the various stadiums were in short supply; there was an inadequate pool of available producers, directors, and on the air talent.

Hylan enthusiastically supported the proposal. Jack VanVolkenburg, president of the Television Network, was noncommittal and passed the responsibility for making the decision off to the chairman of the board, William S. Paley. The chairman was worried about the scope of the commitment. He had an uncanny feel for entertainment programs but no similar feel for sports. A commitment to carry 72 football games averaging approximately 3 hours each meant the network would have to commit itself to carrying some 216 hours of professional football during one season. Only Arthur Godfrey, who was then programming a daily one-hour daytime program and another hour at night, had more hours on the air annually than football would consume, and Godfrey was operating from a single studio.

Paley wanted to know what CBS's "total exposure" would be; how much would the corporation lose if sponsors refused to support the package and it did not generate a penny of revenue? A quick calculation indicated that it would probably amount to approximately $5 million, a relatively modest sum compared to the prices commanded by some of the most popular entertainment programs, but it apparently seemed an extravagant expenditure for Sunday afternoons. Paley wanted time to think about it.

A more detailed analysis suggested that the $5 million estimate would not be far off the mark. A little more than $1 million would probably be required for rights; about $720,000, or $10,000 each, for pickup and production for 72 games; another $1 million for talent and travel; and still another $1 million for the overlapping maze of AT&T circuits. Add in a contingency and the total for a twelve-week season would amount to about the $5 million estimated on the spur of the moment. Sales, promotion, and advertising costs would be extra.

We saw him again about a week later. In the meantime he had talked to an old classmate at the University of Pennsylvania, Carroll Rosenbloom, then the owner of the Baltimore Colts and later of the Los Angeles Rams. Rosenbloom had apparently convinced him that the risk was minimal and the rewards might be enormous. Somewhat reluctantly he gave his approval. With the chairman voting yes the television network could hardly say no.

Now it was time to start negotiating in earnest. Although the commissioner was the key, it was necessary to work out separate agreements with each of the twelve teams and with the advertisers with whom they had firm commitments. The twelve in 1956 were the New York Giants, Philadelphia Eagles, Baltimore Colts, Washington Redskins, Pittsburgh Steelers, Cleveland Browns, Detroit Lions, Chicago Bears, Chicago Cardinals, Green Bay Packers, San Francisco Forty Niners, and Los Angeles Rams. The New York, Washington, Chicago, and West Coast negotiations were relatively uncomplicated. Their networks were large and the territories relatively well defined. Philadelphia, Baltimore, Pittsburgh, Detroit, and Cleveland, however, presented a tangled web of overlapping territory and sponsors who would have to be mollified. Green Bay was such an unattractive prospect that MacPhail told Bell we would bypass it, Bell's reply, "No Green Bay, no deal." MacPhail settled for a $50,000 fee for the Packers' season; it paid off handsomely a year later when under Vince Lombardi they began to win championships.[3]

Selling the schedule to advertisers proved relatively uncomplicated but maddeningly time-consuming. The advertisers who had contracts with the clubs were, for the most part, willing to switch to CBS outlets, but it was a tedious process. It took so long, in fact, that Stanton at one time in spring 1956 wondered whether we might have to abandon the whole program.[4] Once the disparate pieces began to come together, however, it wasn't long before there was enough revenue in sight to meet our commitments, including payments to affiliates for carrying the games.

Arranging for a crazy quilt pattern of microwave circuits to bring all away games to each of the clubs in the league, however, was bewildering. There were no satellites in the sky; the first satellite service was still a decade away. AT&T's first transcontinental circuit was less than five years old. As recently as the 1952 election there was only a single channel available from New York to Los Angeles, from West Coast to East Coast, and from New York to the Southeast and the Southwest. There had been dramatic progress by 1956 in extending the coverage pattern of microwave circuits and coaxial cables, but some areas were still served by single-channel links and return paths to network headquarters were still limited.

The most complex problem involved building a schedule that would meet Bell's mandate that all away from home games be transported back for release in the home market. It clearly required recruiting a specialist. A wizard at solving complicated traffic problems, Randy Brent, was brought in from the Television Network Broadcast Operations department to help solve the puzzle.

Chicago remained a special problem because of Bell's seventy-five-mile blackout policy. This was rectified a couple of years later when, in part as a result of CBS pressure, the Chicago Cardinals moved to St. Louis. This opened up Chicago for the six games a season when the Bears were not at home. It blacked out St. Louis on six Sundays but in audience terms was a good trade.

Recruiting on the air talent was another problem. Red Barber had withdrawn from CBS assignments and was too busy with other commitments to participate. What was needed now were sports broadcasters able to adapt to the television age, more communicative and less bombastic in approach than run-of-the-mill talent, skilled more in interpretation than in description. It was agreed that efforts should be made to recruit Frank Gifford, Pat Summerall, and Kyle Rote from the New York Giants as soon as they were available. Johnny Lujack, the former Notre Dame quarterback, became one of the regulars. As soon as Jim McKay was free of other commitments he signed on to do color. Chris Schenkel came with the New York Giants.

Rights fees kept rising over the years but so did ratings. The arrival of the AFL on NBC in 1960 did little damage. There turned out to be enough demand for football that ratings held up even when the number of games available to the viewer was doubled. The NFL had a substantial advantage in ratings competition since it was well positioned in the nation's larger markets, those with more television homes and thus potentially greater audiences; furthermore, the national set count was growing so rapidly that new television homes alone were sufficient to keep it growing. In fact, competition probably helped create the football craze that still dominates the fall season. And CBS kept riding the crest until Fox surprised everyone by slipping in with a higher bid for the 1994 season.

With the football schedule in place, CBS for the first time since the beginnings of television a decade earlier had moved into position to become a serious factor in the race for broadcast sports supremacy. It now, for the first time, had a full sports program. In addition to twelve Sundays of professional football, it had the baseball "Game of the Week," the "Triple Crown" of horse racing, and the Orange Bowl and would soon add the Masters' golf tournament. It was the football, though, that captivated the masses and converted Sunday afternoons into mandatory television time for millions of fans.

Professional football not only proved to be a triumph for CBS News; it was a phenomenon that would revolutionize behavior patterns during fall weekends. It not only raised Sunday afternoon ratings to new highs and drew substantial advertising revenues, but also filled football stadiums and increased gate receipts. It elevated the income of star players to levels previously paid only to Hollywood stars. It created an environment that a few years later made Monday night football a national institution. By the end of the decade television's coverage of professional football had stimulated a stunning change in American behavior patterns. It happened almost by accident but it was another example of the changes in American life-style generated during the 1950s by television.

18 ·

Carrying the Olympic Torch
to Television

As in the case of professional football it was television that rocketed the Olympic Games, both summer and winter, from mildly popular international events to superspectacle status and it was television's news operations that took the initiative. Newspapers had given extensive coverage to the games, particularly the summer series, from their first modern revival in Athens in 1896. Names of Olympic heroes had struck chords the world over: Paavo Nurmi, the Flying Finn; Joey Ray, the American sprinter; and perhaps more than any other, Jesse Owens, the sprinter and broad jumper from Ohio State University. The coverage, however, lacked the rich overtones, human drama, suspense, and immediacy provided by television. There was some radio coverage, but for the most part the world learned about the games through print. Newsreels covered them but their reports were not available until several days after the event. They caught the spectacle but not the suspense of the live report.

The 1936 games in Berlin in particular were given intensive coverage by the press. The increased attention stemmed partly from the pageantry introduced by the German dictator, Adolf Hitler, and partly from curiosity concerning the Third Reich and its Aryan chauvinism. Tensions in Europe were growing rapidly and Hitler's master race theories were being given widening exposure. The whole world held its breath to see how Hitler would react if the black American, Jesse Owens, were to win a gold medal. Owens did not win only one; he won four in the stadium that Hitler had dedicated to Aryanism. Much of the world awaited Hitler's reaction, which would have been a major international event had there been television coverage. His failure to recognize the American athlete caught the attention of people the world over but not with the dramatic impact that would have resulted from television coverage of the snub. The only live coverage was on radio; it was principally a newspaper story. Pictorial coverage was limited either to still pictures in newspapers and magazines or to newsreels seen several days after the event.

There were no Olympic Games in the war years of 1940 and 1944. When they were resumed in London in 1948 the BBC was able to broadcast some events on television but there was no cross-channel coverage and obviously none across the Atlantic. The big breakthrough came in 1960 at the winter games in Squaw Valley, California, followed by the summer games in Rome the same year. Television was present at both. It created for the first time in Olympic history a vicarious feeling of presence that could never have been achieved without the electronic camera. And it focused attention on the quadrennial games far exceeding anything seen previously.

The winter games were seen live throughout the United States and Canada and on videotape elsewhere; the Rome games, live in Europe and on videotape reproductions in the United States. Some morning and early afternoon events in Rome were seen by American audiences the same day, evening events the next day. Since they were recorded by batteries of interlocked electronic cameras they had the same fluidity of motion and variety of angles as a live television picture.

Olympic coverage began on American television almost by accident. CBS was the first to cover the games, both winter and summer. The first Olympic telecasts slipped into the CBS schedule without any long-term planning. As he had with professional football, Tex Schramm played a significant role.

In his new capacity as assistant director of sports, Schramm urged during autumn 1958 and winter 1959 that CBS negotiate for rights for the winter games scheduled for Squaw Valley in February 1960. Satellites were still not available but microwave circuits by this time had proliferated across the country, making it possible to pick up the games from the site in the valley near the California-Nevada border and feed the signal to the full network. Cameras were no smaller nor lighter than earlier, but their quality was improved and new long lenses had been perfected to record distant scenes. Portable microwave dishes could pick up signals from remote points and the process of laying cable had been simplified, making it possible to station cameras in the remote areas that would be required to cover downhill and slalom ski events and ski jumping. The signal could be carried into Reno or San Francisco and there join the transcontinental network.

Schramm set out to investigate the prospect. He drew up a coverage plan and prepared a proposal for consideration by the television network. CBS, though, was slow to respond. ABC moved more rapidly and by early spring 1959 tied up exclusive rights to the games, scheduled to take place the following February. That ended Schramm's dream of being the first to furnish live coverage of any Olympic event to viewers in North America. Within weeks he had been approached by the owners of the new National Football League franchise in Dallas to become the club's general manager; he quickly accepted the job and resigned from CBS Sports.

Almost simultaneously with Schramm's efforts to interest CBS in the winter games the Gardiner Advertising Agency of St. Louis, through its New York office, began urging the network to consider bidding for rights to cover the summer games in Rome. Robert Lang, who had joined the staff of CBS News to exploit new opportunities in marketing the CBS News product, had struck up a warm relationship with senior staff at Gardiner. One of the key executives at the agency was a well placed Italian from Rome who had participated on the Italian ski team in the winter games at Cortina d'Ampezzo, Italy, in 1956. Giancarlo Rossini had a wide range of acquaintances in Rome, including members of the Italian Olympic Organizing Committee (CONI), which had accepted the responsibility for organizing and producing the summer games. Rossini and his superior at the agency, Roland Martini, convinced Lang that they could get the summer Olympics for CBS if the company wished. By midwinter 1959 the Rome committee was sufficiently interested in a CBS relationship that members expressed an interest in talking about a possible contract. I had planned a European trip for the spring of 1959 and would be in Paris at the beginning of the trip. It was agreed that members of CONI would meet me in Paris for preliminary discussions about a rights purchase.

There was some question at this point whether we would be prepared to undertake a project of this magnitude. Transporting pictures across the Atlantic was still a problem. As in the case of the coronation of Queen Elizabeth in 1953 they would have to be carried by aircraft. The process would not have to be quite as complicated, however, as it was then.

There had been two technological developments since 1953 that promised to simplify the project. Jet aircraft were now flying regular commercial schedules across the North Atlantic, cutting transit time almost in half, and videotape had been in use since mid-1957, replacing the much more cumbersome motion picture film that had caused so many problems in 1953. Videotape recording was still in a primitive stage, but its use would still be incomparably simpler than the kinescoping system used in recording the ceremony at Westminster Abbey seven years earlier. Jet aircraft still had relatively restricted range but there was a sufficient number of jets in service by 1960 that there would be numerous optional times for dispatching shipments. It would not, as in 1953, be necessary to depend on a single military aircraft. A commercial jet, allowing for a refueling stop en route, would make the trip from Rome to New York in about nine hours. A nine-hour flight, when measured against the six-hour time difference between the two cities, would place the videotape package at Idlewild Airport only three clock hours after departure from Rome. It would clearly be a complicated venture, but at least superficially the project looked feasible.

Soundings with the television network indicated at least mild enthusiasm for the innovative gamble. The Sales department was optimistic that advertising support would be forthcoming. There was sufficient optimism that technical operations personnel began to draw preliminary plans for the highly complex recording and editing operation. The reaction throughout the company was sufficiently favorable that it appeared expedient to agree to meet the CONI delegation in Paris in mid-April.

The negotiating session took place at the Plaza Athenee hotel. Neither CONI representatives nor I would make an explicit commitment, but it was evident that all were favorably disposed toward further negotiations. The meeting concluded with an agreement to carry on with the planning process and to signal when we would be ready to proceed to the next step. I continued my Europe trip without making a recommendation to New York. The more I thought about the project, however, the more enthusiastic I became.

Shortly after returning to New York I accepted an invitation to a luncheon at Columbia University's Faculty Club. By chance CBS's president, Frank Stanton, was also there. He invited me to ride back with him to CBS headquarters, approximately a twenty-minute trip. This gave me an uninterrupted opportunity to report on my Paris meeting. By the time we arrived at Fifty-second Street and Madison Avenue, the site of CBS headquarters, he was favorably inclined toward the project and I sensed that we could count on his support. That support reinforced the television network leadership's growing enthusiasm for the project. Neither program nor sales executives could overlook the higher ratings and revenues that would accrue from introducing fresh, attractive programming in what would normally have been the slowest season of the year.

Meanwhile ABC's hold on rights for the winter games at Squaw Valley appeared a little less secure than a few months earlier. In late July IBM executives who were working with CBS News personnel in preparing for coverage of the November 1960 election scheduled a meeting to discuss election coverage plans at the IBM facility at San Jose, California, in which equipment was being built to assist in coverage of the November national election. The computer manufacturer had agreed to large-scale cooperation with CBS News in gathering, compiling, and displaying nationwide election returns and in projecting results.

As we drove down from the San Francisco airport to San Jose I asked Gil Ahlborn of the IBM staff whether a rumor I had heard suggesting that ABC was abandoning its hold on rights to the winter games was true. I assumed that Ahlborn would be a good source since IBM had made a commitment to the organizing committee to time all events with IBM equipment. Ahlborn said he had heard the rumor but could not verify it; he added that he would find out.

Later in the day, as we were finishing our San Jose visit and preparing to return to San Francisco, he reported that the rumor was accurate. In anticipation of our possible interest in acquiring the rights, he had booked transportation for CBS special events director Paul Levitan and me to accompany him to Squaw Valley the next morning. He had also arranged appointments with members of the Squaw Valley organizing committee. They would meet us at the site of the games to view the facility under construction and discuss the possibility of acquiring the rights.

The temperature was in the high 90s as we inspected the venue and talked with members of the organizing committee. They confirmed that ABC had thrown in the sponge and that they were receptive to new bids. The climate was not conducive to thinking seriously about downhill skiing, ice hockey, and bobsledding. It was hard to visualize snow on the mountains and ice on the ponds as we stood, sweltering in the heat, at the top of the ski lift, where the giant slalom was booked to start only seven months later.

Despite the heat the prospect was enticing, doubly so because it would complement coverage of the summer games should CBS elect to go forward. We agreed tentatively on a rights fee of $50,000, subject to CBS Television Network approval, and went on our way. We now had a reasonable chance of carrying both the summer and winter games. All we had to do was sell the television network on agreeing to both ventures. The rights fee was ultimately approved and detailed planning could begin. With the winter games in hand, an agreement with the Rome committee seemed more likely.

By early October CONI was ready to negotiate. Any skepticism among CBS executives had now faded. In order to facilitate conversations in Rome with the organizing committee Rossini offered to go along as guide and translator. In mid-October the CBS delegation set out for the Italian capital. Two senior representatives of the network Technical Operations department were assigned to the trip to evaluate operational problems, begin the facilities planning process, and help in developing a final estimate of costs.

After tramping through a number of Olympic venues in various stages of completion and being wined and dined by CONI and Italian television executives we concluded that the project was feasible. By recording the Italian television signal on videotape at or near the Fiumicino airport we could put edited videotape on jet aircraft leaving Rome in mid- to late afternoon. Allowing for nine hours of flying time and subtracting the six hours for the time change we assumed we could cover events taking place in the morning and early afternoon and have them in New York in time for release on the nighttime program schedule. This would give CBS viewers Olympic programs every night for the nearly two weeks of the games. What few night events there were could be programmed for airing during late afternoon hours the next day and repeated if warranted at night. By setting up a tape projection facility at what was then Idlewild Airport (now JFK) it would be possible to eliminate almost an hour of travel time on New York streets, thus subtracting another sixty minutes from the time lag. Since the recordings were made on tape, not motion picture film, no film processing time was required.

From an advertising sales point of view the games could not have been scheduled at a more favorable time of the year. The last two weeks of August were the "dog days" of summer for television advertising; this was the month when television ratings hit absolute rock bottom. Preemption costs (the cost of making good on commercial spots preempted from long-term advertisers) would be at a minimum. Many advertisers would be happy to have relief for the two weeks of the games.

It was still necessary to negotiate a price for the rights. The CONI group quoted three prices: a figure of $675,000 for rights alone; $750,000 for rights plus partial access to the signal that would be delivered by RAI-TV, the Italian state television network; or $835,000 for full RAI-TV coverage of all events. Even though there was some element of risk involved these figures seemed within reason. They contrast dramatically with the $2.3 billion NBC in 1996 contracted to pay the International Olympic Committee for rights to the summer games in 2004 and 2008 and the winter games in 2006.[1]

It was decided to opt for the middle figure, $750,000 for rights with limited access to the RAI signal. CBS's own film camera personnel would be available for coverage around the periphery of the game venues, and CBS announcers would describe the events from the audio booths. The technical operations personnel estimated that it would take another half million dollars to set up a production center with tape recording and editing facilities in rented space on the airport grounds, pay all talent fees, transport personnel and equipment to the site, and cover meals and lodging and personal expenses. The Sports department would assume the responsibility for assigning directors, producers, on the air talent, and expediters and estimating the costs involved. Allowance would have to be made for transporting from New York a number of bulky videotape recorders and space would have to be rented to house the operations. It would also be necessary to estimate charges for air expressing tapes to Idlewild.

In the event some tape packages might be delayed, causing shipments to miss outbound flights from Rome, a backup facility at Orly airport in Paris was written into the estimate. Any item that missed a flight from Rome, with a facility available in Paris, could be transmitted to the French capital by microwave and recorded there. It could then be shipped to New York on a flight from the French capital. Only a single tape unit would be required at Orly under the assumption that the editing would already have been completed in Rome. Since preemption costs would be minimal a final estimate suggested that approximately $1.5 million would be an adequate cost budget.

There was more than a slight gamble involved. No one could foresee how interested American viewers might be. Since there had been no previous televised Olympic broadcasts there were no precedents to indicate what kind of ratings might be expected, particularly for prerecorded coverage.

The first effort to interest U.S. television in Olympic coverage was made in early 1950. The chief engineer of Finnish television visited New York in February of that year to try to interest the American networks in coverage of the Helsinki games in 1952, but unfortunately for Finland the events were scheduled at precisely the same dates as the American national political conventions. Olympic coverage was out of the question. Television was still too primitive in 1952 to contemplate doing anything but such limited news reporting of the Helsinki games as could be obtained from newsreel sources.

The 1956 games in Melbourne, Australia, were too far away and the time difference was too great to build any interest. Jet airplanes were still some three years in the future and air schedules would not permit coverage in less than three days after the event. Videotape machines had been demonstrated but no production units were yet available, and they would not be in use until early 1957. An American entrepreneur, Paul Talbott, who operated a film company called Freemantle, obtained rights for film coverage but failed to get network orders. The networks, on the other hand, intended to rely on newsreel coverage. Since they were unwilling to pay fees for rights to report public events, they joined in writing and enforcing what they called the "three by three" rule: The networks insisted on being permitted, without payment of rights fees, to show three-minute news clips three times a day during the course of the games. Each was to arrange for its own source of newsreel coverage. Consequently, there was some delayed film coverage but not enough to indicate potential public interest had live coverage been available.

Videotape, available for commercial use by early 1957, put recorded coverage into an entirely new perspective. The fluidity of the television cameras functioning in a live television mode would create the illusion of live action even with a few hours of delay. It seemed a reasonable gamble and the fact that the programs preempted would be summer replacements or repeats made it even more attractive.

Before leaving Rome, we shook hands on a deal. There was still ten months remaining to perfect plans, recruit personnel, select equipment, and market the program, but now the die was cast. It was only a handshake

A handshake with the chairman of the Italian Olympic Committee after the signing in 1959 of an exclusive contract for television coverage of the Rome games in 1960. Photo courtesy of Sig Mickelson. Used by permission.

agreement, but there was little doubt that a contract that both sides would accept could be drafted.

Once agreement was in hand on the Rome games the immediate problem was Squaw Valley and the winter events. They were scheduled to open on February 19, in less than four months. Paul Levitan, who had visited Squaw Valley with me on that blistering day the previous summer accompanied by television network technicians, had clawed his way up and down mountains, searched for camera positions where long lenses could catch the action in the slaloms or the ski jumps without letting the participants out of sight, and puzzled about methods he might use to haul cameras up to mountainside positions and string cable to enable them to feed out a signal. He had to anticipate heavy snow and plan to keep his cameras and cable lines secure from the weather. Thirty or forty years later this was old hat but in 1960 it called for innovation.

Walter Cronkite was selected as the anchorman. He was supported by Bud Palmer, who had called both hockey and basketball games for CBS; by Chris Schenkel, an all-around sports reporter and the voice of the New York football Giants; and by Andrea Mead Lawrence and Dick Button, former winter Olympics medal winners.

By the time the opening ceremony was under way the night of February 16 personnel and hardware were in place. Competition started the morning of February 17. American viewers had never seen anything like it before. They saw ski jumpers soaring through the air, leaning forward so they were almost parallel with their skis, and downhill and slalom skiers whizzing through the gates and spinning around the turns. Nothing excited American fans, though, as much as the final hockey contest of the games, the United States against the USSR. The Soviets were heavily favored as the underdog U.S. team took to the ice on the last Saturday night of the games.

Stands in the arena were full. If the American team upset all the odds and won, they would be Olympic champions, an eventuality that no one had expected as the games opened. The two teams fought to a virtual standstill in the first two periods. Midway into the third and last periods the American team still had not collapsed.

In the Capitol Hilton in Washington, D.C., scores of American political leaders and journalists, all attired in black tie, were gathering at cocktail parties in suites on the upper floors awaiting the opening of the annual dinner for the president of the United States, sponsored by the Radio and Television Correspondents Association. Supreme Court justices, senators, congressmen, broadcast executives, and famous correspondents were present. Every television in every suite was tuned to the hockey game in progress at Squaw Valley, half a continent away. Roars of approval followed every successful effort of the American team to stave off a Soviet rally and sighs were audible as the Soviets threatened. The dinner was delayed until the result was in. When, within minutes of the final whistle, the Americans broke a tie and took the lead the corridors almost erupted in roars of approval. It was a near anticlimax when the whistle ending the contest blew with the United States the unexpected champion. There was a closing ceremony the next day but after the raising of the American flag and the singing of the national anthem all else was redundant. The first live television coverage of any Olympic games had been an unqualified success.

The summer games in Rome offered an entirely different set of problems for television coverage. The winter games were based on live coverage. That meant a premium was placed on camera and microphone locations, camera personnel who could follow the fast-moving events with their long lenses, directors who were skilled in intercutting camera shots, and announcers in the master control booth who knew the events well enough to add interpretation and expertise. Most of the coverage was live and did not permit second-guessing.

Rome was hardly comparable. The television picture came from Italian television, RAI-TV, except film shot around the periphery of the stadiums. The burden was on RAI for camera shot selection. CBS's responsibility was to select the RAI picture it wished to record and to edit the material selected into packages for shipment to New York within the time frames allotted by the network schedule. Personalities selected by CBS described the events and added commentary. Bud Palmer, the former Princeton and New York Knickerbocker basketball star, was the lead voice. He was assisted by Bob Richards, at one time holder of the international pole vault record. Their audio reports, transmitted from the stadium where the events were taking place, were blended with the RAI picture.

The number of venues from which to select was vast. Olympic games are in some respects similar to three-ring circuses, except there are normally many more than three rings in action at once: track and field stadiums, soccer fields, natatoriums, wrestling and boxing areas, marathon and long-distance speed walking courses, archery and pistol ranges, and rowing and sailing venues. The CBS producer, at the control room at Fiumicino airport, was responsible for selecting the events he would cover and the portions of the events he would incorporate within the assigned running time. The process would have been relatively simple with late-twentieth-century technology using multitrack digital electronic editing. The editing equipment available in 1960, however, was primitive in 1990s terms. Three two-inch quad head Ampex tape recorders were set up in the vacant motion picture theater. The signal from RAI-TV was recorded on one or more of the recorders, depending on how many events of interest to American viewers might be taking place simultaneously. The editing was accomplished by using a razor blade to slice diagonally across the recorded material. Splicing was done with Scotch tape. It was a tedious and time-consuming process and required a delicate touch.

Disaster almost struck on opening night. The producer of the program failed to maintain a log of the opening ceremony, an event running for approximately two and a half hours that had to be cut to fit a one-hour time slot, or approximately fifty-four minutes to allow for commercials. The entire program was recorded on videotape from the RAI-TV signal in the make-shift studio at the Fiumicino airport. Cutting to less than one third of its total running time had to be completed in time to ready the final cut for shipment in midmorning the next day. Without a rough log the tape editors would have to start from scratch in constructing the abbreviated version. Timing for midmorning shipment was critical; the program was scheduled for release to the network from New York the next evening.

Fortunately as I sat alongside the producer watching the ceremony I had kept notes on the proceedings including a rough schedule of the running times of individual features, including the entry marches of the USSR and U.S. teams. On discovering there was no log available I quickly selected from my notes those portions of the ceremony that seemed most interesting to an American audience, noted the number of minutes each consumed, added them up, and found that the components I had selected would approximately round out the time available for the network program. I took my notes to the tape editors and spent the remainder of the night working on program production. The heat was intense. It was a typical August night in Rome and there was no air-conditioning in the old unused cinema house.

At five o'clock in the morning all three tape machines suddenly gave out. They simply quit. Fortunately the job was virtually completed. It would only take a few minutes for editors in New York to complete the final touch-up. There was concern, though, that major repairs would be required. That would create a grim situation. Competition would start later in the day and without tape machines there would be no program material. It turned out, however, that the extreme heat and long hours of operation had simply exhausted the equipment. After a few hours of rest all three machines were pronounced in good working order.

After that first nearly calamitous night, operations ran relatively smoothly. Some of the burden on Rome was removed by expanding the operation at Idlewild. An experienced producer-director and tape editors were assigned to the facility along with additional tape machines. Pressure on Rome to deliver finely cut programs was reduced. Editors there could ship rough cuts and the Idlewild facility could apply the final touches.

It turned out that same day coverage was more limited than expected. Midmorning flights arriving in New York in early afternoon were numerous but midafternoon flights that could deliver program material featuring same day events edited for nighttime exposure were limited. It was more expedient to aim for finely edited nighttime programs even if they were delayed by a day.

The whole venture was enough of a success that NBC quickly bid on and won rights for exclusive coverage of the Tokyo games in 1964. A pattern had been established. The Olympic Games had become an international spectacle. Set counts in Europe and the Far East were rising rapidly, to the point where an international audience could now be a reality.

The games themselves, except for one feature, changed very little after the Rome experience. The opening ceremony that CBS had struggled so hard to deliver with the aid of its balky tape machines suddenly took on new importance as a signature of the games. The unidimensional parade of the athletes to open the games as recorded in Rome gradually went through a metamorphosis and became a grand pageant staged largely for a world audience. The opening and closing ceremonies became opportunities to display the most attractive talents of the host nation. The increasing attention paid to these pageants since 1960 can be credited to television and the primitive tape-recorded efforts in Rome. The extent to which television has influenced the games in the intervening years is reflected in a critical review in the *New York Times* in July 1996: "The Olympics, of course," the critic Caryn James writes, "are as much about television and show business as they are about sports."[2]

19 •

In Pursuit of the Dollar

It was comfortable for broadcast executives in the 1950s to boast at public forums and before congressional committees that they were investing large sums of money in news and public affairs without hope of significant return. It was at least implied that news and news-related programs were carried as loss leaders in response to an obligation to "serve in the public interest."

As in many claims made by industry spokesmen there is some element of truth in such assertions but also a large element of exaggeration. The record shows that many loss leaders were carried on television network schedules and that senior corporate executives who had final authority over accepting or rejecting programs frequently agreed to finance programs that promised public benefit but little or no financial return. The public was left to draw the inference that news and public affairs were largely a charitable enterprise of broadcast networks. Nothing could be further from the truth; financial controls actually were firm. Willingness to open up the corporate purse for some efforts to serve the public in no way encouraged or even permitted free spending behavior by news personnel. Even the early "See It Now," for example, was constantly under pressure to cut back costs and live within its budget. Only the prestige of Ed Murrow, his disdain for financial controls, and the critical success of the program saved it from the budget cutter's knife. Ultimately it was policy problems rather than over-spending alone that caused the program's demise.[1]

Budgets for news and news-related programs were not nearly as lavish as those for entertainment. Their spending base was much lower and thus lacked much elasticity. Most programs that succeeded in winning sponsorship were sold at discounted prices that further reduced spending flexibility. And there was little prospect of striking a bonanza as occurred with such attractive entertainment programs as "I Love Lucy" and the "Jackie Gleason" show. Producers of informational programs, unlike those of entertainment ventures, were severely restricted in rehearsal time, set design, expenditures on sets and props, and talent fees for writers, directors, and performers.

Budgetary controls were strict. Producers and directors were forced to do with less and there was less elasticity. It was much easier to condone a budget overrun on a successful entertainment show than on a low-budget sustaining program that had little hope of ever catching the attention of a sponsor. The lack of resources stimulated a vicious circle. It was hard to attract a sponsor to a program that was produced with only a bare minimum of the resources required to make it a crowd pleaser, and without adequate resources it was hard to create programs that would attract commercial interest.

Additional financial support was frequently only grudgingly approved. It took nearly two years of planning, budgeting, and pruning, for example, to win approval of a plan in 1952 and 1953 to establish a film reporting unit to support the News department. (The effort to win corporate support for establishing CBS Newsfilm is described in detail in Chapter 11.)

After the merger News controlled its own administrative budget. Program budgets, however, remained under the control of the broadcasting division showing the program. Administrative costs, theoretically the responsibility of news executives, came under direct scrutiny of senior corporate executives. As the department gradually moved toward divisional autonomy there was more freedom to make administrative decisions, but pressure from corporate executives to control costs intensified.

As long as costs were held at "reasonable" levels pressures were not onerous. The corporation was quite willing to absorb without flinching the cost of carrying a number of public service–oriented programs including "Adventure" so long as the weekly expenditure remained reasonable. It similarly supported other noncommercial ventures, including "Let's Take a Trip," "Air Power," and "The Search," without protest as long as program budgets were held at minimal levels and producers demonstrated concern for costs. Every year end throughout the decade it was happy to bring five or six News department correspondents back from their foreign posts for the "Years of Crisis" series. Costs for transportation and food and housing were considerable, but there was a substantial pay-off in publicity, government relations, and general public goodwill. It was an invaluable opportunity to showcase a superior reporting staff and promote the entire news and public affairs function. The network was likewise willing to support a number of relatively high-budget documentaries including "Where We Stand" if they seemed to serve a significant national purpose.

It was made clear to news management, though, that expenses had to be justified, budgets had to be held at the lowest level consistent with delivering a high-quality product, and there had to be an obvious value to the corporation accruing from any program requiring corporate support. As costs continued to rise and homes with television continued to increase, pressures were intensified. Competition grew stiffer. ABC programs began to show up in network ratings, adding a third factor in the ratings competition. Entertainment programs with their larger budgets and ratings appeal began to encroach on hours previously available for so-called public service programming. Football preempted most of the Sunday afternoon time that once belonged to public affairs.

It became obvious that some effort would have to be devoted to improving quality, increasing entertainment value, and targeting higher ratings. One possible cure would involve building increased advertising support.

No matter how much the critics derided television advertising there were valid reasons for trying to attract commercial sponsors to "public service programs." Sponsorship would help improve the quality of program output. It would make greater resources available for research, scripts, on the air talent, set design and construction, and promotion. There was also evidence that a program supported by a sponsor carried an additional stamp of approval, the endorsement of a major advertiser. With the commercials came a larger promotion budget, the support of the advertising agency that placed the order, and more prestige within the network and corporate headquarters. There was probably another more subtle effect, one that would be impossible to measure. There was reason to think that the average viewer regarded a program supported by an advertiser as more important and of higher quality than one without commercials. If an advertiser is willing to support the program with his money, the reasoning went, he must regard it as a significant contribution to the program schedule.

There was, however, a tricky problem involved in selling serious programs. Advertising agency personnel had a tendency not to see beyond highly rated, low-cost-per-thousand viewers programming. Network salesmen were similarly committed to the sure thing; it was very difficult to stimulate a high degree of enthusiasm among them for a nonentertainment program and equally difficult to persuade an agency account executive that he might create a climate with an informational series that would give the sponsor a degree of prestige not possible with run-of-the-mill entertainment. Few advertisers, without recommendations from their agencies, were likely to take the gamble. Alcoa had with "See It Now," Oldsmobile with the Douglas Edwards news programs, and Westinghouse with conventions and elections, but, by and large, there was little commercial interest in most news and public affairs programs. Such successful public affairs ventures as "Adventure," "The Search," "Air Power," "Let's Take a Trip," and "Face the Nation" had been unsponsored. Had they had advertising support it is likely that they would have been more heavily promoted, better supported financially, and watched by larger audiences, thus serving the public more effectively.

As television penetration of American homes began to near a saturation level, some change in strategy seemed to be called for. Too few news and information programs were attracting sponsors in any measure consistent with the value they might bring to an advertiser. As long as they remained unsponsored it was unlikely they would be able to command budgets at a level at which they could be more attractive to viewers. Benefits accruing to advertisers who had gambled on information programming suggested that good buys were to be found. Nonentertainment programs would never draw the mass audiences that entertainment would, but costs were lower and corporate public relations goals could be better served.

The key to exploiting the potential market lay in finding the proper method of approach. It was apparent that one of the road blocks impeding sales was a lack of confidence among both advertising agency account executives and network television salesmen in any option but highly rated entertainment programs. If it were possible to discover a formula that might short circuit the normal selling pattern there might be an increased chance of directly approaching senior corporate executives. A query from a CEO to his advertising manager encouraging him to look into a specific program would almost certainly start wheels turning.

The key was finding a route to the senior executive. If interest could be created at this level, it was quite possible that the account executive at the advertising agency would jump to attention and the CBS salesman on the account become more enthusiastic. There was a risk in this approach; the strategy would call for going over the heads of the network salesmen, agency account executives, and corporate advertising managers and proceeding directly to senior management. It would require employing as the point man for news and informational programming an individual with broad acquaintanceships at the top corporate level and enough brass to complete an end run around lesser executives to put the scheme in motion.

I talked to Frank Stanton about trying the strategy. He listened but said nothing. Several months later he called to invite me to his office, where he introduced me to Robert Lang and suggested that Lang might be able to do the sales job I had previously described to him. Lang had just returned to the United States after serving several years with Radio Free Europe, much of that time as its director. In that assignment and with the Office of Special Services (OSS) during the war he had rubbed shoulders with scores of business leaders who were presidents and chairmen of major corporations. He had many acquaintances among the corporate executives we hoped to target.

Within less than a month, by January 1956, Lang was on the job. There was no immediate upsurge in commercial orders for informational programs. It took months of cultivation before results were apparent. But then orders began to trickle in. Prudential Insurance was one of the first to become a major supporter of news and public affairs programs. It began with the thirty-minute program covering Chancellor Adenauer's trip to Moscow in October 1956. "The Twentieth Century," a weekly half hour chronicling recent history through film clips, followed. Lang maintained a close relationship with the Reach McClinton advertising agency, which handled the Prudential account, and with Carroll Shanks, chairman and CEO of Prudential.

Shulton broke precedent by buying sponsorship of the ninety-minute program on mental health "Out of Darkness," one of the few times that a one-shot documentary had succeeded in winning advertiser support. A science series, "Conquest," was sponsored by Monsanto through the Gardiner Agency's New York office. Lang's relationships with Gardiner were so cordial that Gardiner was largely responsible for helping CBS News win rights to the 1960 summer Olympics in Rome. Firestone Tire and Rubber was sufficiently intrigued by its sponsorship of a one-hour program built around President Eisenhower's trip to Germany in 1959 that it ordered a weekly year-round series, "Eyewitness to History," beginning in 1960. Bell and Howell and Goodrich shared sponsorship of "CBS Reports" and Olin Matthieson bought full sponsorship of "Small World."

A new day had dawned in News and Public Affairs programming. Not all the sales made were at a level guaranteeing substantial profits, but there was now income rather than dead loss and with it promotion and advertising. The strategy as carried out by Bob Lang was working well.

The encouraging sales efforts did not fully succeed, however, in dissolving all pressures on the News and Public Affairs department budget. The economic downturn that struck the country in 1957 left its mark on the new television industry. Revenues fell but costs kept rising. Under pressure from its Wall Street directors CBS embarked on a strict cost cutting campaign. Whether true or not, it seemed to News and Public Affairs personnel that the burden fell most sharply on them. The News department, in particular, had grown exponentially since the Newsfilm project was undertaken in 1953. The handful of 14 employees in 1951 and 1952 had grown to some 350 by 1957. Full television news bureaus were operating in London, Paris, Bonn, Rome, Beirut, and Tokyo and in Washington, Chicago, and Los Angeles. Full-time news personnel were stationed in Boston and

Atlanta and in Vienna, Cairo, and Saigon. CBS Newsfilm, the syndicated service, was by 1959 serving every major market in the United States and thirty-nine cities in twenty-seven countries.[2]

There was, however, very little fat in the organization, very little superfluous manpower. That point did not influence the budget cutters. Two sharp cuts, in particular, were severely damaging. One affected news film assignments; the other, leases of private lines capable of carrying a television signal.

The cancellation of a leased AT&T television link between CBS News headquarters and the United Nations struck the News department a devastating blow shortly after the service was dropped. Serious civil disturbances in Lebanon in May 1958 involving the possible overthrow of the nation's president persuaded President Eisenhower to send five thousand United States Marines ashore near Beirut in a major peacetime invasion. Tensions were running so high in the Middle East and the move was so daring that the UN Security Council was quickly convened, but CBS had no circuit into the UN capable of carrying a television signal. Both ABC and NBC did and used their facilities to good advantage. Worse, AT&T was unable on short notice to make one available to CBS. The network was forced for lack of facilities to grind away with soap operas and an occasional audio report while both NBC and ABC were carrying the proceedings live. Newspaper critics were unsparing in flaying CBS for lagging behind the competition and the news staff was embarrassed by its inability even to try to compete.

AT&T finally found a line in early evening, but by that time it was early morning in the eastern Mediterranean and activity was effectively suspended for the night. The Security Council had scheduled a nighttime meeting so, in an effort to play catch-up, the news staff arranged to cover it, using the precious broadcast line to switch to the UN for live coverage. To do so, it had to preempt the prestigious and highly rated "Playhouse 90," a drama program running a full ninety minutes. The CBS special coverage was barely under way when the Security Council suddenly recessed without taking decisive action. There was no way of reinstating "Playhouse 90" so the special coverage had to stay on the air for the full ninety minutes with virtually no action to report either at the Security Council or in the Middle East, where it was early morning.

In short, the day was a calamity and a costly one. Coming as it did so soon after the Middle East war of November 1966 while tensions were still running high, the defeat was painful. CBS was a distinct loser.

More serious was the imposition of strict budgetary controls on the television assignment desk. Personnel on the desk decide which stories should be covered, which crews should be assigned, how much footage should be exposed, and which method of transportation should be used to carry the crew to the story and exposed film and commentary back to headquarters.

Most other costs—salaries, rent, acquisition of equipment, production, and direction—could be budgeted in advance with some reasonable expectation that they could be adhered to but no one could fully anticipate what news was going to break and when and where. Personnel attached to the assignment desk had to make the decision, frequently with little time to spare, where to send the reporting crew, how large the crew should be, and how much coverage was required. The safe way to perform was to over-assign, gamble on sending personnel to cover stories that might justify coverage but were not sure things. But a mistake could be costly. There were travel and subsistence costs to be considered and allocations for raw film stock, shipping, laboratory processing, and finally editing. The best means of control was employment of personnel with judgment and an acute news sense that would enable them to assess the potential importance of a story before the assignment was made, then to give them free rein.

The ultimate result of the devastating budget cuts of 1957 was that staff members became gun-shy. Assignment editors were under instructions to keep detailed records of assignments made, costs incurred, and disposition of the stories covered. Attention was frequently focused more tightly on budgets than on news. Confidence gave way to indecision; courage to timidity.

There was apparently ample justification for company-wide reduction of costs. President Frank Stanton announced publicly that profits from continuing operations had declined sharply from preceding years and "We shall have to work and work hard."[3] But the cuts were most damaging in the news division. No matter how much it had grown, there was little fat to spare.

Stringent new financial reporting systems were put into effect without protest, but their impact stultified news operations for months. Assignment personnel became more concerned with keeping records and avoiding mistakes of judgment than with moving aggressively to whip the opposition and deliver a superior news report. Timidity with regard to taking risks became the prevailing theme. Financial controls curbed much of the swash-buckling gung-ho attitude that had characterized the operation in previous years. Fortunately the pressure was limited largely to the assignment desk and to the regularly scheduled news broadcasts. The most devastating effect was the impact on News department morale. Confidence was giving way to indecision and imaginative planning to record keeping.

It was unfortunate that the budget axe had to fall just as the department was completing a transition from corporate department to autonomous division. Once the transition was completed it would achieve a status on organization charts as one of eight autonomous divisions of the corporation, a status that would put it administratively, at least, on the same level as its three customers, the radio and television networks and the television stations division.

In a sense the news division would function as an outside program packager. Its role would be to develop program ideas, offer them to the appropriate broadcasting unit, and once the offers were accepted undertake full responsibility for production within budgetary limitations laid down by the division accepting the product. Creative personnel, including producers, directors, writers, reporters, and news executives, would continue to be members of the news division staff. Production and facilities would be bought from the appropriate broadcasting division at prices set by the division and recorded on "rate cards." Sales and promotion would be handled by the respective outlets for the programs, but Bob Lang would function as sales liaison. Legal, personnel, and labor relations functions would be purchased from the corporation. The divisional status in a sense offered new freedoms but simultaneously imposed sharp restrictions. The customers were all in-house. There was no opportunity to shop programs among several potential buyers.

This left two functions that the autonomous division would have to develop on its own: financial management and public relations. It would have to create a department adequate to plan its annual budget and establish effective controls. There would be no more ad hoc personnel additions or extraordinary equipment acquisitions without preliminary budget approval. Expenses directly related to programs would have to be included in program budgets expressly approved by the appropriate broadcasting division.

Prices to be paid by the broadcasting divisions either for single programs or for series to be produced by the news division were to be negotiated. The negotiation process could lead to stalemate unless corporate executives adjudicated disputes concerning programs in which the corporation had a vital interest, as in the case of "CBS Reports." In pricing that series, after its initial year, the corporation agreed in effect to overlook any loss incurred although the television network was reluctant to sell at anything below the full market price.

Once the mechanism for autonomy had been worked out all that was required was for the corporation to announce formally that the News and Public Affairs department would henceforth be recognized as the CBS News division of the corporation. That announcement was made in early October 1959. The company's annual report for 1960 reported, "CBS News became fully established as a separate operating division of CBS." The note added that the new division "provided 18 per cent of the programming of the CBS Television Network and 30 per cent of that of the CBS Radio Network."[4] The paragraph concluded with a salute to the new division that reflected its successful efforts to increase the volume of its sales. "News and public affairs broadcasting is becoming increasingly important, and increasingly popular, with an encouraging growth in commercial sponsorship."

Full divisional status was good for prestige. It put CBS a step ahead of the other two television networks. But it did nothing to improve its relations with its customers, the corporation's broadcasting divisions. Negotiations over pricing programs became more difficult. As customers, the network and television stations felt they could become more demanding and more critical of both on the air product and client relations.

One of the sensitive issues in client relations was the timidity among sponsors regarding the broadcast of sensitive items. Most sponsors understood that they could not be identified with programs without serving as targets for inevitable protests. Charles Percy, the Bell and Howell chairman, expressly acknowledged the likelihood that there would some vigorous complaints when he agreed to sponsor "CBS Reports." When Murrow and Friendly scheduled a program on integration under the title "Who Speaks for the South?" I called Percy to warn him that he could expect to hear from a swarm of angry supporters of the status quo. He replied that he had told us when he signed the contract that Bell and Howell was buying the commercials and CBS was delivering the program.

Firestone was not as relaxed about a one-hour, year-end news roundup program that it had agreed to sponsor in connection with its purchase of the weekly "Eyewitness to History." During the 1960 calendar year Fidel Castro had confiscated a Firestone plant. Since the Castro phenomenon was one of the most significant news stories of the year there was no way that the producer, Les Midgeley, could overlook either the island country, its new dictator, or its confiscation of American-owned property. On the day the program was scheduled for broadcast, January 1, 1961, a senior Firestone representative demanded that the item be excised or the company's commercials deleted. It took an entire day of telephone calls before the rubber company relented and the program went on the air as planned.

Controversies with sponsors had been relatively few. A potentially devastating story moved on the news wires in 1955 that could have jeopardized relations with the only sponsor of the Douglas Edwards news. The program ran five times a week at 7:30 P.M. sponsored by the American Tobacco Company for Pall Mall cigarettes. One midafternoon Don Hewitt called while he and the program staff were assembling the program for that night. He had some disturbing news: A report had been delivered to the American Medical Association meeting in San Francisco that day suggesting that cigarette smoking was a likely cause of cancer. "What do we do about the story?" Hewitt wanted to know.

My reply was "Use the story, but play it straight. Don't give it any unusual play."

I then called the CBS Television Network president, Jack Van Volkenburg, to tell him about our decision. He did not object but suggested that I call Pall Mall's advertising agency, Sullivan, Stauffer, Colwell and Bayless, to inform the account executive there that the story would be on the air that night. The agency did not protest and the story took its spot in the broadcast, the first time a link between smoking and cancer had been publicly aired on a network and, ironically, on a program sponsored by a tobacco company.

A potentially damaging situation was smoothed over without any serious repercussions when the noted Irish poet Brendan Behan offended many viewers of the Murrow-Friendly program "Small World." The sponsor was Olin-Matthieson, the big chemical company. The program format normally called for two guests, one on each side of the Atlantic. It was recorded on film by 35-mm cameras, one focused on the guest in New York, another on the guest in Europe, and the third on Murrow. Since the reel on a 35-mm camera would only accommodate approximately ten minutes of running time, breaks were required to reload. Once the filming was completed film editors shaped the package into a sixty-minute unit. Behan was filmed in the same New York studio as Murrow but they were seated on separate sets.

The Irish poet had been notorious for his uncontrolled alcoholism but Murrow and Friendly had been assured that those days were over and that there would be no problems. The program started out smoothly. After the first break filming was resumed, but rather than sit quietly and participate in the conversation, Behan stood, reached for the microphone on a boom above him, pulled it down, and shouted, "Edward, Edward, where are you?" He was eventually seated and the conversation went on normally with no further disruptions.

The next day during an editing session Friendly called and asked that I come to the viewing room to watch a portion of the program with him. He showed me the episode in which Behan reached for the mike and shouted for Edward. We watched it several times. Apparently it did not look nearly so demeaning to Behan in the small viewing room with the large screen as it would on Sunday afternoon in the living room. We decided on a few relatively minor changes in which the most ludicrous actions were eliminated and approved the program for air.

On Sunday afternoon at home it looked quite different. It was shocking to see the noted poet so out of control and hard to understand why we had been so complaisant in the screening room. It was clear that Friendly and I would have to pay a call on the advertiser and the agency the next morning to apologize and promise no more bad taste in the future. It was a humiliating call. The sponsor was clearly disturbed but decided to remain with the program rather than abruptly withdraw support.

As 1959 came to a close, broadcasting news and information had progressed to the point where it was light years ahead of that in the early 1950s, when it was just beginning to establish a foothold; the ragtag News and Public Affairs department had become an autonomous corporate division on a level with the radio and television networks. News broadcasts of the two television networks, CBS and NBC, were regularly being viewed five nights a week in more than 14 million homes. A pattern for television documentaries had been established and television had played a significant role in bringing down Senator Joseph McCarthy. The new medium, an expensive toy as the decade opened, was well along the way to establishing equal rights with the written press in covering the news. And it was building massive audiences. Progress had been breathtaking. In 1960 it would be in a position to round out the decade in triumph.

20 •

The End of the Decade

As the decade of the 1950s ended, news and information programs on television would have been almost unrecognizable to a viewer who had been in a deep sleep since January 1950. The fifteen-minute early evening news was still the staple but now there was news on network television between seven and nine o'clock weekday mornings and early Sunday evenings. Special half-hour news programs followed virtually every major national or international news event. Still photographs had largely given way to motion picture film. The quality was still not very good, but film stocks had improved markedly and professionally trained camera personnel had replaced the eager learners of the previous decade. Informational (or public affairs) programs had proliferated as producers, directors, and writers honed their skills and the networks began to deliver profits rather than the red ink of the early fifties. CBS boasted in its 1960 annual report that its newest autonomous division, CBS News, had produced 15 percent of the CBS Television Network's program schedule in the previous year.[1]

The total homes viewing the two early evening network news programs had risen from approximately 5 million in the 1950–51 season to more than 15 million. This meant that more than 30 percent of all American homes with television were regular followers of the news programs on the two networks. NBC had led the ratings by a two to one margin in 1950, had been overtaken by CBS in 1956, but by 1960 had edged ahead again by a narrow margin. ABC was becoming more aggressive but still was not an important factor in the ratings race.[2]

The personnel complement of the newly designated News division at CBS had risen from the fifteen employed in producing news in early 1950 and the additional twenty producing public affairs and sports programs for both radio and television (mostly radio) to nearly four hundred with a large majority working in television. A professional cadre of producers, directors, writers, researchers, cameramen, sound technicians, film editors, and scenic designers had grown up with the business.

Sports broadcasts had become a major drawing card for both CBS and NBC. Professional football was firmly established on CBS, and NBC had just arranged to carry a full schedule of games of the new American Football League. The CBS Sports department had won the rights to both the winter Olympics in Squaw Valley and the summer Olympics in Rome to go along with the Master's golf tournament, the Triple Crown, the Orange Bowl, and the Cotton Bowl. NBC had rights to college football and the baseball World Series.

"CBS Reports" had replaced "See It Now" and was winning critical praise. A special news unit was grinding out long-form, thirty-minute news programs with increasing frequency and attracting sponsors.

The 1960 calendar year would provide opportunities for head to head competition with NBC and an increasingly aggressive ABC in coverage of the quadrennial election year, including primaries, conventions, and the election. The conventions and elections were, in effect, the World Series or Super Bowl for the television networks, providing opportunities to test themselves directly against the other networks on a single broad-gauge news event with the A. C. Nielsen Company keeping score with its ratings system. NBC had won in 1952, largely because of its preponderance of affiliations in the major single-station markets; by 1956 the playing field had been leveled and CBS had come out the winner. The question now was, Could it hold its dominant position?

There were some ominous signs. CBS had clearly won the ratings contest at both conventions in 1956, but critics noticed an interesting departure from established convention coverage patterns. NBC fielded a team of unknown anchormen, Chet Huntley and David Brinkley. Huntley had been a local news broadcaster at CBS and ABC stations in Los Angeles and Brinkley a member of NBC's Washington staff; neither had attracted much national attention. The two now functioned as a team: Huntley the straight reporter, Brinkley the sardonic commentator, fast with the irreverent quip. It was a radical departure from the conventional pattern but well adapted to a political convention with a plethora of party pageantry but very little news.

CBS, as it had in 1952, had approached both 1956 conventions as serious news events. But there was little serious news to cover. Adlai Steven-

Douglas Edwards interviewing Eleanor Roosevelt at the Democratic National Convention in 1956. Elliott Roosevelt is in the center. Photo courtesy of Sig Mickelson. Used by permission.

son was a shoo-in for the Democratic nomination weeks before the party faithful convened in Chicago on August 13, 1956. The only serious question involved the nomination for vice president. After his nomination for the presidency, Stevenson threw the convention into an uproar when he violated tradition by announcing that he would not designate a vice presidential candidate but leave the choice to the delegates. The result was a free-for-all, and a debacle for CBS.

CBS went to the convention with an inadequate supply of coaxial cable, an essential ingredient in deploying electronic cameras in the era before hand-held portable units that could transmit by shortwave. The contest for the vice presidential nomination quickly settled into a two-man race between Senator John Kennedy of Massachusetts and Senator Estes Kefauver of Tennessee. Once the balloting began both awaited the results in their headquarters suites in the Stock Yards Inn, adjacent to the convention venue at the International Amphitheater. Since CBS had sufficient cable for only one location, it was decided to deploy its camera outside the Kefauver suite in the expectation that he would be the winner.

As the balloting proceeded Kennedy was making a surprisingly effective run. After consulting some presumed experts I made the personal decision to strike the camera at the Kefauver suite and move it to Kennedy's in a nearby corridor. It appeared to be a wise decision as Kennedy's total mounted. After the last state had been called it appeared that he might be ahead. Then a torrent of requests arose as state banners waved in the air calling on the chair to be recognized for permission to change the state's vote. One by one the changes were recorded and it was soon evident that Kefauver would be the winner. But it was too late for CBS to move its camera. As the newly nominated smiling vice presidential candidate opened the door to his suite to make his statement of acceptance his image appeared full face on the ABC and NBC monitors. CBS had nothing better to show than delegates milling about aimlessly on the convention floor. It was a humiliating blow to the CBS staff.

The Republican convention the next week in San Francisco offered even less prospect of hard news. There was some speculation that President Eisenhower might dump Vice President Richard Nixon from the ticket and substitute Harold Stassen, but the president squelched those rumors the second day by formally announcing that he was supporting the vice president.

That step stifled the last possible chance of controversy and left the networks, in essence, with no story to cover. It was a situation made to order for Huntley and Brinkley. Brinkley's sardonic wit enlivened the proceedings and created an attitude of mild amusement among viewers. CBS continued to view the proceedings as a serious news story long after there was no news remaining. Its sober-sided staff was prepared for ferreting out hard news, but there was none to be found. Bill Leonard, still working the con-

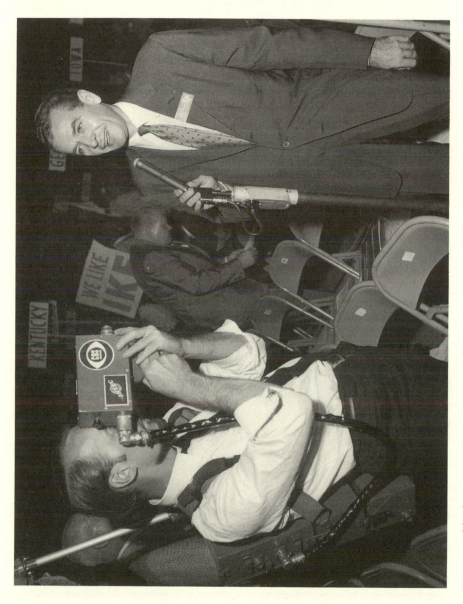

New portable shortwave television camera photographs Charles Collingwood on the floor at the Republican National Convention, San Francisco, 1956. Photo courtesy of Sig Mickelson. Used by permission.

vention floor tirelessly, found the only intriguing news story at the convention, one that puzzled both delegates and media. Who was Joe Smith, who had been nominated for the presidency by Terry Carpenter, a Nebraska delegate? Carpenter admitted to Leonard that Joe Smith was fictitious; he had nominated him because something had to be done to add life to the dull proceedings.

CBS won the ratings war but had proved inadequate at shifting gears from its traditional serious approach to the light touch that NBC had introduced. The real damage occurred, later. Before the end of the year John Cameron Swayze, who had presided over NBC's early evening news since its introduction in 1948, was removed to make way for Huntley and Brinkley. It was an innovative approach. The network created a two-person anchor team with Huntley in New York and Brinkley in Washington. Their customary "sign-off," "Good night, David. Good night, Chet," quickly became recognizable across the nation.

The Huntley-Brinkley team didn't at first do much damage to CBS ratings, but the approach was so different it soon attracted attention. The competition now pitted the earnest and somewhat humorless Edwards against the offbeat pair with straight news from the more sober Huntley and quick-witted barbs from Brinkley, who, in addition to being an effective quipster, was a first-class reporter. Edwards held the ratings lead for many months but it was inevitable that eventually he would be knocked off his perch. It had taken him seven years of dogged pursuit from his first broadcast in 1948 to catch and pass Swayze, but now the handwriting was on the wall. In time he would fall back to a runner-up position.

It was not until ratings were compiled for the 1955–56 season that Edwards had reached the top spot. He held the lead through 1957–58, but by 1958–59 Huntley and Brinkley had returned NBC to the number one position, which they held until they were dethroned by Walter Cronkite late in the 1960s.[3]

By early 1960, with Huntley and Brinkley now firmly established as the leader in the ratings, the time seemed appropriate to make a change. I had an opportunity at a senior management retreat at Absecon, New Jersey, to spend some time alone with chairman Paley. I told him that I thought it imperative that we replace Edwards. It was doubly urgent now that we were running behind NBC in the ratings. As a replacement I recommended Cronkite. Paley approved, provided I clear it with James T. Aubrey, who had taken over the television network presidency several months earlier.

Aubrey flatly refused. He was willing to remove Edwards but wanted no part of Cronkite for what reason I had no notion, nor did he tell me. He insisted that if I wanted to make a change I choose from among Clete Roberts, Baxter Ward, and Mike Wallace. Roberts and Ward were West Coast news broadcasters whom he had known during his tours of duty for

CBS election studio on election night 1956. Walter Cronkite is listening to a phone message, far left. Photo courtesy of Sig Mickelson. Used by permission.

CBS and ABC in Los Angeles. Wallace had been working in New York since the late 1940s in a variety of assignments but not in straight news.

I balked at selecting any of the three. Roberts and Ward, I thought, were successful West Coast personalities but would have been ill fits in the elite CBS staff. I had great respect for Wallace, but his reputation had been made largely as a hard-hitting interrogator in half hour interview programs on DuMont and ABC. In the early 1950s he had performed with Buff Cobb, then his wife, in a daily afternoon CBS Television talk show, "Mike and Buff." I had thought enough of Mike and Buff to invite them to join our team to do features at the 1952 conventions in Chicago, but I did not see him moving into the showcase news position at CBS.

It is obvious that I should have fought Aubrey on the issue, but I was not spoiling for a fight so I let it ride and Edwards remained in his anchor position for another two years before Cronkite finally took over.

Huntley and Brinkley were a major factor in winning back NBC's early evening news lead, but NBC's resurgence went well beyond the news series. It suddenly turned more aggressive in programming news specials and in breaking into established program schedules to report fast-breaking significant news. And CBS began to look sluggish.

There were a number of apparent reasons for the reversal of positions. One stemmed in part from the rigorous financial squeeze that had been forced on the CBS News division in 1957. Some of the swashbuckling attitude of the television news staff, the "we can beat anybody at this game" attitude, was lost when financial controls began to stifle initiative. Too much effort went into maintaining detailed financial records and not enough into initiative and chance taking.

The geographical diffusion of its facilities also tended to make it cumbersome. CBS simply had no central location where it could house the whole organization and its diverse components. The radio and television news departments were theoretically integrated in 1954 but remained physically separated, Radio News at 485 Madison Avenue, Television News on the third floor of a wing of Grand Central Terminal at 70 East Forty-fifth Street. The television news studio, at the time the newsroom was installed on Forty-fifth Street, was moved from Liederkranz Hall on Fifty-eighth Street to a studio complex on the third floor on the Forty-second Street side of Grand Central Terminal. It was no longer necessary to make the long trek from Fifty-second and Madison to Liederkranz Hall at Fifty-eighth and Park once the script was prepared, but the show staff still had a complicated trip from newsroom to studio. They either had to travel through the crowded terminal's main waiting room or cross over the waiting room by way of a narrow catwalk, high above the main floor where commuters were milling around waiting for outbound suburban trains. It was not unusual to see the entire team, Edwards, Hewitt, writers, film

CBS Chairman William S. Paley with the author in the CBS studio on election night 1956. Photo courtesy of Sig Mickelson. Used by permission.

editors, and graphic artists, rushing across the catwalk single file a few minutes before air time, carrying film cans, scripts, and program graphics.

The awkward separation between news headquarters and studio was not the only problem involving work space. After delicate negotiations the corporation's Labor Relations department had helped break the monopoly of the International Brotherhood of Electrical Workers (IBEW) over CBS film operations. The modified contract allowed the employment of a number of cameramen and film editors from the much more film-oriented International Alliance of Theater and Stage Employees (IATSE). Union regulations, however, prevented members of the two unions from being housed in the same quarters. Consequently, space was rented in a building several blocks away from news headquarters for the newly hired IATSE crews.

The film laboratory, through which all film had to go for processing, was all the way across Manhattan on West Fifty-fifth Street. There were editing rooms for other CBS News programs in a half dozen other locations in midtown Manhattan. The director of news remained with the Radio News department at Fifty-second Street and Madison Avenue and the Public Affairs and Sports departments were housed at Fifty-fifth Street and Madison. Coordination of activities could be achieved only by the expenditure of both time and effort and countless telephone conversations. The creation of geographically separated compartments both inhibited exchange of ideas and fostered rivalries. The demolition of the East Fifty-fifth Street building in 1959 forced a move, but the new news headquarters on the thirty-second floor of the Graybar Building at Forty-third and Lexington, though adjacent to Grand Central, offered only a marginal improvement. The new space required a thirty-one floor elevator ride, a walk through the same crowded Grand Central lobby, and another elevator ride to the third-floor studio. There was not even a catwalk alternative.

I remained at 485 Madison Avenue with a small headquarters staff, too far removed from the operating units to exercise much influence. It was a relatively central location with respect to the scattered news and public affairs components but made for unwieldy relationships with departments and for an excess of contacts by telephone rather than in person.

The combination of these awkward circumstances made CBS News vulnerable to the aggressive and broad-based attack that NBC was beginning to launch. The CBS invulnerability began to crack when Huntley and Brinkley were introduced at the 1956 conventions. The stage was set for fierce competition when they replaced Swayze as the twin anchors of the "NBC Evening News" only weeks after the conventions.

Another major change at NBC intensified the attack. Robert Kintner, president of ABC, had joined NBC in autumn 1956 as a free-floating executive, but he was clearly hired for a larger purpose, the eventual succession to the presidency of the NBC Network. Before joining ABC he had been a journalist with a national reputation as a syndicated columnist.

When he arrived at NBC he determined to strike CBS at the point at which it would be most vulnerable: As a journalist he chose news as his target. CBS had built such a commanding lead in its entertainment program schedule that it would take years and millions of dollars to knock it off. Huntley and Brinkley, however, were already gnawing at the CBS lead in the early evening news when he finally took over the NBC presidency in mid-1958.

CBS had dropped the ball with Gulf Oil in early 1957 when it refused to sell Gulf its news special on Kuwait because of a possible conflict of interest. Kintner quickly signed up the oil company as a stand-by sponsor for "Instant News Specials." That was defeat number one.

Reuven Frank, later NBC News president but at that time producer of the Huntley-Brinkley show, points out in *Out of Thin Air* how patterns at NBC changed when Kintner took charge. "His first ukase," Frank writes, "was to have the head of NBC News report directly to him as President of NBC. . . . No longer would it take four phone calls and two meetings to ask leave to interrupt a soap opera to give Americans the news that the sky had fallen."[4] Frank adds that "he (Kintner) had an obsession to beat CBS."[5]

One of his first moves was to lure Irving Gitlin away from his position as director of Public Affairs for CBS News and set him up as a premier documentarian at NBC. The increasing exposure being given to Fred Friendly within the organization, especially Friendly's selection as executive producer of "CBS Reports," had left Gitlin vulnerable to approaches from the outside. He was also disappointed at what he regarded as loss of interest of both Stanton and Paley in CBS News. The Kintner approach was well timed to cater to his bruised ego.

Kintner's next target was a longtime CBS News executive, Elmer Lower. Lower had joined CBS in 1953 as manager of the News department's Washington television bureau. A year later he moved to New York to be, in effect, general manager of News and Public Affairs operations. As such he was second in overall command of the department. His defection was a total surprise to me. When I arrived at Los Angeles International Airport in early 1960 for a meeting regarding our plans for the Democratic National Convention in Los Angeles that summer I was pleased that Lower had been thoughtful enough to meet me with a limousine. As soon as we were en route to the meeting site, however, I learned the reason for his solicitous behavior. He told me that he had been recruited by Bob Kintner to move to NBC. When I asked how far the negotiations had gone, he replied that he had accepted Kintner's offer and would be leaving as soon as he could get back to New York and clean out his office. This made two defections to NBC of the four principal operating executives in the News division, and two big acquisitions for Kintner and NBC.

Lower's defection created the most immediate concern. He had been working virtually full time as manager of a small task force directing preparations for the 1960 political year. His departure would leave an enormous gap that we had no one to fill without reaching outside the organization. There was also a concern that NBC would now have automatic and instant access to all our planning to that date, and the opening of the Democratic Convention in Los Angeles was only weeks away.

All three networks approached the political season as they had in 1952 with the exception that the equipment available was vastly more sophisticated, staffs were larger and better trained, and senior corporate managers were now more concerned about the outcome of the ratings contest. Competition among the networks had been increasing in ferocity each year. Kintner's fervent desire to beat CBS at any cost added a new element that assured a fierce battle for supremacy.

Relentless competition started with the primary elections in West Virginia and Wisconsin. CBS and NBC fought it out toe to toe, with NBC having a slight edge in West Virginia and CBS in Wisconsin. In Wisconsin CBS introduced a new device aimed to determine which way various special interest segments of the population were voting. Advance data were gathered from selected precincts representing a broad variety of Wisconsin voters including Polish Catholic laborers in the Milwaukee area, wealthy German Catholic farmers in the soil-rich Fox River valley, Scandinavian farmers in the less desirable farmland in the northwestern corner of the state, and other less well-defined population groups. The data were assembled to be fed into IBM's most powerful new computer (the 7090) on primary election night and matched with results coming in from the polls. It was expected that this would furnish invaluable clues to the sources of support for the two principal contestants for the Democratic delegates from the state. The data, broadcast on election night, showed that both normally liberal-voting laborers in the Catholic precincts in and around Milwaukee and the more conservative Catholic farmers were turning out strongly for Kennedy. Humphrey's main source of strength was not labor as expected but the Scandinavian Lutheran farmers in Wisconsin's far northwestern lake area. The Kennedys were furious about what they described as the introduction of the religious issue into the campaign and called CBS with vigorous protests. The protests were listened to but no apologies were given, and a new device for reading meaning into early election returns had been implemented. It was CBS's night.

By the opening date of the conventions, three months later, the pendulum had definitely swung NBC's way. All three networks had massed millions of dollars' worth of sophisticated hardware, hundreds of staff personnel, and the most up-to-date electronic resources for event coverage, and were prepared to give the viewers a show comparable to that in Chicago eight years earlier when television firmly established itself as a news medium on a level with newspapers, newsmagazines, and radio. There were hand-held shortwave cameras, cameras on fish pole booms that could peer over a twelve-foot fence or into a second-floor window, mobile units maneuverable enough to pursue candidates or their supporters in dense traffic and parades. Videotape recorders would enable news teams to record events and hold them for release at opportune times. And there were scores of writers, editors, reporters, on-air personalities, and technicians to support the effort. The only weakness was that there wasn't much of a story to cover.

The Democrats were first. Kennedy was not a sure first-ballot winner but the odds against anyone's dislodging him were slight. Harry Truman, Adlai Stevenson, and Lyndon Johnson were all on the scene and participating in what maneuvering for position there was, but there never was much doubt that Kennedy would ultimately be the nominee. The question for the networks was, How do you make a spectacle out of an event whose outcome seemed so obvious?

CBS approached it seriously and solemnly as it had the conventions in 1956 and 1952 except it didn't have the inner drive and enthusiasm it had then. The first shock occurred on the Tuesday morning after the convention opened. The overnight television ratings showed NBC a clear winner. Subsequent overnight ratings were only marginally better. On Sunday, July 17, in the *New York Times*, Jack Gould explained why. "The National Broadcasting Company's team of Chet Huntley and David Brinkley swept away the stuffy, old-fashioned concept of ponderous reportage on the home screen. They talked as recognizable humans, sprinkled their observations with delightful wit and were easily the TV hit of the week."[6]

Gould later in the same piece pronounced the end of an era. "The preeminence of CBS in news coverage which has been something of a tradition in broadcasting no longer exists. . . . The sophisticated bite of CBS in large measure has slipped away."[7]

Bob Chandler, in the show business weekly *Variety*, picked up on the theme in his column on July 27: "There's a growing belief," he wrote, "that the solemn, sometimes stuffy and always let's-make-it-look-important technique of CBS has finally had it."[8] From the point of view of ratings for the Democratic Convention, Chandler was right.

By the third day CBS was becoming more aggressive and better harnessing the talents of its correspondents. It was obvious, however, that NBC was more alert, better attuned to covering an event with little hard news except a bit of maneuvering behind the scenes. CBS correspondents were much more effective in assaying broad political and economic movements than in ferreting out the nitty-gritty of politics. The best political reporting CBS had done was in Chicago in 1952, when it had virtually no access to the CBS correspondent staff and had to rely on catch-as-catch-can recruitment to get a staff. Bill Leonard from WCBS radio in New York, Jim Bormann from WCCO in Minneapolis, and Grant Holcomb from KNXT in Los Angeles were indefatigable and sufficiently knowledgeable about politics and politicians to burrow into the most complicated thickets and emege with accurate stories of the most obscure maneuvers. Leonard was involved again in both 1956 and 1960 but was now one of a large corps of regular CBS reporters, many of whom had neither the experience nor the inclination to excel in political reporting.

CBS was guilty of another critical strategic error. Since Huntley and Brinkley were whipping Cronkite in the ratings books, Don Hewitt, whose judgment was normally impeccable, approached me before the opening of the Wednesday session and suggested that we try Murrow in the "anchor studio" to work with Cronkite. Since we were becoming desperate at that point I agreed with the provision that Murrow be seated at the opposite side of the room from Cronkite and have a separate microphone. I was afraid of chaos if the two constantly overrode each other. Murrow, however, the moment he walked into the studio, asked the technicians to move him alongside Cronkite and arrange for him to work from the same microphone. The two were courteous to each other. There were no conflicts but they did not mesh as a team. They were no Huntley and Brinkley.

The Republican Convention in Chicago convened after a week's respite. There was even less of a story than in Los Angeles. There was not the slightest doubt that Vice President Nixon would be nominated for the presidency. Platform conflicts had been resolved by an agreement between Nixon and Nelson Rockefeller negotiated during a visit by the vice president to the New York governor's New York office the preceding week. The only question to be resolved was, Who would be the GOP's vice presidential nominee?

Ratings were generally lower than for the Democratic meetings two weeks earlier but again NBC maintained a clear although a narrower lead. Jack Gould, in the *New York Times* of July 26, envisioned the possibility of a close ratings race. "If CBS catches on to the format of informality to relieve the serious moments of the convention and, perhaps, more apparently sharpens up its floor interviews, it could be nip-and-tuck between CBS and NBC albeit Mr. Brinkley at his best is still going to take a lot of catching."[9] Gould was right. Brinkley was going to take a lot of catching, more than CBS was able to accomplish. NBC came home a clear winner. It was apparent that after a period of CBS ascendancy NBC had moved into the lead and that Bob Kintner was in the process of achieving his goal.

There was a significant trend, however, that foretold a notable shift in television viewing. In 1952 when television was still in its infancy, the total number of stations across the entire country had been restricted largely to the 108 that were on the air in 1949, the year in which the FCC imposed its freeze on granting new licenses. Set owners except in the nation's three largest cities had no choice concerning the programs available to them. They took what the networks offered or went dark. Options were available in New York and Los Angeles with seven stations each and in Chicago with four. Otherwise the viewer got the conventions whether he wanted them or not. By 1960, 673 stations had been authorized and by the end of 1959, 573 were already on the air.[10] Many of the 573, obviously, were network affiliates, but independents were growing in numbers. And they had to scramble for programs of their own. Baseball games and reruns of motion pictures began to appear in ratings books in competition with the conventions and were showing surprising strength. It was clear that political convention coverage would no longer benefit from the shortage of television stations that had given it a virtual monopoly in 1952.

Election night would offer the next opportunity for hand to hand combat among the networks. Before the election, however, there was a possibility that the broadcast networks, both radio and television, might be able to bring the candidates of the two major parties into the ring for a series of face to face debates. There had been desultory discussion of presidential debates since Senator Blair Moody of Michigan had urged in 1952 on the CBS public affairs program "Peoples' Platform" that General Eisenhower and Governor Stevenson be invited to meet on a debate platform. CBS president Stanton quickly followed up the senator's suggestion, but General Eisenhower's advisers flatly refused. There was little chance that the general, now a president, would accept in 1956.

Stanton had kept the debate possibility alive, however, over the years between 1956 and 1960, but there were two compelling impediments to implementation of the suggestion. One was a provision in the Federal Communications Act of 1934 mandating that if time were given by a licensed broadcaster to one candidate for a political office, equivalent time had to be given to each other candidate for that same office. Since there were normally from fourteen to sixteen candidates running for the presidency, such as the Vegetarians, the Prohibitionists, the Socialist Labor party, the Poor Man's party, and the Communists, the autumn season would have been filled with appearances by candidates who had not the slightest chance of drawing more than a handful of votes. The only solution seemed to be a repeal of Section 315, but members of the Congress who did not look forward with delight to having to take on a host of candidates looking for national TV exposure to help oust them from their seats were not enthusiastic about making a change. Incumbents running for second terms in the presidency were also unlikely to have any enthusiasm for standing on a platform and slugging it out with an opponent, no matter how ineffectual.

In 1960, however, there was no incumbent in the race. If Section 315 could be deleted or at least suspended for one election, a debate might be possible. Stanton saw the opportunity and began a campaign to win elimination or suspension of the offending clause. Before a bill could be passed both Senator Kennedy and Vice President Nixon had agreed in principle to participate in a series of joint appearances. In late August the House finally passed the bill for a one-time suspension and the way was cleared for negotiations over time, place, and format.[11]

The author talks with presidential candidate Richard Nixon in the television studio prior to the first 1960 Kennedy–Nixon debate. On the right is director Don Hewitt. Photo courtesy of Sig Mickelson. Used by permission.

Negotiations were not easy. Negotiators for the broadcasters, principally John Daly from ABC, William McAndrew from NBC, and me, were concerned almost up to the time that the moderator, Howard K. Smith, introduced the two candidates in a CBS Chicago studio on the night of September 26, 1960, that one or the other might find an excuse to bow out.

There were four joint appearances in all. Reliable estimates suggested that more than 100 million persons saw some part of at least one of them. More than 70 million were estimated to have seen the first in Chicago.[12] It is generally assumed that his appearance in that first debate in Chicago gave Kennedy the impetus he needed to win the presidency.

The debates constitute one of the defining moments in television news history. If there was any doubt of the role that television played in public life, they were thoroughly dispelled. In that sense the debates took their place with the 1952 political conventions, the "See It Now" broadcast on Senator McCarthy, and the Khruhschev interview on "Face the Nation" as events in which television established itself as the equal of the press in informing the public and furnishing raw material for formulating public opinion. Except for the political conventions the initiative for each of these events came from within the television industry. They were both of such overwhelming importance that the printed media could not avoid enhancing their impact by featuring them with page 1 banner headlines.

Election night coverage from a ratings point of view was a rerun of the conventions, NBC a clear winner. Reporting, however, was vastly more sophisticated than it had been in 1952 or 1956. IBM put the use of its gigantic new computer, the 7090, and its system of collating data on punch cards at the disposal of CBS. Unfortunately the system IBM devised for the receiving and collating of data in the studio broke down and forced the network to rely on a backup system using adding machines and hand written reports. The big computer, so big that it could not be moved to the studio, however, performed impeccably. Its first printout, timed at 8:12 P.M. EST on election night, with 4 percent of the nation's precincts reporting, forecast a Kennedy victory with odds calculated at 11 to 5.[13] Notwithstanding the computer's confident forecast of a Kennedy victory, the race was so close that the network was not certain of the result until mid-morning the next day.

Again NBC was the clear ratings winner. ABC, too, made a respectable showing, suggesting that the two-network news contest that had prevailed during the first full decade of television would soon become a three-way battle. CBS was boasting that its early evening news program had a greater circulation than *Life* magazine and a Roper poll conducted during 1959 indicated that television had almost caught newspapers as the source of most news for the American public. At the end of 1959 the poll showed 51 percent of respondents reported that they got most of their news from

TV versus 57 percent for newspapers. By 1963, TV had forged ahead.[14] Its news and information broadcasts had come a long way from their primitive beginnings only a little more than a decade earlier.

By the end of 1960 television news had moved light years ahead of those early days. Edward R. Murrow, Walter Cronkite, Chet Huntley, David Brinkley, John Cameron Swayze, and Douglas Edwards had become names almost as familiar to American citizens as the most popular Hollywood movie stars'. Newspapers were changing patterns to interpret news and add background as a complement to television rather than assume that TV was only a supplemental source of news. Television set density in American homes had soared to nearly 90 percent. Television would continue to grow but the patterns were established. From now on changes would be evolutionary. The revolution was over.

Notes

INTRODUCTION

1. Statistics are taken from data compiled by the Research department of CBS Television, available in the writer's files.
2. Ibid.
3. Ibid.

CHAPTER 1

1. *Broadcasting*, February 9, 1961, p. 91.
2. Ibid.
3. Ibid., May 11, 1961, p. 77.
4. Most of the information about the early postwar efforts of CBS to build a news service is derived from a lengthy interview with Chester Burger. An audiotape of this interview is in the author's files.
5. *CBS, Inc. Annual Report*, 1953.
6. *Broadcasting*, March 18, 1981, p. 231.
7. Burns W. Roper, *A Ten-Year View of Public Attitudes toward Television and Other Mass Media, 1959–1968* (New York: Roper Organization, 1979), p. 2.

CHAPTER 2

1. *Broadcasting*, February 16, 1961, p. 106.
2. Ibid.

3. *CBS, Inc. Annual Report*, 1948.
4. An account of this episode was related to the writer by Chester Burger. It was recorded on audiotape and may be found in the writer's files.
5. After leaving CBS some years later Schaffner went to Hollywood, where he won an Oscar for directing *Patton*.

CHAPTER 3

1. *Broadcasting*, February 16, 1981, p. 108.
2. Ibid.
3. These figures are included in a summary of audience ratings of network television early evening news broadcasts, 1950–51 to 1960–61, prepared for the writer by the Research department of CBS Television. They are available in the writer's files.
4. *CBS, Inc. Annual Report*, 1950.
5. Stanley Cloud and Lynne Olson, *The Murrow Boys* (Boston: Houghton Mifflin, 1996), p. 291.
6. A. M. Sperber, *Murrow: His Life and Times* (New York: Freundlich Books, 1986), pp. 346–48.
7. Joseph E. Persico, *Edward R. Murrow: An American Original* (New York: McGraw-Hill, 1988), pp. 290–92.
8. Estimate made by CBS Television Research department in connection with plans for covering the 1952 political conventions.
9. *CBS, Inc. Annual Report*, 1950.
10. CBS Television Research department data.

CHAPTER 4

1. *New York Times*, September 4, 1951, p. 1.
2. Leonard Mosley, *Dulles: A Biography of Eleanor, Allen and John Foster Dulles and Their Family Network* (New York: Dial Press/James Wade, 1978), p. 261.
3. *New York Times*, September 5, 1951, p. 1.
4. Ibid., September 7, 1951, p. 1.
5. *Broadcasting*, September 15, 1951, p. 14.

CHAPTER 5

1. Long after Friendly had left CBS and Don Hewitt had begun producing "60 Minutes" Palmer Williams was still on the CBS News payroll, serving as Hewitt's second in command and senior producer of "60 Minutes."

CHAPTER 6

1. Interview with Phil Scheffler recorded on audiotape and available in the writer's files.

2. Ibid.
3. *CBS, Inc. Annual Report*, 1959.

CHAPTER 7

1. John Cogley, *Report on Blacklisting*, vol. 1, *Movies* (New York: Fund for the Republic, 1956), p. 93.
2. I have a copy of this list in my files.
3. Many years later I asked Dr. Stanton where it might have come from. He replied that he was not sure but thought it had probably been delivered to CBS by either the Young and Rubicam advertising agency or Clarence Francis, the chairman of the General Foods Corporation.
4. *New York Times*, November 3, 1952; a detailed version of the Sloane episode may be found on p. 12.
5. For a detailed report on the Burdett episode see Cloud and Olson, *Murrow Boys*, pp. 314–29.
6. Statement made by Cowden in an interview. The text is available on audiotape in the writer's files.

CHAPTER 8

1. Gould's column is reprinted in full in James F. Fixx, ed., *The Mass Media and Politics* (New York: Arno Press, 1972), p. 17.
2. Ibid.
3. Data furnished by CBS Television Research department available in the writer's files.
4. Ibid.
5. *CBS, Inc. Annual Report*, 1953.
6. Fixx, *Mass Media and Politics*, p. 19.

CHAPTER 9

1. The original of the letter signed by Schoenbrun is in the writer's files.
2. Ibid.
3. The information cited is included in a memorandum to the writer from Schoenbrun regarding an off-the-record interview with General Lucius Clay dated May 28, 1952. The original is in the writer's files.
4. The full content of Mullen's conversation with General Eisenhower regarding the CBS move into the theater may be found on an audiotape in the Mickelson Archive, Wisconsin Historical Society, Madison.
5. Press release from the CBS Television Network, June 19, 1952, in the writer's files.
6. Gould's column was reprinted in Fixx, *Mass Media and Politics*, p. 19.
7. Kurt Lang and Gladys Engel Lang, *Politics and Television* (Chicago: Quadrangle Books, 1968), p. 137.
8. Data supplied by the CBS Television Research department available in the writer's files.

9. Ibid.
10. Fixx, *Mass Media and Politics*, p. 23.
11. Ibid., p. 24.

CHAPTER 10

1. The original cablegram received aboard the BOAC Stratocruiser is hanging on a wall in the writer's home office.
2. *New York Times*, June 7, 1953, p. 11.
3. Ibid.
4. This episode is described in a detailed but unpublished report on the coronation venture written by the author. It may be found in his files.

CHAPTER 11

1. *CBS, Inc. Annual Report*, 1953.
2. A copy of this memorandum may be found in the Mickelson Archive, Wisconsin Historical Society, Madison.
3. Details concerning this meeting may be found in a CBS Television memorandum from Mickelson addressed to VanVolkenburg, Robinson, Harrison, and Falknor in the Mickelson Archive, Wisconsin Historical Society, Madison.
4. CBS Television press release, April 8, 1953, available in Mickelson Archive, Wisconsin Historical Society, Madison.
5. Memo from Mickelson to TV News and Public Affairs staff, April 8, 1953, Mickelson Archive, Wisconsin Historical Society, Madison.
6. Memorandum from Mickelson to Van Volkenburg, Mickelson Archive, Wisconsin Historical Society, Madison.
7. Ibid.
8. Full text of this memorandum is available in Mickelson Archive, Wisconsin Historical Society, Madison.
9. Ibid.
10. *CBS, Inc. Annual Report*, 1953.
11. Memo, Donghi to Mickelson, January 11, 1954, copy in Mickelson Archive, Wisconsin Historical Society, Madison.
12. Ibid.
13. The Paley speech is quoted in a memorandum, Mickelson to Van Volkenburg, June 7, 1954, available in Mickelson Archive, Wisconsin Historical Society, Madison, as is the full text of the Paley speech.

CHAPTER 12

1. Interview with Don Hewitt in New York, February 1997. Notes are in the writer's personal files.

CHAPTER 13

1. "Public Broadcasting" was first identified by that term in a report issued in 1967 by a task force set up by the Carnegie Corporation. The report made a clear distinction between classroom "instructional television" and the broader cultural type of program, which it identified as "public television."
2. An extensive exchange of memoranda between Columbia University executives and the writer may be found in the Mickelson Archive, Wisconsin Historical Society, Madison.
3. Memorandum from Irving Gitlin and Irving Meltzer to "all writer-producers and directors, The Search," Mickelson Archive, Wisconsin Historical Society, Madison.
4. *New York Times*, November 6, 1954 p. 17. The clipping is in the writer's personal files.

CHAPTER 14

1. Persico, *Edward R. Morrow*, pp. 291–92.
2. *CBS, Inc. Annual Reports*, 1951, 1954, 1961.
3. A detailed account of the Radulovitch episode may be found in Fred W. Friendly, *Due to Circumstances beyond Our Control* (New York: Random House, 1967), pp. 3–20.
4. Ibid., p. 3.
5. Ibid., p. 4.
6. Unpublished manuscript, "An Objectivity Study of Three CBS News Broadcasts," prepared by the University of Wisconsin investigative team assigned to analyze CBS News scripts, dated November 21, 1954. The original manuscript may be found in the writer's personal files.
7. Ibid., p. 55.
8. Friendly, *Due to Circumstances beyond Our Control*, p. 92.

CHAPTER 15

1. Chairman Paley's role in suggesting the procedure was described to the writer personally by the chairman.
2. *CBS, Inc. Annual Report*, 1954.

CHAPTER 16

1. The memo from Friendly to Mickelson, June 13, 1959, may be found in the Mickelson Archive, Wisconsin Historical Society, Madison.
2. Ibid., June 15, 1959.
3. Ibid.
4. Ibid., June 18, 1969.
5. The memo referred to is in the Mickelson Archive, Wisconsin Historical Society, Madison.
6. *New York Times*, October 20, 1959, p. 1.

7. A detailed account of this episode may be found in Sperber, *Murrow*, pp. 574–83.

CHAPTER 17

1. Memorandum, Dorothy Boyce, Program Statistics department, CBS Reference department, to Mickelson, October 28, 1955. A copy is in the Mickelson Archive, Wisconsin Historical Society, Madison.
2. Apparently both the league and CBS were surprised it turned out to be as popular as it did. The asking price for rights started a dizzying climb almost immediately. By 1960, the price paid by CBS had risen to more than $9 million. By 1993 Fox was paying more than $393 million annually, or $1.58 billion for four years.
3. By 1963 Bell had left the commissioner's post and was succeeded by Pete Rozelle. Rozelle saw no sense in continuing to permit each team to control its own rights and theoretically do its own negotiating. He assumed the responsibility for negotiating on behalf of the entire league, with the proceeds to be divided among the member teams. His first negotiating effort raised the fee for the season to $9.3 million.
4. Memorandum, Stanton to Lower, March 28, 1956, Mickelson Archive, Wisconsin Historical Society, Madison.

CHAPTER 18

1. The *New York Times* reported on December 13, 1995, p. B1, that NBC had won the rights for a package of three Olympic Games for prices of $793 million for the summer games of 2004, $894 million for the summer games of 2008, and $613 million for the winter games in 2006. The $793 million for 2004 amounts to approximately 112 times the asking price of $675,000 for rights only in 1960, or more than 100 times the price, including some pickup fees paid by CBS in 1960.
2. James Caryn, "Foraging for Cracks in the Olympic Spirit," *New York Times*, July 31, 1996, p. B1.

CHAPTER 19

1. The budget overages of "See It Now" were of such magnitude that they overshadowed losses recorded by other news and public affairs programs. An analysis of costs and revenues for the series in 1956, for example, shows that income totaled $232,125 against costs of $1,085,130, for a loss of $862,005. The same year the weeknight news broadcast featuring Douglas Edwards sustained a loss of $272,456 on income of $1,085,460. This analysis may be found in "CBS Television Network, CBS Radio Network Commercial Show Costs and Income, Year 1956," in "CBS Organization Chart—Budget," in the writer's files.
2. *CBS, Inc. Annual Report*, 1960, "To the Stockholders."
3. *New York Times*, January 14, 1958, p. 17.

4. *CBS, Inc. Annual Report*, 1960.

CHAPTER 20

1. *CBS, Inc. Annual Report*, 1960, "To the Stockholders."
2. The statistical data are derived from an untitled report and analysis prepared for the writer by members of the CBS Television Research staff. They are based largely on Nielsen reports.
3. Ibid.
4. Reuven Frank, *Out of Thin Air* (New York: Simon & Schuster, 1991), p. 134.
5. Ibid., p. 136.
6. "TV's New Convention Look," *New York Times*, Radio section, p. 2.
7. Ibid.
8. Bob Chandler, "Convention Coverage Sparking Some Soul Searching among CBS Brass on News Styles, Techniques," *Variety*, July 17, 1960, p. 1.
9. Jack Gould, "TV: Fine Studies of Nixon in Chicago," *New York Times*, July 26, 1960, p. 16.
10. *Broadcasting*, May 4, 1961, p. 87.
11. A detailed description of the campaign to win congressional support for the bill and of the negotiations leading up to the actual debates may be found in Mickelson, *From Whistle Stop to Sound Bite* (New York: Praeger, 1989), pp. 119–34.
12. Untitled report from CBS Television Research compiled for the writer from data furnished by Nielsen reports.
13. A copy of the printout is available in the writer's files.
14. Burns W. Roper, *Public Perception of Television and Other Mass Media: A Twenty Year Review, 1959–1978* (New York: Roper Organization, 1979).

Bibliography

BOOKS

Barnow, Erik. *The Image Empire, A History of Broadcasting in the United States from 1953*. New York: Oxford University Press, 1970.
————. *A Tower in Babel*. New York: Oxford University Press, 1966.
————. *Tube of Plenty: The Evolution of American Television* (second revised edition). New York: Oxford University Press, 1990.
Bliss, Edward, Jr. *Now the News, The History of Broadcast Journalism*. New York: Columbia University Press, 1991.
Bower, Robert T. *Television and the Public*. New York: Holt, Rinehart & Winston, 1973.
Brown, Les. *Television, The Business behind the Box*. New York: Harcourt, Brace, 1974.
Cloud, Stanley and Lynne Olson. *The Murrow Boys*. Boston: Houghton Mifflin, 1996.
Cogley, John. *Report on Blacklisting*. New York: Fund for the Republic, 1956.
Cox, Geoffrey. *Pioneering Television News*. London: John Libbey, 1995.
Cronkite, Walter. *A Reporter's Life*. New York: Alfred A. Knopf, 1996.
Diamond, Edwin. *The Tin Kazoo: Television, Politics and the News*. Boston: MIT Press, 1975.
Faulk, John Henry. *Fear on Trial*. New York: Simon & Schuster, 1964.
Fixx, James. *The Mass Media and Politics*. New York: Arno Press, 1972.
Frank, Reuven. *Out of Thin Air*. New York: Simon & Schuster, 1991.

Friendly, Fred W. *Due to Circumstances beyond Our Control*. New York: Random House, 1967.

Halberstam, David. *The Fifties*. New York: Villard Press, 1993.

——. *The Powers That Be*. New York: Alfred A. Knopf, 1979.

James, Doug. *Walter Cronkite: His Life and Times*. Brentwood, Tenn.: J. M. Press, 1991.

Kendrick, Alex. *Prime Time: The Life of Edward R. Murrow*. Boston: Little, Brown, 1969.

Kisseloff, Jeff. *The Box: An Oral History of Television, 1920–1961*. New York: Penguin Books, 1995.

Lang, Kurt and Gladys Engel Lang. *Politics and Television*. Chicago: Quadrangle Books, 1968.

Leonard, Bill. *In the Storm of the Eye*. New York: G. P. Putnam's Sons, 1987.

McCabe, Peter. *Bad News at Black Rock: The Sell-Out of CBS News*. New York: Arbor House, 1975.

McCullough, David. *Truman*. New York: Simon & Schuster, 1992.

MacDonald, J. Fred. *One Nation under Television: The Rise and Decline of Network TV*. New York: Pantheon Books, 1990.

MacNeill, Robert. *The People Machine*. New York: Harper & Row, 1968.

Matusow, Barbara. *The Evening Stars*. Boston: Houghton Mifflin, 1983.

Mayer, Martin. *Making News*. Garden City, N.Y.: Doubleday, 1987.

Metz, Robert. *CBS, Reflections in a Blood Shot Eye*. Chicago: Playboy Books, 1975.

Midgeley, Leslie. *How Many Words Do You Want?* New York: Birch Lane Press, 1989.

Mosley, Leonard. *Dulles: A Biography of Eleanor, Allen and John Foster Dulles and Their Family Network*. New York: Dial Press/James Wade, 1978.

Murrow, Edward R. and Fred W. Friendly. *See It Now*. New York: Simon & Schuster, 1955.

Paley, William S. *As It Happened: A Memoir by William S. Paley, Founder and Chairman, CBS*. New York: Doubleday, 1979.

Paper, Lewis J. *Empire: The Making of CBS*. New York: St. Martin's Press, 1987.

Persico, Joseph E. *Edward R. Murrow: An American Original*. New York: McGraw-Hill, 1988.

Reasoner, Harry. *Before the Colors Fade*. New York: Alfred A. Knopf, 1981.

Roper, Burns W. *Public Perception of Television and Other Mass Media: A Twenty Year Review, 1959–1978*. New York: Roper Organization, 1979.

——. *A Ten-Year View of Public Attitudes toward Television and Other Mass Media, 1959–1968*. New York: Roper Organization, 1968.

Schoenbrun, David. *America Inside Out*. New York: McGraw-Hill, 1984.

Schorr, Daniel. *Clearing the Air*. Boston: Houghton Mifflin, 1977.

Schrauth, Raymond A. *The American Journey of Eric Sevareid*. South Royalton, Vt.: Steerforth Press, 1995.

Smith, Sally Bedell. *In All His Glory, The Life of William S. Paley*. New York: Simon & Schuster, 1990.

Sperber, A. M. *Murrow: His Life and Times*. New York: Freundlich Books, 1986.

PERIODICALS

Broadcasting. "The First 50 Years of Broadcasting."
  1946. February 2, 1981. pp. 77–81
  1947. February 9, 1981. pp. 87–91
  1948. February 16, 1981. pp. 103–11
  1949. February 23, 1981. pp. 89–95
  1950. March 2, 1981. pp. 93–97
  1951. March 9, 1981. pp. 161–65
  1952. March 16, 1981. pp. 231–35
  1953. March 23, 1981. pp. 101–5
  1954. March 30, 1981. pp. 77–81
  1955. April 6, 1981. pp. 147–51
  1956. April 13, 1981. pp. 159–63
  1957. April 20, 1981. pp. 99–103
  1958. April 27, 1981. pp. 99–103
  1959. May 4, 1981. pp. 83–87
  1960. May 11, 1981. pp. 77–81
CBS, Inc. Annual Reports. 1946–1960
New York Times

Index

About the Author

SIG MICKELSON is a Research Fellow at the Hoover Institution at Stanford University and Distinguished Professor of Journalism at the Manship School of Mass Communication at Louisiana State University. He has served as vice president of CBS, Inc., and was the first president of CBS News. He is the author of *America's Other Voice* (Praeger, 1983) and *From Whistle Stop to Sound Bite* (Praeger, 1989), and the editor of *The First Amendment—The Challenge of New Technology* (Praeger, 1989).